Borderline Personality Disorder

Borderline Personality Disorder

John G. Gunderson, M.D.

*Director of Psychotherapy, McLean Hospital,
Belmont; and Associate Professor, Harvard Medical
School, Boston, Massachusetts*

American Psychiatric Press, Inc.

1400 K Street, N.W.
Washington, D.C. 20005

Cover design by Tom Jones and Jane Kearns, Inc.
Text design by Tim Clancy and Richard E. Farkas
Typeset by VIP Systems, Inc.
Printed by R. R. Donnelley & Sons Co.

Copyright © 1984 by John G. Gunderson
ALL RIGHTS RESERVED
Manufactured in the United States of America
First printing—October 1984
Second printing—August 1985

Library of Congress Cataloging in Publication Data

Gunderson, John G., 1942–
Borderline personality disorder.

Bibliography: p. 185
Includes index.
1. Borderline personality disorder. I. Title.
[DNLM: 1. Personality Disorders. WM 190 G975b]
RC569.5.B67 G86 1984 616.89 84-18411
ISBN 0-88048-020-3

To my father,
Sherman Edward Gunderson

Contents

Preface

This book is primarily intended for use by those who have clinical responsibility for the care of borderline patients. Although I am both a clinical researcher and a psychoanalyst, this book predominantly derives from my experience as a hospital psychiatrist and psychotherapist. As such, my incursions into the extensive empirical and psychoanalytic literature about borderline patients are harnessed by an effort to cite only what has proven helpful for informing clinical considerations. In addition to presenting my own viewpoints throughout the book, I try to provide an even-handed review of the major contributions and the persisting controversies about treatment as found in the literature.

In the initial chapter, I review the historical developments which brought borderline patients to the forefront of clinical interest and describe the means by which borderline patients can be identified and differentiated. Chapter 2 offers a dynamic formulation by which the clinical syndrome of borderline patients can be seen to have coherence and organization and reviews the competing formulations offered by others. The chapters which follow review in depth the major treatment problems posed by borderline patients. Chapters 3 and 4 discuss general issues related to structuring and studying individual psychotherapy—most of which occurs in outpatient office settings. Chapters 5, 6, and 7 focus on the specific therapeutic problems of self-destructiveness, rage, and psychotic regression. These occur in both inpatient and outpatient settings. The next two chapters address the interactions between components of broader social and therapeutic contexts—namely, the structure and problems of residential treatment programs and the interactions between different therapeutic modalities. Chapter 10 distills from the rest of the book the predominant clinical dilemmas presented by borderline patients. In this final chapter, I present the thesis which is woven into and unifies this book: The treatment problems posed by borderline patients are sufficiently distinct that the evolution of a distinct psychiatric diagnosis for them is warranted.

Acknowledgments

It is customary for authors to acknowledge the valuable support provided to them by their families. In this instance, I can only say that this book was written despite my family who, throughout its preparation, consistently presented a lovable alternative in which I could invest my time and energy. It is similarly vexsome to acknowledge my patients as a source of support for this effort. Although providing the problems around which this book revolves, they have uniformly fostered in me more humility than confidence in what I might understand about them.

To a very large extent, I am indebted to the many contributors to the literature who are cited throughout the book. If this book is as good as its bibliography, then it will have accomplished my highest ambition. Each of these contributors has provided a reservoir of information, experience, and opinion which has helped me to shape and inform my views on the diagnosis and treatment of borderline patients. Of special note are the seminal contributions of Roy Grinker, who provided an example of good sense and intellectual integrity, and of Otto Kernberg, whose work was in large measure the backdrop against which I organized my own clinical and theoretical development. To these Elvin Semrad and Otto Will must be added, since their examples steered me toward the heart of this book—the effort to understand the experience of patients.

Finally and most importantly, I am grateful to the institutions and individuals with whom I have been fortunate to interact and learn. My interest in this subject began during my residency at

Massachusetts Mental Health Center. Next, while at the National Institute of Mental Health, Loren Mosher encouraged me to think critically and write clearly. Most particularly, since 1973 McLean Hospital has provided a complex and rich clinical resource in which to develop clinical insights and skills. Its leaders, Dr. Shervert Frazier and Dr. Francis de Marneffe, as well as the late Alfred Stanton, have fostered an atmosphere which allows creative clinical work to join academic scholarship. A most pivotal part of this institutional context has been the tolerant, cheerful, and skillful secretarial support provided during the preparation of this manuscript by Sue Busa.

John G. Gunderson, M.D.

Borderline
Personality Disorder

1

Diagnosis of Borderline
Personality Disorder

The diverse and often confusing literature on borderline patients that led to the current development of this diagnostic category has been reviewed quite extensively (Grinker and Werble 1977; Grinker et al. 1968; Gunderson 1982; Gunderson and Elliott 1984; Gunderson and Singer 1975; Kernberg 1975; Liebowitz 1979; Mack 1975; Meissner 1978a; Perry and Klerman 1978; Stone 1980). In the following review, a broader brush is used to isolate the major recurrent themes. To do this, I have selected pivotal contributions that help put the current status of this diagnosis and the controversies that continue to surround it into perspective. In keeping with the general purpose of this book, the review is anchored in clinical phenomenology and the practical issues of differential diagnosis.

HISTORICAL DEVELOPMENTS

The confluence of four relatively distinct clinical observations formed the backdrop for the interest in developing the borderline diagnostic category. The first of these observations was that a type of patient was identified who, despite the appearance of healthier functioning, revealed unsuspecting evidence of primitive thinking on unstructured psychological tests. Rorschach (1942) was the first to identify this phenomenon in patients whose performance on more structured tests was normal. A second observation concerned patients who, when referred for psychoanalysis on the basis of their presumed

1

neurotic level of function, revealed primitive regressive transferences that eventually required the termination of their analysis, sometimes even requiring hospitalizations. Hoch and Polatin (1949) called such patients "pseudoneurotic schizophrenics." This regressive predilection in both unstructured testing and unstructured clinical situations was elaborated on as a central feature by Knight (1953) in his seminal description of borderline patients.

A third observation relevant to the later identification of borderline patients derived from staff working within psychiatric hospitals. They, too, observed a group of patients who regressed into primitive and highly destructive behaviors within the supportive confines of hospitals, which had proven helpful to other patient groups. Although not initially identified in the literature as a phenomenon specific to borderline patients, this was a well-established and familiar part of the clinical lore on active inpatient services by the late 1950s. A fourth clinical observation that helped stimulate interest in defining borderline patients rose out of the intense countertransference reactions these patients generated in therapists—countertransference responses characteristically marked by feelings of helplessness and rage. These commonplace reactions were important insofar as they suggested that the problems in treatment were not understandable simply as misapplications of the concepts of either psychoanalysis or therapeutic communities, but reflected something perversely troublesome within the nature of these patients themselves.

Against the backdrop of these four distinct and independent clinical observations, three major studies reported in the late 1960s further focused attention on borderline patients. As with the clinical observations that preceded them, these studies were done independent of each other and involved very different lines of investigative interest: Kernberg (1967) was interested in the internal psychological structure, Grinker et al. (1968) were interested in the descriptive characteristics, and Kety et al. (1968) investigated the genetic transmission of schizophrenia.

Kernberg used the term *borderline personality organization* to identify a group of patients with severe character pathology who were neither psychotic nor neurotic. The identifying features of these patients were their unstable identities, their use of primitive defenses, and their generally intact reality testing. Despite the fact that their reality testing could fail transiently in unstructured or stressful circumstances, Kernberg departed from his psychoanalytic predecessors by indicating that a psychoanalytically oriented psychotherapy was specifically indicated and potentially curative for these patients. His efforts to delineate a concept of borderline personality and his therapeutic optimism became strong impetus for generating a renewed search for the dynamic and developmental understanding of such patients. This impetus was given much momentum by the enthusiastic reports of residential treatments for these patients that came at about the same time from Masterson (1971) and Rinsley (1965).

Grinker et al. (1968) undertook the first prospective and systematic collection of observations and subsequent data analyses on borderline patients. They concluded that four characteristics identified what they called the "borderline syndrome." These were (a) failures in self-identity, (b) anaclitic relationships, (c) a type of depression based on loneliness, and (d) the predominance of expressed anger. The approach made by Grinker et al. to diagnosis was a dramatic departure from the many preceding descriptive efforts, and marked the introduction of modern and more sophisticated psychiatric research methods to the study of these patients. This work would serve as the springboard for a whole series of empirical descriptive studies in the 1970s (for review, see Gunderson 1982).

A third impetus for defining borderline patients derived from the landmark series of adoption studies (Kety et al. 1975; Rosenthal et al. 1971; Wender et al. 1971). In the efforts to delineate the genetic transmission of schizophrenia, these investigators introduced the idea of a schizophrenia "spectrum" and identified a group of persons called "borderline schizophrenics" who had severe character pathology and various schizophrenia-like forms of cognition and who clustered in the biological relatives of adopted-away schizophrenic persons. The impact of this work was to suggest that the riddle of schizophrenia's genetic transmission might be resolved only by the better definition of these so-called borderline cases. More generally, this work became a cornerstone for the rise of biological psychiatry, which revived attention to the possible biogenetic substrates to various forms of severe character pathology (for review, see Siever and Gunderson 1983).

BORDERLINE PERSONALITY DISORDER: PRESENT STATUS

These three very different, but highly influential investigations gave rise to the modern era in which the borderline personality has become a major focus for psychiatric investigations. This concentration of interest has created a broad awareness of this syndrome among mental health professionals and a far clearer and more uniform employment of the borderline diagnosis. It has been recognized within the standard diagnostic nomenclature of the *Diagnostic and Statistical Manual of Mental Disorders*, Third Edition (DSM-III 1980) and has been cited as one of the major achievements in that process (Spitzer et al. 1980). In the following section, I will describe the criteria that have emerged from the past decade of study as best defining this syndrome, and place this syndrome in some relation to the other concepts that have been offered for this category.

As suggested above, considerable consensus has been achieved with respect to the characteristics of the borderline syndrome (see Table 1). These characteristics largely echo those identified from a review of the descriptive accounts found in the literature prior to 1975 (Gunderson and Singer 1975). They have undergone revision and further refinement as a result of the series of empirical investigations conducted during the 1970s (for a review, see Gunderson 1982). Most of these advances were incorporated in the criteria listed in DSM-III. In some aspects, however, the criteria that follow are based on more recent research and on further developments in my interpretation of the existing empirical and clinical evidence. I believe these criteria represent the best available means for identifying borderline patients. They are presented in the approximate rank ordering of importance.

Intense Unstable Interpersonal Relationships

Devaluation, manipulation, dependency, and masochism characterize and cause the intensity and instability of interpersonal relationships of borderline patients. Devaluation refers to the tendency to discredit or undermine the strengths and personal significance of important others. As noted elsewhere (see Chapter 3), it emerges as an expression of an angry response to separations. Manipulation refers to those efforts by which covert means are used to control or gain support from significant others. Typical ways include somatic complaints, provocative actions, or misleading messages, as well as self-destructive acts (described as a separate criterion below). Masochism refers to the pattern in which borderline patients repeatedly, knowingly, and seemingly avoidably find themselves hurt in their close relationships. It is commonplace for borderline patients to see themselves as having been repeatedly victimized and mistreated in a long series of previous relationships, often beginning with their parents. The dependency of borderline patients is frequently manifest in receiving actual caregiving or compliantly (at times) following direction from their important others while denying their neediness.

As shown in Table 1, with the exception of idealization which has appeared in some criteria sets (DSM III; Kernberg et al. 1981; Sheehy et al. 1980), there has been little disagreement about the diagnostic importance of these features of the borderline patients' interpersonal relationships. Idealization has not been found in other studies—especially those in which a narrower concept of borderline personality is used (for further discussion, see Chapter 2). With this exception, these characteristic disturbances in interpersonal relations uniformly provide the most distinguishing aspect of the borderline syndrome vis-à-vis a variety of other diagnoses.

Manipulative Suicide Attempts

Manipulative attempts refers to those suicide efforts or gestures that seem designed to exact a "saving" response from a significant other. This most commonly occurs as wrist slashing or overdosing, and is the most frequent precipitant for hospitalization. Investigations of a series of patients who made repeated suicide attempts (Crumley 1979) or who were self-mutilators (Grunebaum and Klerman 1967) document that this characteristic comes closest to answering Mack's (1975) appeal for a "behavioral specialty" to fix the borderline diagnosis in the clinician's mind alongside other major forms of personality disorder. These suicide gestures are the most problematic expression of the manipulativeness of borderline patients (see Chapter 5).

TABLE 1. Empirically Derived Criteria for Borderline Personality

	Grinker et al. 1968	Gunderson and Kolb 1978	Spitzer et al. 1979	Sheehy et al. 1980	Kernberg et al. 1981	Perry 1984
Affect	1. Anger 2. Depression, loneliness	1. Heightened affectivity • anger • depression (nondiscriminating) • chronic dysphoria	1. Anger 2. Unstable affect • depression • irritability • anxiety 3. Chronic feelings of emptiness/boredom	1. Poor affect 2. Intense feelings and impulses	NA	1. Angry responses to crises 2. Chronic emptiness
Identity	3. Poor self-identity	NA	4. Identity disturbance	3. Unstable sense of self	1. Identity diffusion	3. Disturbed identity and self-perception
Interpersonal Relationships	4. Anaclitic relations	2. Disturbed close relationships • devaluation • manipulation • dependency • masochism 3. High socialization • intolerant of aloneness	5. Unstable intense relationships • devaluation • manipulation • idealization • shifting attitudes 6. Intolerant of aloneness	4. Devaluation and idealization 5. Periodic social isolation	Devaluation and idealization (These are considered defenses; see 3 below)	4. Angry relationships • manipulation • controlling • exploitative 5. Dependent relationships • stormy, unstable • masochistic • intolerant of aloneness 6. Unstably perceives others

TABLE 1. Empirically Derived Criteria for Borderline Personality (*continued*)

	Grinker et al. 1968	Gunderson and Kolb 1978	Spitzer et al. 1979	Sheehy et al. 1980	Kernberg et al. 1981	Perry 1984
Impulsivity	NA	4. Impulsivity • drug and alcohol abuse • promiscuity 5. Manipulative • suicide • mutilation • overdoses	7. Impulsivity • drug and alcohol abuse 8. Physically self-damaging acts • mutilation • suicide gestures • fights, accidents	6. Impulsivity 7. Drug and alcohol abuse 8. Unstable sex (promiscuity) NA	NA	7. Self-destructive impulses • impulsive • mutilation • suicide attempts (manipulative) • overdoses • destructive acts
Psychosis	NA	6. Mild psychotic experiences • dissociation • paranoid ideas • regressions • absence of any severe or widespread psychotic symptoms	(Dissociative experience, ideas of reference, and paranoid ideas became part of the schizotypal item list.)	9. Projection and poor sense of reality	2. Intact reality testing • vulnerable to brief psychotic experiences • altered sense of reality • projection (These are considered defenses; see 3 below)	8. Regressions in treatment 9. Anxiety and intolerance • loss of control • depersonalization • transient psychotic experiences
Miscellaneous		7. Low achievement		10. Absence of hypochondriasis 11. Absence of obsessions and compulsion 12. bizarre sexual fantasies	3. Primitive defenses • splitting • denial (See also above)	Splits self and object images

Unstable Sense of Self

The problems in establishing and maintaining a stable and coherent sense of self are central to borderline patients, and have been features of most criteria sets for this diagnosis (see Table 1). Despite its centrality, this is a very problematic criterion on which to base the borderline diagnosis because of the difficulties in its accurate identification without sustained exposure to a patient. Real disagreements about what constitutes evidence for identity problems exist. In addition, it lacks specificity for borderline patients vis-à-vis other forms of serious character pathology.

Two phenomena closely related to this faulty sense of self may be more reliably distinguished features of borderline patients that give evidence for this criterion. One is intolerance of aloneness, which is thought to reflect failures of object constancy (Adler and Buie 1979a, 1979b). Borderline persons tend to be compulsively social because their sense of their own coherence and value depends on the presence of others. The second phenomenon is abandonment anxiety. The acute sensitivity and the preoccupation with abandonment (Masterson 1971) are also reflectors of their vulnerable sense of self when alone.

Negative Affects

The affect of borderline patients is definitely not flat; these patients display multiple intense and negative affects. Of these, anger, expressed more or less directly, is clearly the most discriminating. Bitterness, demandingness, and sarcasm, and more direct expressions of rage that erupt readily during interaction with borderline patients, are a major reason for the difficulties many mental health professionals have in treating such patients (Chapter 6).

Other characteristics of affect helpful in identifying borderline patients include the absence of sustained periods of satisfaction or well-being, and, conversely, the presence of sustained dysphoric feelings—most notably boredom and emptiness. As will be discussed, depression is very characteristic of borderline patients. Its value as an indicator for the borderline diagnosis does not lie in its specificity as an affect (many other diagnoses have associated depression) but may be in the specific dynamic meaning of the depression (i.e., in borderline patients it reflects intolerable convictions of basic "badness").

Ego-Dystonic Psychotic Experiences

These experiences most commonly take the form of drug-free paranoid ideation and a history of regressive phenomena appearing in the course of previous treatment. They may also take the form of dissociative experiences (depersonalization or derealization) or exaggerated psychotic-like responses to drugs. Neither the response to drugs nor the presence of dissociative experiences is sufficiently common to make a very helpful criterion for the borderline diagnosis; when they occur, however, they should be considered as strongly suggestive of this diagnosis.

In general, the occurrence of any mild or brief ego-dystonic psychotic-like experiences in the absence of severe, widespread psychotic symptoms at any time in the patient's past life is a strong indicator for the borderline diagnosis.

In DSM-III, psychotic experiences are included only as an ancillary feature in the criterion set. Frances et al. (1984) found these psychotic episodes infrequent in an outpatient borderline sample and not very discriminating. As noted above, its value in diagnosis is not so much because of its frequency in borderline samples (i.e., its sensitivity); its value derives from its specificity. As a criterion, it is perhaps the reverse side of the failures in identity that are quite characteristic of borderline patients (although hard to discern), but lack specificity. It is argued elsewhere (see Chapter 7) that the hazards and problems in managing psychotic experiences when they occur may be sufficiently important that this criterion should be included as a way of alerting clinicians to the fact that patients diagnosed borderline—perhaps on the basis of other characteristics—may be vulnerable to these regressions in unstructured settings.

Impulsivity

The principal form impulsivity takes is a pattern of periodic, but serious, alcohol or drug abuse. The young borderline person is apt to use a variety of drugs impulsively. Problems with alcohol often get worse as borderline patients age. Substance abuse is one of the most common presenting problems in the young adult group where the borderline diagnosis is usually first established. Sexual deviance is highly related to impulsivity because it consists largely of promiscuous behaviors of borderline patients under the influence of alcohol or other drugs. As described elsewhere (Chapter 2), these and other impulsive actions such as accidents, fights, or destructive acts are likely to occur under circumstances in which borderline patients would otherwise feel alone and abandoned.

Low Achievement

The typical level of school and work achievement is quite low in borderline patients. This is so despite apparent talent and ability to do better, and is quite similar to the achievement levels attained by schizophrenic patients.

Many clinicians, especially those in outpatient psychotherapy practices, have mistakenly utilized the diagnosis of borderline personality for patients whose external function is fine but who they believe internally primitive (for example, see Abend et al. 1983). Certainly poor functioning should not be a requirement for the borderline diagnosis, but it remains, as Koenigsberg (1982) noted, a useful indicator for the diagnosis in outpatients as well as inpatients because it reflects the usual "cost" for having this infantile type of personality organization. Dysfunction in role performance helps distinguish this group from patients who appear similar but who have higher levels of personality organization.

A review of the criteria sets that have been put forth in the series of empirical studies during the last decade (see Table 1) demonstrates the impressive concordance in features which each study has concluded best define this patient group. Although various investigators have rearranged the criteria set in different ways, there are almost no major disagreements among them despite the utilization of different assessment techniques, comparison groups, treatment settings (including both inpatient and outpatient samples), and even conceptual orientations. Not only is the concordance in these criteria sets impressive, but the degree of discrimination from a variety of comparison groups has been uniformly high in these and other studies (Conte et al. 1980; Frances et al. 1984; Kobele et al. unpublished; Koenigsberg 1982; Koenigsberg et al. 1983; Kroll et al. 1981, 1982, 1983; Perry 1984; Soloff and Ulrich 1981; Willett et al. 1973). All studies have reported sensitivities and specificities for the borderline diagnosis routinely in the mid-70th percentile or above. Such levels of discrimination compare well with those achieved for other, presumably better established, diagnoses. It was by no means evident at the outset to those of us who were involved in these investigations that a criteria set would emerge with so much consensus and that would prove so discriminating.

CONTROVERSIES

The results of the series of descriptive investigations done in the past decade have clearly supported the concept of a borderline syndrome—that is, a cluster of characteristics which occur together with greater-than-chance frequency and which can be differentiated from other patient groups. Despite this consensus of clinical and research opinion supporting the criteria set provided above and supporting its inclusion in DSM-III, it is still true that controversies persist. To a considerable extent, the current controversies can be seen as extensions of conceptual issues found in the earlier contributions by Grinker, Kety, and Kernberg and their colleagues.

How this syndrome relates to these historical forebearers is illustrated in Figure 1. Borderline personality disorder (BPD), as described above and as found in DSM-III, clearly represents a group between psychoses and neuroses in the midlevel range of severity of psychopathology. There it has taken its place next to other major forms of character pathology. This was the concept initially introduced by Grinker (1979), and which differs from his definition, as shown in Figure 1, only by having had its boundaries become moderately narrower (Perry 1981).

The concept of the borderline as a type of personality disorder is at distinct variance with that concept of borderline represented by Kernberg's designation of "borderline personality organization" (BPO). Kernberg employed the diagnosis of borderline personality organization as one of three major forms of character pathology. As such, it is bounded on the one side by persons with "psychotic personality organizations" and on the other by those with "neurotic personality organizations." It is meant to include all major forms of character pathology. Because as much as 25 to 30 percent of the general population (perhaps 40 percent of the psychiatric population) could be expected to evidence severe character pathology, this is clearly a much broader and inclusive usage for the term *borderline*. Even the most modest estimate recently provided by Kernberg (1983) would put the prevalence figure at 15 percent of the general population.

A third concept of the borderline that remains extant and still

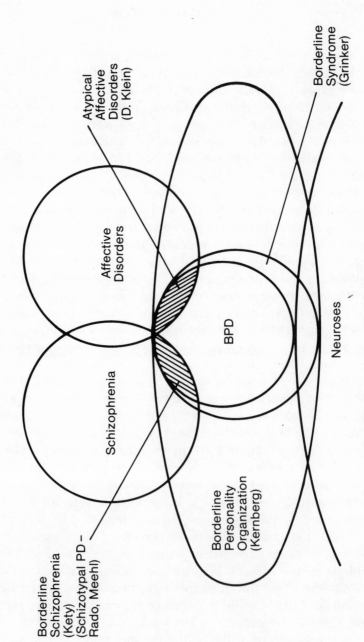

FIGURE 1. Concepts of Borderline Disorders

causes skepticism about the modern meaning of the borderline category is traceable to its usage to designate "adjacent to" or "an atypical form of" psychosis. Kety, and most of his predecessors (McCully 1962; Weiner 1966) who had used borderline in this way, were making reference to the margin of schizophrenia. In recent years, Klein (1975) and Stone (1980) have retained this usage, but they came to view the more important "border" of the borderline category as being with affective disorders.

In the following section, these controversies will be examined with special reference to the issues in differential diagnosis that highlight these competing concepts for clinicians. First the border with the schizophrenic psychoses will be examined, then the border with affective disorders, and finally the boundaries with other personality disorders. Obviously, the first two categories bear on the question of borderline personality disorder as an atypical variation of one of the major psychoses, whereas the latter issue (i.e., differential diagnosis with other personality disorders) bears on the question of the value of the broad, overarching concept of borderline personality organization (BPO) as opposed to the more discrete category of personality disorder (BPD) delineated by Grinker, advocated here and found in DSM-III.

Borderline as Part of a Schizophrenia Spectrum

As noted earlier in this chapter, linkage to schizophrenia for the patients who are now called borderline has been suggested both by the psychological test literature, in which such patients revealed primitive cognitions similar to those of schizophrenics, and by the psychoanalytic literature, which identified patients who regressed into a schizophrenia-like psychosis in unstructured treatment. In addition, the adoptive studies suggested a genetic link between schizophrenia and the nonpsychotic characterologically disturbed group. A fourth linkage to schizophrenia was suggested by a comparative study of a 3- and 5-year course of matched samples of borderline and schizophrenic patients (Carpenter et al. 1977; Gunderson et al. 1975a). This study showed surprising similarities in the course of borderline and schizophrenic patients in terms of symptoms, recidivism, employment, and even in social relations, although borderlines appeared modestly more sociable. These four observations suggested a linkage between schizophrenia and the so-called borderline patients that was psychological, genetic, and prognostic, and supported the notion that the borderline designation was identifying an important but atypical variant of schizophrenia.

More recent descriptive studies have shown overlap between borderline and schizophrenic subjects in terms of dysfunctional role performance, poor sense of identity, and psychotic-like ideation. With respect to role performance, the borderline patient, unlike many schizophrenic patients, will typically appear to have the social or intellectual abilities needed for better role performance.

Most recent studies on the psychological test performance of borderline patients repeated the earlier observations about the primitiveness of thinking in this patient group, but have also clarified and underscored major differences from schizophrenic patients in both the quantity and quality of reality testing or other cognitive deficits (Carr et al. 1979; Singer and Larson 1981). The problems in reality testing of borderline patients are more transient and ego alien than for schizophrenic patients. However, under certain stressful circumstances, many borderline patients will transiently show evidence of psychotic thinking similar to that of schizophrenics. That this thinking may be assisted by phenothiazines (see Chapter 9), I believe, reflects the nonspecificity of phenothiazine action and the nonspecificity of psychotic symptoms rather than indicating a more basic linkage between these two categories. Still, the problems in reality testing can occasionally present a subtle distinction vis-à-vis schizophrenia, and it is best to rely on the other aspects of the overall clinical picture for differentiation.

The areas in which the differences are consistently clear in descriptive accounts are the intense, affectively laden, interpersonal relationships of the borderline patients. The overt dependent neediness, the manifest anger, and the manipulativeness of borderline patients are rarely seen in schizophrenic patients and usually make the clinical distinction quite obvious.

Further work has also clarified the presumed genetic linkage between borderline patients and schizophrenia. Efforts to define the characteristics of those called "borderline schizophrenics" in prior research (the adoptive studies) led to the development of a new category (Gunderson et al. 1983; Spitzer et al. 1979). Rado (1962) and Meehl's (1962) old term *schizotypal personality* was revived to name this category (for review, see Siever and Gunderson 1983). Evidence accumulating supports the familial (Baron 1983; Kendler et al. 1981) and genetic (Torgersen 1984) link of this group to schizophrenia and fails to show any such linkage to borderline personality. The lack of a familial-genetic connection between borderlines and schizophrenia has been further indicated by a series of studies looking at the prevalence of psychiatric disorders in relatives of borderline patients (Gunderson and Elliott 1984). All have failed to show any evidence of an increased frequency of schizophrenia.

Studies on the course of borderline patients have failed to show any significant shift toward the schizophrenic diagnosis (Akiskal 1981; Carpenter et al. 1977; McGlashan 1984; Pope et al. 1983; Stone 1980; Werble 1970). McGlashan has reported that borderline patients have a better prognosis than schizotypals, and the latter group is more similar to schizophrenics. Koenigsberg et al. (1983) has noted that some recompensated schizophrenics may fulfill criteria for borderline personality disorder. This could represent a psychometric problem with structured diagnostic instruments that could easily be averted with good clinical judgment. It is also possible that some borderline patients may develop schizophrenia and then resume functioning in a typically borderline style after the flagrant signs of psychosis recede. If so, in my clinical experience, this is unusual.

Viewed in the light of this accumulating knowledge, there remains only weak support for the notion of a close linkage between borderline patients and schizophrenia. Despite earlier reservations (Siever and Gunderson 1979) about the development of a new category, schizotypal disorder, it has proven to be a helpful step toward the separation of the old "borderline schizophrenia" concept from the borderline personality category. Nonetheless, it is true that a patient diagnosed borderline by current criteria may occasionally go on to develop schizophrenia. In addition, in rare cases, schizophrenic patients may recompensate and appear to have a borderline personality.

Borderline as Part of an Affective Disorder Spectrum

The possible linkage of borderline personality to the affective disorders developed considerably later than the idea of a linkage to schizophrenia. Donald Klein (1975) was the first to suggest that the major linkage between borderline patients was to affective disorders—most notably to atypical forms of depression. Stone (1977) picked up this idea on the basis of his observations that many borderline patients from his practice had affectively ill relatives. Finding support in each other's work, and the subsequent preliminary reports from Akiskal (1981), both Klein (1977) and more extensively Stone (1979, 1980) and Stone et al. (1981) further explored this linkage. The development of DSM-III gave further impetus to this shift by restricting the usage of the schizophrenia diagnosis to an essentially Kraepelinian concept, while greatly expanding the criteria for affective disorders. By DSM-III definition, an estimated 40 percent of psychiatric patients now qualify for diagnoses of affective disorders (Spitzer et al. 1982).

In fact, the rapidly expanding data on both borderline personality and affective disorders suggest a complicated but peripheral relationship between these areas of psychopathology. To review this literature, I will summarize the state of information in a variety of areas from a much more extensive review available elsewhere (Gunderson and Elliott, 1984). Figure 2 illustrates an overall view of the interfaces between these categories.

Although there is enormous variance in the levels of concurrence between the disorders found from study to study, in most instances the levels are higher than expected by chance. The prediction that many borderline patients go on to develop more overt classic forms of affective disorder with time has failed to be confirmed by the recent follow-up studies. Most investigators have found that the borderline syndrome is stable over time. At present, it is still unclear whether the overall prognostic picture for borderline patients is closer to that of schizophrenia (e.g., Gunderson et al. 1975a) or affective disorders (e.g., McGlashan 1983b). Pope et al. (1983) showed that the presence of a concurrent affective disorder placed the prognosis somewhere in between.

The substantial series of studies that have examined the prevalence of psychiatric disorders in the relatives of borderline samples document some increase in the prevalence of affective disorders. However, the increase is not consistent from study to study, and generally is less than that found in relatives of affectively disordered probands. Moreover, the studies suggest that the affective disorders found in the relatives are unipolar depressions and specifically not in the bipolar categories, which have the heavier biogenetic implications.

Probably the most common form of affective disorder found in borderline patients is unipolar nonmelancholic depression (Charney et al. 1981). Nevertheless, there are borderline patients who do

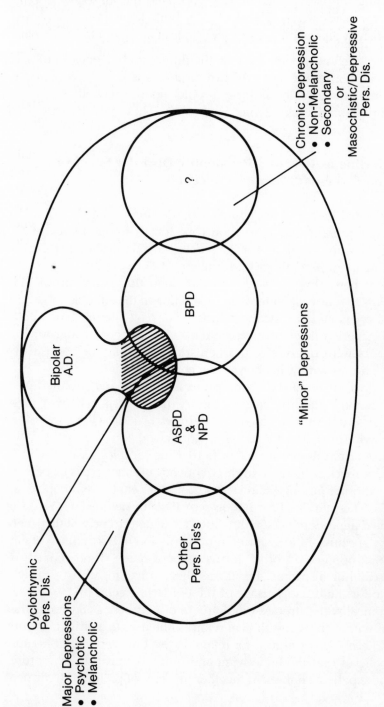

FIGURE 2. Borderline Personality Disorder and Affective Disorders

not have evidence of much depression, and thus the borderline syndrome cannot be understood simply as epiphenomena of, or secondary to, an underlying depression; that is, the syndrome can occur in the absence of any evidence of depression.

From a clinical point of view, the differential diagnosis problem between borderline and affective disorders is largely restricted to two subgroups of the latter—chronic, nonmelancholic dysphoric conditions and cyclothymic personality. These will be discussed later.

Borderline as Part of a Personality Disorder Spectrum ("Broad" versus "Narrow" Concepts)

As noted earlier (see Figure 1), borderline personality disorder would represent only a fraction (one-fourth to one-tenth) of the patients who would be considered to have borderline personality organization, as defined by Kernberg (1967). He has likened the present borderline category in DSM-III to that subgroup of BPO patients that he calls "infantile." In addition to the infantile subgroup, Kernberg would include most antisocial, "as-if," narcissistic, schizoid, cyclothymic, "impulse-ridden," and selected subgroups of patients with depressive-masochistic, histrionic, or compulsive personalities within his borderline concept.

In favor of Kernberg's concept, expert psychoanalytic therapists have noted little difference in the treatment responsivity of these patients, whether diagnosis is defined broadly (BPO) or more narrowly (BPD) (Waldinger and Gunderson 1984). Moreover, the studies of family prevalence of borderline samples have now indicated a marked increase in the frequency of other types of personality disorder among the relatives (Loranger et al. 1982; Pope et al. 1983). These studies have not been sufficiently detailed with respect to the diagnoses of personality disorder to determine whether there is any specificity in the familial transmission of borderline personality as opposed to other forms of personality disorder such as antisocial or histrionic. Insofar as they "travel together," it might argue for the broader usage of the borderline concept.

Ironically, the strongest indictment of Kernberg's concept comes from within the same clinical realm as he uses to justify it. On one side, Kernberg has argued for retaining this broader concept because he believes that the underlying and unifying intrapsychic features of these patients link them together in terms of preferred treatment techniques and what their course of psychotherapeutic treatment is likely to entail. I agree with many other psychoanalytic authors (Abend et al. 1983; Dickes 1974; Giovacchini 1979; Mack 1975; Meissner 1978a, 1978b; Robbins 1976) that this broad concept overlooks important distinguishing psychological features of these various subgroups that in turn have important therapeutic and prognostic implications. Even while impugning the overinclusiveness of the BPO concept, Abend et al. (1983) illustrated its hazards by drawing theoretical and therapeutic implications from patients with BPO that would be confusing and misleading when applied to patients with BPD. In fact, Kernberg (1975) himself identifies major prognostic differences for various subgroups of BPO patients, such as the general unresponsivity to psychotherapy of antisocial and cyclothymic patients. Elsewhere, there are other suggestions that BPD patients require quite different treatment techniques than those with narcissistic personality (Kohut 1971) and schizotypal personality (Stone 1983a).

There is also a growing number of studies outside the psychotherapeutic realm that are looking at the interface of BPD with other personality disorders. They have uniformly indicated that the borderline patients are descriptively discriminable (Frances et al. 1984; Koenigsberg et al. 1983; Sheehy et al. 1980; Spitzer et al. 1979). From a developmental point of view, there are suggestions that a narrower definition of borderline personality may identify patients with more pathological use of transitional objects (Morris et al. 1984). Finally, the narrow concept defines a group with a profile of defenses and conflicts that are discriminable from other personality disorders included within the broad BPO concept (Perry and Cooper 1983). These emerging data generally point to the value of the narrower concept of BPD. Whatever merits exist for a more inclusive concept, it is less confusing to use the term *severe character disorder* than to retain the BPO term.

DIFFERENTIAL DIAGNOSIS

In the following discussion, the relationship of borderline personality to other major forms of character pathology with whom differential diagnostic issues are common will be discussed. Figure 3 illustrates my impressions about the relationship of BPD to some of the categories that are discussed. It is difficult to do justice to

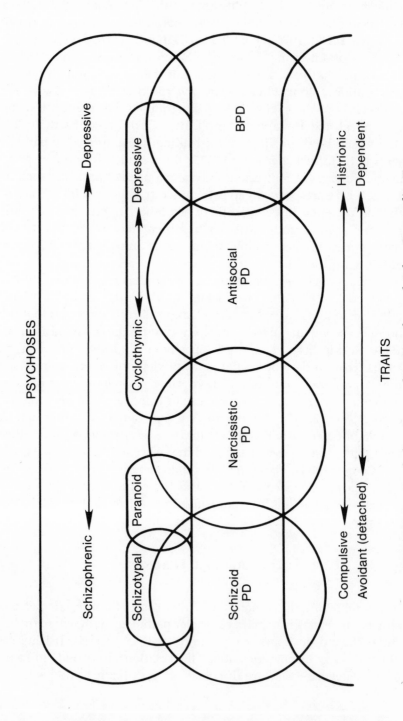

FIGURE 3. Borderline Personality Disorder and Other Personality Types

the complexity of this given a two-dimensional picture and the still-incomplete and rapidly expanding amount of information in this area.

Schizotypal Personality Disorder

Spitzer et al. (1979) originally separated the new schizotypal group from the borderline category. Their study and a later study by myself and colleagues (Gunderson et al. 1983) indicated a high frequency with which borderline patients fulfilled DSM-III schizotypal criteria. Both patient types have common problems in cognition and communication. Nevertheless, other work has suggested the overlap may not be as large as first expected (Frances et al. 1984; McGlashan 1983b). It is not common for schizotypal patients to have the borderline patient's dependent manipulative features. Moreover, newer data suggest that a shift in the emphasis within the DSM-III criteria for the schizotypal group provides for easy differentiation from borderline patients (Gunderson et al. 1983; Kendler 1984; Torgersen 1984). This work suggests that criteria of social isolation, affective detachment, somatic complaints, and aloof, suspicious relationships—rather than cognitive peculiarities—readily divides schizotypal from borderline patients. These revised criteria shift the differential diagnostic problems of schizotypal persons to the border with schizoid and avoidant (phobic) personality categories.

Nonmelancholic Depression

In terms of phenomenology, it is clear that the depressions of borderline patients will appear similar to those of patients with pure depression in many ways. These patient groups have in common the additional features of dependency, object hunger, and an awareness of social proprieties. Both may have transient, even dystonic, psychotic-like symptoms. Both are likely to have sustained feelings of worthlessness or hopelessness.

However, borderline patients are more apt to experience chronic feelings of boredom, loneliness, and emptiness than patients with other forms of depression. Moreover, the guilt, remorse, and failures in self-esteem of borderline patients reflect an unmodulated attack on the self as totally bad, thus lacking any of the partial or reasoned aspects of nonpsychotic depression based on either unconscious fantasy or real failure. Such overwhelming attacks on the self do not tend to be sustained as in psychotic depressions, but are much more likely to be reacted to impulsively, especially self-destructively, and by reactions in which the depression is alleviated by externalization or projections. These defenses cause failures to be attributed to mistreatment by significant others. These distinctions indicate that careful evaluation of the phenomenology and the dynamics of depressions in borderline patients may allow a sophisticated clinician to distinguish them from other depressions. Examining for the presence of other more divergent components of the borderline syndrome usually makes the differential diagnosis quite apparent.

Once again, the major differentiating feature of the borderline group vis-à-vis the depressive group is likely to be in their interpersonal relations, which are apt to be more stormy and marked by much clearer manipulativeness and hostility. Secondly, the borderline patient differs from the depressive in the use of impulsive activity, including the pattern of repetitive self-destructiveness. The latter is unusual in depressive patients—regardless of whether one's dynamic formulation emphasizes the self-destructiveness as an expression of a depressive experience or as a means of gaining control over an important object. Finally, most depressive patients are more comfortable acknowledging their wishes for (or actually having) a nurturant and supportive relationship with an idealized other. For borderline patients, such a longing is usually explicitly denied even while the longing is being enacted.

As noted elsewhere (Gunderson 1983c), DSM-III has lacked a category that reflects a dependent orientation but which did not have either the sexual overtones of the histrionic group or the angry, impulsive characteristics of the borderline category. Along this line, Kernberg (1981a) has advocated the restoration of a "depressive/masochistic" form of personality disorder. Kernberg noted that both the excessive superego and the social functioning of this group define a better prognosis for insight-oriented treatment than exists with most forms of personality disorder. In line with these recommendations, a masochistic personality category has been recommended for inclusion in the revisions of DSM-III. It remains to be seen whether this category can do for the boundary between borderline and depressive disorders what proved successful under similar circumstances with respect to the boundary between borderline personality and schizophrenia; namely, whether this category will allow the patients who sit on this boundary to be more cleanly discriminated from borderline patients descriptively while also helping to sort out those who have some familial, pharmacological, and prognostic affiliation to the depressive disorders. I suspect it may identify analyzable patients but will not help much with the borderline-chronic depressive boundary.

Cyclothymic Personality

The second area in which the affective disorders pose a problematic differential diagnosis is cyclothymic personality (bipolar type 2). In the presence of a clear history of intermittent hypomania, the differential diagnosis here is not too problematic. Nevertheless, many patients have periods of agitation and excitement not easily identified as cyclothymic. Akiskal (1981) first pointed to the overlap in this area while observing that many clinicians overlooked, and therefore underdiagnosed, cyclothymic disorder in patients they called borderline. Others, such as Jacobson (1953) and Kernberg (1967) saw striking intrapsychic similarities. From a phenomenologic point of view, both borderline and cyclothymic patients have enormous instability in their relationships, marked mood changes, frequent substance abuse, and other impulsive behaviors.

Intrapsychically, Perry and Cooper (1983) have suggested that the cyclothymic person is more apt to accept an explicit dependency on an idealized other and have far less separation or abandonment conflict than borderline patients. Moreover, their life is more apt to be filled with stable friendships and they will have less difficulty finding appropriate expressions of their anger and be less likely to feel that they are being unfairly thwarted.

Cyclothymic patients will often be consciously preoccupied with issues of self-control manifested in speech, sleep, food, and relationships. While the need of borderline patients for control in relationships can be inferred or can be convincingly found in uncovering treatments (see Chapter 3), this feature is more sustained, more conscious, and more directed toward symptoms like mood in cyclothymic patients. In addition, cyclothymic patients will have intermittent periods in which they have maintained grandiose views of themselves very similar to those of narcissistic patients. As a result, the cyclothymic person is likely to experience sustained feelings of well-being and to lack chronic dysphoric feelings of boredom or emptiness.

Narcissistic Personality Disorder

A great deal has been written in the recent literature seeking to clarify similarities and distinctions between borderline personality and narcissistic personality. In attempting to explain this, Millon (1981) has pointed out "as presented in contemporary psychoanalytic literature, both syndromes . . . lack clear clinical referents. . . . Difficulty of this sort does not exist in the diagnostic criteria spelled out in DSM-III. . . . Each is clearly delineated and comprehensible even to the clinical novice" (p. 174). Despite the distinctiveness between these syndromes as defined in DSM-III, the areas of similarity can still make these diagnoses difficult to differentiate in clinical practice. These areas include the predilection to anger and to psychotic ideation, sustained periods of boredom, and the hypersensitivity to personal hurt. In both, failures and rejections can lead to severe depressions. Finally, the exploitiveness that may be evident in the interpersonal relations of both groups adds to the potential for diagnostic confusion. As a result of such areas of overlap, most investigators have found both diagnoses (even by DSM-III criteria) are suitable for some patients (Frances et al. 1984; Kernberg et al. 1981; Koenigsberg 1982).

The overlap found in DSM-III may be less the result of intrinsic similarities than due to the absence of criteria sets that focus on the major areas in which the syndromes diverge. Thus narcissistic patients may show evidence of good role performance in contrast to the poor performance of most borderline patients. The narcissistic patient is likely to be arrogant or disdainful toward others and in constant need for appreciation and admiration by them. In contrast, the borderline patient's need from others is in the areas of availability and nurturance. The narcissistic patient's exploitiveness is part of an overall arrogance and is based on a sense of entitlement, whereas the borderline patient's exploitiveness is likely to be manipulative and based on a perceived need for survival.

Narcissistic patients are likely to have a grandiose view of themselves for which they require considerable admiration or appreciation by others; this view may be sustained through a relationship with an idealized other. Again, in contrast to narcissistic patients, borderline patients are likely to have a devalued view of themselves which is only mollified by the stable presence of a supportive other—someone who, in their case, is not seen in idealized terms.

Antisocial Personality Disorder

Borderline and antisocial personalities often overlap more commonly than has been recognized in the literature (Perry 1984). To some extent this would seem to be a product of overly broad inclusionary criteria for both diagnoses found in DSM-III (see Millon 1981 for an enlightened discussion of this). The preponderance of men among antisocial samples contrasts with the preponderance of women in borderline samples. This suggests that basic developmental problems shared by these groups are finding different manifestations due to the cultural forces that might lead men toward instrumental forms of gratification whereas women are more apt to turn to interpersonal clinging behaviors.

Clinically, both syndromes have in common impulsivity, failures to sustain socially productive roles, an intolerance of frustration, a high frequency of concurrent depressions, and manipulativeness. However, the manipulativeness in the antisocial person may be more calculating and successful than in the typical borderline patient whose manipulative actions are frequently generated by immediate stresses and are thus more desperate and self-destructive in nature. Antisocial acts by borderline patients are likely to be accompanied by either severe shame, if confronted, or justified on the basis of their felt needs for survival, whereas the antisocial person will experience these as ego syntonic. In recent work, Perry and Cooper (1983) showed strikingly heightened abandonment or separation conflict, object hunger, and conflicts about expressing needs and anger in borderline persons compared with an antisocial group. Another difference, highlighted in clinical descriptive accounts of the antisocial person, is the higher level of detachment and disaffiliation in interpersonal relationships compared with the borderline person. This is evident in the antisocial person's counterdependence and lack of personal loyalty.

Schizoid Personality Disorder

In contrasting the schizoid personality with the borderline personality, the outstanding differentiating characteristic concerns interpersonal relations. The schizoid group is socially isolated whereas the latter is typically engaged in intense, stormy relationships. Schizoid persons prefer solitary activity whereas borderline persons will actively try to avoid being alone.

The areas of potential overlap that might be initially confusing include psychotic-like ideation, role dysfunction, and interpersonal suspiciousness that may be apparent for both groups of patients. McGlashan's (1983b) work has suggested that a worse prognosis exists for the schizoid/schizotypal patient, an impression that dovetails with both Giovacchini's (1979) and Stone's (1983b) reports on the relatively poorer responsivity to psychotherapy by patients in the schizoid/schizotypal category compared with borderlines. Giovacchini makes the useful contrast that the schizoid person has largely given up on relationships and presents a treatment problem characterized by hopelessness in contrast to borderline patients who remain hopeful of being helped in a relationship but feel helpless to determine their own fate.

Histrionic Personality Disorder

There is an unfortunate overlap between the criteria in DSM-III for histrionic personality and for the borderline category. These criteria suggest a close relationship between the two in which the borderline group might be considered to be a more dysfunctional variant. Thus both groups tend to be dependent, manipulative, and affectively expressive. This overlap of criteria overlooks valuable and time-honored distinctions that have been set forth as means of differentiating out the hysteric (Chodoff and Lyons 1958; Marmor 1953; Zetzel 1968).

In line with such contributions, the criteria in DSM-III for histrionic category should be revised so as to reflect the greater stability and better function of this group. The criteria for both suicidal behavior and psychotic experiences will no longer be used to characterize the histrionic group. More critically, the central role of sexuality in the regulation of self-esteem and its overt interpersonal expressions in seductiveness, erotization, and rivalry with members of the same sex should become criteria for the histrionic group. The histrionic person's tendency to lose functions as a means of getting others to take responsibility is similar to the manipulativeness of borderline patients, but is less likely to take an explicitly self-destructive form. With respect to affect, the histrionic patient is not predominantly angry as with the borderline patient. Moreover, the histrionic patient may experience some periods of sustained well-being and pleasure.

GENERAL COMMENTS

Implicit in this chapter is an acceptance of the notion of categorical integrity for the borderline syndrome vis-à-vis the other types of disorder discussed. Even within the range of personality disorders, the distinctions in clinical phenomenology are reflecting meaningful differences in personality organization and therapeutic potential. However, in many instances the identifying features for these personality categories can and should be sharpened so as to highlight the discriminations and thereby diminish the unreliability in their use and improve their clinical utility. This does not argue against what Frances et al. (1984) have called a dimensional concept of personality disorders. On the contrary, it seems most reasonable to assume that all forms of psychopathology can only be described as approximations whose boundaries are inherently infirm. Nevertheless, the categorical concept may have validity as well as utility insofar as biological and environmental factors interact in ways for which there may be a discrete number of natural forms by which the serious disorders of character coalesce. This appears to be a viable and reasonable possibility.

The issue of whether the personality disorders are categories also can be raised from the perspective of level or degree of psychopathology. Here again it seems that the major character disorders lie in a midrange of psychopathology shading without a clearly perceptible boundary into the psychoses on the one side and personality trait disturbances on the other. These, in turn, continue to shade off into areas of more neurotic and eventually healthy personality functioning. At each step in this overall hierarchy from healthiest to sickest, the number of discrete options becomes more circumscribed and in some ways the subtlety and complexity of the personality becomes simplified. With respect to the personality diagnoses, there is a basic agreement between this scheme and that offered a decade ago by Kernberg's (1967, 1970) recommendation of a spectrum of character pathology, which he roughly divided into high-, middle-, and low-level subgroups. There is also a basic agreement with Stone's (1980) observations that the critical boundary toward more dysfunctional categories for borderline patients is with affective disorders rather than with schizophrenics. Conceptually, I am in agreement with Grinker et al. (1968) and Millon (1981) in thinking that clarification and understanding of personality disorders should be based on interpretation of observations from biological, genetic, interpersonal, and broader social perspectives of functioning (i.e., require a systems theory).

It remains unclear which forms of personality disorders should be considered "nearest neighbors" to the borderline category. As illustrated in Figure 3, in level of severity, the antisocial, schizoid, and narcissistic seem comparable. Categories such as paranoid, schizotypal, and cyclothymic are disorders mediating the boundary with the psychoses. The clinical discrimination of these groups has been addressed above. The boundary to less severe ("higher level") forms of personality disorder has been given less attention here and elsewhere in the literature. Some have suggested that narcissistic personality disorder should be considered in this direction (e.g., Adler 1981; Kohut and Wolf 1978; Rinsley 1982). I have indicated that I believe the histrionic personality and a type of masochistic personality (still to be established and overlapping with the dependent category in DSM-III) would be the most important neighbors on this side.

In the following chapters, the argument for the validity of the borderline diagnosis is reduced to its clinical utility. The recurrent and predictable clinical problems which clinicians encounter and which lie behind the enormous interest in the development of this category are described. In the final chapter, this point is returned to and expanded on as the critical cornerstone supporting the continued utilization of the borderline diagnosis.

2

Psychodynamic Formulations

A traditional means by which psychoanalysts bring their special perspective to bear on classification is through their efforts to identify patterns to underlying personality that make a clinical syndrome coherent and understandable. Disturbingly little attention was given to these perspectives in the development of the DSM-III psychiatric classification system (Frances and Cooper 1981; Gunderson 1983c; Kernberg 1981a; Michaels 1984; Vaillant 1984). With respect to borderline personality disorder, its inclusion in DSM-III was more the result of the syndrome having been clarified (see Chapter 1) than it was due to the extensive psychoanalytic studies of the intrapsychic characteristics of these patients. The cost for this is that DSM-III criteria are inconsistent in their ability to capture the underlying internal psychological coherence of the borderline person's personality (Gunderson 1983c).

This chapter presents a means of organizing and understanding why the seemingly disparate characteristics of borderline patients cluster together and why they shift in the sequences that are observed clinically. The validity of this syndrome as a diagnostic category can be supported by delineating such underlying psychodynamic features that are specific to the concept of a borderline personality disorder. Because this psychodynamic formulation is tightly linked to the clinical phenomena that compose this syndrome, it offers a means of understanding borderline patients that is intended to be more specific than existing theories.

The central observation in this chapter is that the major clinical characteristics of patients with borderline personality disorder can be understood as reactive to the presence and nature of the borderline person's major interpersonal relationships. This formulation makes the following contributions or revisions with respect to other conceptualizations. First, shifts in phenomenology are considered central to defining the borderline category rather than an emphasis on the more inferential, but more stable, underlying principles of personality organization. Second, the unifying psychodynamic coherence, and therefore the validity of the borderline syndrome as a specific form of personality disorder, is supported by the predictable patterns of interpersonal response. Third, shifts in phenomenology are attributed to changing levels of ego function and shifting types of defense rather than relying heavily on the concepts of splitting or projective identification. Fourth, a broader developmental framework is inferred and the usefulness of a specific developmental arrest as a means of explaining adult borderline psychopathology is challenged.

LINKING DEFINITIONS TO THEORY

As noted in Chapter 1, the syndrome of borderline personality disorder (BPD) represents only one of the several forms of serious character pathology that Kernberg (1967, 1975, 1977) had grouped within the umbrella concept of borderline personality organization (BPO). According to Kernberg, severe forms of character pathology have in common the following three characteristics: (a) identity diffusion, (b) the predominance of primitive defenses, and (c) reality testing. Identity diffusion has to do with the failure to establish some stable internal sense of one's self. This can be manifest in problems of body image, polymorphous sexual activity, and dramatically fluctuating views of one's self, as well as the general dependence of the self view and behavior on contextual determinants. Stone (1982) has adopted this as the central prerequisite feature for the borderline diagnosis. As noted in Chapter 1, problems exist with its assessment and specificity. Concerning the predominance of primitive defenses, Kernberg particularly emphasizes the diagnostic value of the defenses of splitting, denial, and projective identification in borderline patients. In a study of BPD patients, Perry and Cooper (1983) have reported a modest level of specificity of this and other constellations of defenses vis-à-vis two other personality categories, which Kernberg would include as BPO. This work suggests that these types of defenses are more common to a narrower patient population than encompassed by BPO. Patients with severe character pathology have generally intact reality testing in contrast to those with psychosis. However, this ego function may transiently fail in periods of stress in contrast to people with healthier personalities.

These three identifying psychological characteristics of patients with severe character disorders are expected by Kernberg (1977, 1981b) to portray stable patterns of function that allow them to be differentiated from psychotics or neurotics. These features do not provide a basis for differentiating BPD patients from those with other forms of serious character disorder. As noted in Chapter 1, many authors have criticized the broadness of the BPO concept and have called for more specific formulations of borderline patients that would allow them to be differentiated from other forms of severe character disorder (Abend et al. 1983; Dickes 1974; Liebowitz 1979; Mack 1975; Meissner 1978a, 1978b; Robbins 1976; Sugarman and Lerner 1980). It is paradoxical that Kernberg himself (1967, 1971, 1981a) has been among the most articulate observers in pointing out how the various severe forms of character disorder differ from each other descriptively, prognostically, and in response to psychotherapeutic treatments.

The common and still growing number of descriptive and psychological studies noting major differences between the various forms of severe character disorder point to the need for more specific psychological formulations to inform and validate the narrower borderline concept and other major forms of character disorder.

What follows is an effort to describe the specific and discriminating psychological features that discriminate borderline patients from the broader range of patients with severe characterologic disturbances, and to draw from the enormous psychoanalytic literature on this subject those accounts that apply to this narrower group.

DYNAMICS OF BORDERLINE PERSONALITY DISORDER: THREE LEVELS OF FUNCTION

Of the various conceptual approaches to borderline personality cited by Meissner (1978b), the following formulation is within the framework of object relations and ego psychology. It begins with empirically established phenomena and then attempts to take into consideration and account for the unstable and rapid changes in these phenomena. The dynamics of these changes are the material that psychoanalytically oriented therapists are preoccupied with and, as such, the formulation remains closely tied to the clinical situation.

This formulation emphasizes the degree to which the borderline person's manifest psychopathology can be understood in terms of relationships to major objects. The term *major object* will be used to refer to any significant current relationship perceived as necessary. In the following section, the borderline person's current relationships to the three levels of psychological functioning are observed. Lower levels of psychological function emerge regressively and act to preserve a sense of contact with and control over major object relationships (see Table 2).

Level I

When a major object is present and supportive, the depressive, bored, and lonely features predominate. Here the borderline person is at the first and best level of function. It is characterized by considerable conscious longing for closer attachment but considerable passivity and failure to initiate greater sharing within the context of the relationships. There is a capacity here to reflect on past failures and to identify conflicts and resistances realistically. There remains, however, considerable concern about the object's

TABLE 2.   Levels of the Borderline's Function

Subjective Experience of Primary Object	Clinical Phenomena	Therapeutic Response
Supportive	Dysphoria Depression Masochism	Interpret
Frustrating	Anger Manipulation Devaluation	Interpret Confront Limit
Absent	Panic Impulsivity Psychosis	Provide Intrude

fragility and concurrent fears of being controlled by becoming dependent. As Kernberg (1975) has pointed out, such concerns reflect fears of projected hostility. The wary expectation of being controlled can be used as an active attempt to gain control over others. The result is that a dysphoric stalemate exists in relationships, which is periodically disrupted by regressive efforts to provoke reassurance from the other or by progressive initiatives to acknowledge what they want and feel they need from that person more fully.

Two major organizing and sustaining beliefs are: "Should I want more from you, or should I be angry at you, you will leave" and "If I'm compliant, something will be given to me that will make me invulnerable and less destructive." The nature of this "something" is generally not well defined. Behind these conscious beliefs are concerns with the destructiveness of their own aggressive wishes and wishes to find a powerful protector. In any event, the basic tension between wanting more from the object and fearing that less will be received accounts for the sustained dysphoria characteristic of borderline functioning at this level.

Within treatment contexts, these features of the borderline's personality disorder will be evident during uninterrupted phases of therapy (even more evident in the middle of hours), and likewise when such patients are offered considerable autonomy within supportive residential treatment settings. During these periods, patients will generally be able to work collaboratively with an active therapist toward fuller affective expression and insight (i.e., accept interpretations). The resistances most commonly encountered are the patient's passive compliance, accompanied by failure to initiate contact, bring in new material, and so on. This often occurs in response to activity by the therapist that is experienced as directive or helpful. Such compliance and failures to initiate often contain a covert demand that the therapist do more. Another resistance arises after having shared new material or affect; then the patient withdraws and becomes defiant. Such sharing is accompanied by fears that there will be a loss of control, that they will give in to their passive wishes, and that, if either of these fears is actualized, the therapist will then respond exploitatively. These represent threats to the illusion of control over the therapist which sustains the patient on this level. The overt expression of these concerns is an increased fear of being controlled and an openly defiant posture.

Within residential settings, impatience and fears of giving too much gratification (secondary gain) are common feelings among staff working with borderline patients who are functioning within this level. Treatment personnel are likely to overestimate a patient's strengths and try to stir patients into better social functioning and more independence. There is frequently a failure to recognize and interpret, especially to less verbal patients, the degree to which their passivity reflects fears of losing control over their affects and the degree to which their compliance silently hides their belief that their object is under their control. Under such circumstances, it is difficult to appreciate and anticipate the extreme sensitivity to rejection that becomes evident when either greater autonomy or separation is encouraged.

Level II

When a major object is frustrating to borderline persons or when the specter of their loss is raised, a second level of psychological functioning and a different constellation of clinical phenomena are evident. The angry, devaluative, and manipulative features predominate. Although the affective tone of anger is pervasive, it is only occasionally expressed as open rage. More frequently, it takes a modified form such as biting sarcasm, belligerent argumentativeness, or extreme demands. The anger is modified to alleviate fears of losing the object (in reality as well as its mental representation), while it still communicates the wish to maintain a hold on the person. Failing this, the patient can attempt to deny the fear of loss by dismissing the felt need for the object (i.e., devaluation) or attempt to prevent loss by dramatizing the object need. Manipulative suicide gestures are frequent under these circumstances. At its extreme, when there is danger of the anger becoming too uncontrolled, the rage gets projected onto the object and paranoid accusations occur. All of these reactions are best understood as efforts, often conscious, to control or coerce the object into staying.

These issues—to feel the need for a reliably available other and to feel able to control that person—have not changed from the higher level. Rather it is the repertoire of defenses and their behavioral expression that undergo regression and are most specific to the borderline patient. These reactions continue as long as the object is still perceived as accessible or retainable. The disabling effects of anticipated loss can frequently be seen as the patient struggles to find some acceptable expression of its attendant affects.

This can take the form of rather elaborated and poorly connected affective states—giggling, bland dismissals, sudden rages, and, of course, extreme lability. The distinctive feature is the dissembled unsustained quality of the affects.

Within treatment contexts, these features of the borderline's psychopathology become evident only when the treating person, or institution, has assumed the role of a major object (i.e., is felt as needed by the patient). When the object is felt as needed, these regressive phenomena emerge whenever separations are imminent (i.e., terminations, vacations, and end of hours). They also take place within the psychotherapy hours themselves whenever the therapist is seen as being inattentive, withholding, or inaccurate. The borderline patient's elaborate efforts to prevent separations and sudden anger at or withdrawal from frustrations are critical features in the treatment of borderlines. These features have been a focus of most authors who have primarily been concerned with analytic therapy (Adler 1975; Giovacchini 1973; Kernberg 1968; Masterson 1972) (see Chapter 6). Under these circumstances, borderline patients will frequently dismiss a therapist's interpretative or clarificatory efforts (e.g., to point out how this current view of the therapist is discrepant with a previous one). The therapist's primary task is to interrupt the patient's anger enough to draw attention to the provoking incident. This often requires confrontation or limit setting. Such responses address the change of feeling and attitude as a regressive retreat from some reality that the patient wishes to avoid. It preserves and calls on the patient to utilize still intact ego functions of reality testing and self-observation. It is not that the expressions of anger at the therapist's failure are not critically important in themselves; it is that the transformed rage (i.e., devaluation, manipulation, or paranoid accusations) utilizes defenses of denial, acting out, and projection, which prevent the patient's recognition of the feeling response and its reason. I believe this helps understand why many experienced therapists have found it futile to allow borderline patients to spend much time in this preferred mode of angry expressiveness.

Once the regressive efforts are interrupted, interpretative work directed at the devaluation ("You're working hard not to know what you want" or "You're afraid to want things from me which you can't control"), the manipulation ("You're trying to exert control over me without risking that it will provoke my anger" or "You want to prevent me from being unavailable"), or the projection

("You're mad at me for not always being available" or "You're afraid of how enraged you might be with me") can be accepted and worked with. An insistent examination of the importance a patient places on the therapist's presence brings to light separation anxieties and forces a greater awareness of fears of experiencing the impotent helplessness that are a realistic part of relationships.

Because this second level of psychological function occurs within the therapeutic context, and while the patient's communications still remain directed to a specific object, the analysis of its purpose and form is a critical part of psychotherapy.

Level III

When a borderline person feels an absence or lack of any major object, then a third level of psychological function becomes predominant. The phenomena during such periods include the occurrence of brief psychotic episodes, panic states, or impulsive efforts to avoid such panic. These phenomena each represent efforts to ward off the subjective experience of aloneness (Adler and Buie 1979a) and, I would add, total badness.

Under ordinary circumstances, this aspect of the borderline patient's psychology is evident in the need to have people around—even if without any evident emotional contact, in using radio and television as hypnotics, or in heavy reliance on transitional objects (Arkema 1981; Morris et al. 1984). Under the more extreme circumstances when there has been a loss of a specific and essential object relationship, dangerous impulsive acts occur that most commonly consist of taking drugs or alcohol. These serve both to numb the panic and to initiate social contacts. Fights and promiscuity occur under these circumstances—often assisted by the disinhibiting influence of the drugs or alcohol—and reflect desperate efforts to establish contact with and to revive the illusion of control over some new objects.

A second major type of reaction against the experience of aloneness is a prolonged dissociative episode of either the depersonalization or derealization types. These detach the borderline person from either the reality of bodily distress or the reality of the environmental situation that evokes that intolerable distress. During dissociative episodes, nihilistic fears occur ("am I dead, has my body dissolved"), and these may give rise to self-mutilation in order to confirm being alive by feeling pain. Frequently, such self-mutilation is accompanied by restitutive fantasies in which the absent object is either believed to be performing the act or is being punished by the act, but in either event is still involved. These self-mutilative actions are quite different in their intent and subjective experience from the suicidal gestures that occur when ongoing contact with a specific object is still being sought (Chapter 5).

Sometimes nihilistic ideas slip from dystonic fears to become beliefs; they then take on aspects of psychotic depressions. The conviction of being evil and nihilistic beliefs are two extremes that the borderline patient achieves when the usual defenses of action and substitutive objects are not available. Presumably, it is in reference to such phenomena that Kernberg (1967) refers to the borderline's very primitive punitive superego. Masterson (1972, 1976) talks of the underlying, generally avoided, abandonment depression as central to his formulations. Perhaps because of the amount of interpersonal involvement and the borderline person's dramatic responsivity to such involvement, sustained depressions of psychotic proportions are unusual in borderline patients, particularly for those who are in treatment settings.

Occasionally, bizarre imagery, simple hallucinatory phenomena, or transient somatic delusions occur. The object restitutive aspect of these experiences is often painfully evident (e.g., the patient who developed the belief she was pregnant, or the patient who developed anal and urethral retentiveness requiring emergency room care). The most common delusional experience is ideas of reference. Not only do these project unacceptable self-judgments, they sustain a sense of involvement with nonspecific others where none exists. The general point here is that the various phenomena associated with this lowest level of function (desperate impulsivity, substance abuse, dissociative episodes, brief psychotic episodes, and ideas of reference) represent efforts to manage the fear of aloneness and the sense of badness. This badness is related to beliefs that they have failed or wronged their object.

These experiences of alone–badness and the panicky reactions to it are seldom seen within the hospital or psychotherapeutic context. As described subsequently (Chapter 7), they do, however, often come to the attention of clinicians as a reason for seeking treatment or as phenomena described retrospectively by borderline patients. Understanding the context in which they occur is important so that their recurrence can be anticipated and avoided. The resolution of the cause of these phenomena must await a softening of such a person's view of the self as destructive and the acquisition of object constancy.

The borderline patient's felt relatedness to a major object directly reflects relatedness to reality. When the patient feels in contact with an essentially supportive object, the reality sense is intact. When this object tie is threatened, the patient's relationship to reality is shaky but the reality testing remains intact. When, in this third level of function, there is a felt absence of a primary object, the reality-testing function itself becomes shaky or, as in the dissociative reactions, the feeling of reality is disrupted. Here, however, the reality-testing function is readily recovered in the presence of a sustaining object. A related issue is the borderline patient's relationship to external structures. Here too, fluctuations in the borderline patient's phenomenology can be directly affected by the current status of external structures—structures can serve the same ameliorating effect as an object relationship. Such observations are critical in terms of managing the therapeutic situation so as to respond sensitively to the patient's changing relationship to objects and the changing capacity for reality testing (see Chapter 7). Thus the patient experiencing prolonged dissociative reactions should be contained in a residential setting where involvement is required. If a patient can experience hallucinatory phenomena in the therapist's office, it is a signal that the therapist's leverage as a primary object tie is not established. Kernberg (1971) noted how the transference psychosis of borderline patients can be reversed by increasing structure either in therapy or in the patient's life situation. Similarly, transference distortions can be diminished by increasing the degree of object contact by conjoint meetings with the primary objects from the nuclear family (Shapiro et al. 1977).

RELATIONSHIP TO OTHER FORMULATIONS

The phenomena described as part of the three levels of functioning and the shifts between them are easily recognized by persons who have worked extensively with borderline patients. They derive from the same background of clinical observations from which previous attempts to formulate theories about borderline patients have been drawn.

By its emphasis on the observable changing patterns seen in the clinical situation, it has little to add to what Kernberg has said about more stable but more inferential underlying organization of such personalities. Problems with identity and the vulnerability in reality testing are clearly persistent. Even the central issues of interpersonal control, object availability, and convictions of badness do not change; rather it is the repertoire of defenses and resulting phenomenology that change dramatically and predictably. These regressive changes provide a means of managing these persistent central issues in the face of interpersonal frustration or loss. This formulation rests closer to the surface phenomenology and is more interpersonal than Kernberg's. As described later, it does not rely as heavily on defenses of splitting and projective identification. Moreover, it gives less emphasis to the innateness and the pervasiveness of aggression than does Kernberg, and it gives more credence to the positive object-directed motives of borderline patients.

In addition to Kernberg's effort to describe underlying features of the borderline personality organization of these patients already noted, this formulation obviously has a great deal in common with Mahler's (1971) and subsequently Masterson's (1972) emphasis on the role of libidinal availability and abandonment experiences of borderline patients. From yet a third theoretical perspective, this formulation easily joins the emphasis given by Buie and Adler (1982) to the central problems in tolerating aloneness and failures of object constancy. Thus in many respects this formulation represents more of a reshuffling or reordering of the same set of observations drawn on by others rather than a radical departure from them. Having said this, there remain some ideologic differences. This formulation gives the aggressive motives a far more central role than do Buie and Adler. By fitting between the extremes offered by Kernberg and Buie and Adler, it partially bridges a gap noted in the previous reviews of these theories by Robbins (1976) and Shapiro (1978a)— namely, the need for a theory that adequately encompasses both the angry, aggressive behaviors and the compliant masochistic behaviors of borderline patients. Some of the clinical implications of this way of viewing aggression are spelled out elsewhere (see Chapter 6). It departs from Masterson by not utilizing either the concepts of withdrawing and rewarding part object representations and by not positing an underlying warded-off abandonment depression.

At first glance, the alternation between the first and second levels of function described in this formulation bears some descriptive similarity to the alternation between the "depressive position" (Klein

1950; Winnicott 1958) and the "paranoid" or "schizoid position" (Klein 1932, 1946; Fairbairn 1946). However, despite the fact that the first and highest level of function described above involves capacities for introspection, ambivalence, and concern, these masquerade the borderline person's underlying dependency on the presence of a supportive major object and the coexisting failures to achieve object constancy. Clearly this is not the depressive position that Klein and Winnicott had in mind. Moreover, the attachment even on this level of function involves beliefs in omnipotent control over a supportive object. This observation suggests the applicability of the concepts of either a concurrent self-object form of attachment (Kohut 1966, 1971) or a form of transitional object relatedness (Winnicott 1953). In other words, existing side by side with these changes in phenomenology that are related to the presence and quality of the person's relationship to major objects is an attachment to an object based on its positive soothing potential.

Modell (1963) offered a theoretical perspective on borderlines that emphasized their developmental arrest at the level of transitional object relations. His efforts to correlate the transference phenomena of borderline patients to a specific primitive form of object relatedness agrees with many of the observations made in this chapter. The theory, however, is based on a developmental fixation that seems too specific and hence fails to account for the broad range and specific pattern of phenomena in patients with this disorder. Recent empirical studies support the idea that borderline patients actually have heavier usage of transitional objects in their lives than do other personality-disordered patients (Arkema 1981; Morris et al. 1984). Thus Modell's theory receives indirect empirical support and offers a means of understanding why borderline patients are more apt to seek treatment and cling dependently to a therapist than are the other equally dysfunctional forms of character pathology.

Ekstein and Wallerstein (1954) referred to a group of borderline children characterized by shifting levels of ego organization. These children fluctuate between a reality-oriented, although painfully troubled form of ego organization in which objects exist outside the self to a more primitive form or ego organization in which there is a loss of self–object differentiation and a withdrawal into idiosyncratic fantasy. Ekstein (1966) pointed out how the higher level of ego organization appeared when the child was in contact with a benign object (therapist), but the movement to fantasy occurred when contact was lost with the object (therapist). Pine (1974) subsequently noted, as I have here, that the lower level of organization serves as a regressive defense from painful inner or outer realities and serves to avoid panic. These processes are clearly similar to the observations on adult borderline patients I have described, except that the regressive dedifferentiation is not associated with retreat into fantasy so much as a retreat into typical behavioral efforts to control objects omnipotently or to replace them magically. Pine stated that such children form one subgroup of those who have serious personality problems (i.e., those children whose disorder is neither psychotic nor neurotic). Obviously, it seems to parallel that subgroup of adult characterologically disturbed patients whose syndrome and dynamic characteristics are described above.

Frosch (1964, 1970) paid particular attention to the psychotic vulnerability in such patients and what makes them different from patients who are psychotic. The only addition I have offered to what he has said about the ego's position vis-à-vis reality is to highlight the contextual determinants of this position and to define further the defensive purposes for which this position changes. Although Frosch paid less extensive attention to examining other areas of fluctuating but highly related functioning such as object relations, I believe the patients he calls psychotic characters would usually be included within those who fit the descriptive and dynamic characteristics of patients with BPD. However, it is likely that other patients with severe character pathology—including some schizoid, "as if," "false self," paranoid, narcissistic, and schizotypal persons—could have problems with reality similar to what Frosch described without the characteristic object relations of borderline patients.

DEVELOPMENTAL CONSIDERATIONS

Mahler (1971) first drew attention to. the parallels between the adult borderline's transference relationships and the childhood issues in the rapprochement subphase. She and later other object-relations theorists (Masterson and Rinsley 1975; Rinsley 1977; Zinner and Shapiro 1975) have emphasized the central role of maternal libidinal availability as the developing infant seeks to become autonomous. The observations on adult borderline patients operating on the first and second levels of function clearly document such hypersensitivity to separation experiences. Masterson and Rinsley (1975) and Zinner and Shapiro (1975) have indicated that this failure to navigate successfully through the rapprochement subphase reflects failures of the maternal object to provide sufficient libidinal support. While agreeing with the importance of this phase, Kernberg (1980) noted that the developmental failure can be due either to insufficient maternal support or to excessive, perhaps constitutional genetically based, needs on the part of the child.

A thoughtful review of the levels of function observed in borderline patients indicates developmental issues must be extended both earlier and later than the rapprochement subphase. Mahler (1971) herself recognized this and subsequently documented instances in which children with severe developmental problems in the rapprochement subphase failed to grow up to be borderline, whereas others who had no discernible problem during this subphase grew up to be typically borderline (Mahler and Kaplan 1977). In this respect, the phenomena observed during Level III specifically point to the need to encompass a role for unresolved symbiotic issues in developmental theory. A central role for symbiotic issues has been identified by a number of authors (Giovacchini 1973; Horner 1975; Robbins 1976; Searles 1977). Moreover, whatever the impairments in psychic function derived from early development, important strengths that reflect later developmental learning coexist. In this regard, the observations on families have suggested their important ongoing role throughout the course of development in shaping the personality that becomes borderline (see Chapter 9). The role of the family appears to include at least two major patterns, one of which involves major, lifelong libidinal unavailability, that is, neglect (Gunderson et al. 1980; Walsh 1977). The other, as noted above, may involve the active withdrawal (Masterson and Rinsley 1975) or the inconsistent presence (Shapiro et al. 1975) of libidinal availability at critical times in development.

In summary, developmental theories that attempt to explain the pathogenesis of borderline personality disorder on the basis of a phase-specific, parent–child interactional failure are bound to be inadequate. The nature of the borderline patient's psychopathology is such that the shaping influences extend to multiple phases of development. Kohut and Wolfe (1978) closely approximate these impressions by citing the overwhelming importance of chronic familial ambience and attitudes compared to events—even events that are traumatic—on the developing personality.

OBSERVATIONS ON SPLITTING

The concept of splitting is defined as the inability to synthesize contradictory good and bad self or other representations. Much of the borderline patient's psychopathology has been attributed to this (Kernberg 1967; Masterson 1975; Shapiro et al. 1975). The rapidly changing phenomenology of borderlines is seen as the product of a developmental fixation in object relations, which determines grossly discrepant attitudes or behavior.

Since 1967, Kernberg has written most persuasively about the central role of splitting as a defense in borderline patients, which is a primary cause of their ego weaknesses. He notes four major forms in which splitting is clinically manifest: (a) as alternative expressions of complementary sides of a conflict combined with bland denial and lack of concern over the contradiction in behavior and internal experience; (b) a selective lack of impulse control with episodic breakthrough of primitive impulses that are ego-syntonic during the time of their expression; (c) the division of external objects into "all good" ones and "all bad" ones; and (d) extreme and repetitive oscillation between contradictory "all good" and "all bad" perceptions of others.

Regrettably, the concept of splitting has become widely and sometimes indiscriminately applied both to the clinical phenomena that Kernberg has identified and to others as well. Clinicians need to be alert to this and, especially with respect to the latter three of these clinical manifestations, they should consider alternative explanations for these clinical phenomena. With respect to the second of Kernberg's four clinical manifestations of splitting (selective lack of impulse control), there is a danger that the concept of splitting leads one to view impulsive behaviors as relatively unpurposeful breakthroughs of impulses driven from behind by instincts, rather than as multidetermined reactions to identifiable contextual events (see Frosch 1977), which are specifically, if unconsciously, designed to diminish the experience of object loss or frustration. With respect to the third manifestation (dividing members of an object field into good and bad), it remains unclear whether the borderline patient randomly selects people for either the "all good" projections or the "all bad" projections, as opposed to being exaggerated responses to either gratifying or frustrating qualities within the object itself (see Chapter 8). The latter possibility is clinically significant insofar as, if it is true (as I believe), it means that neither the good nor the bad perceptions of others are failures to recognize and respond to realistic qualities in others.

Kernberg's fourth clinical manifestation of splitting involves extreme vacillations between seeing others in idealized "all good" and devalued "all bad" terms. The impression this conveys is of two totally oppositional views of the object, which alternate depending on unclear but dramatic shifts in the patient's intrapsychic regulation and which do not allow the patient any neutralized area in which to view the other in terms other than "all good" or "all bad." The major difficulties with this view are its failure to describe what accomplishes this shift (i.e., some form of ego regulatory mechanism) and what precipitates the shifts (i.e., the environmental context). It also gives an impression that idealization is more common in borderline patients than, in my experience, actually occurs. Several studies have indicated that, in fact, idealization is not common among borderline patients (Gunderson and Kolb 1978; Lerner and Lerner 1980). It may well be that the attention given idealization in the earlier literature reflects the overly broad application of borderline concept to patients who might better be classified as having narcissistic personality in whom such idealization is more typical. A final reservation about the use of splitting to explain rapid alternations in the view of significant others by borderline patients has already been noted; namely, in periods of extreme frustration and anger, borderline patients retain perception of the object as valued and important and thus more ambivalently perceive their object than the concept of splitting implies.

The concept of splitting, when erroneously applied, can lead clinicians to oversimplify the phenomena they are observing and invalidate the complex interaction between external reality and internal projections that commonly exist. This may be the most harmful when the borderline patient's perception of "badness" in others is invalidated by its being written off as manifesting a primitive expression of drive or as a primitive defense against reality (see Chapter 6).

DISCUSSION

A formulation of borderline personality disorder that emphasizes the dynamics of shifting levels of psychological function seen both within and outside the psychotherapeutic context is offered. This contribution helps define the specific contextual determinants for these shifts. It attempts to explain the occurrence of the major discriminating characteristics of borderline patients and to specify the ways in which such patients differ intrapsychically from patients with some other major form of character pathology. This chapter suggests that the borderline category should be reserved for persons with a specific, stable form of personality disorder that is discernible descriptively and whose descriptive characteristics can be understood dynamically.

Unlike other psychoanalytic theories for borderline patients, the framework for this contribution began with empirical efforts to define an adult syndrome and has secondarily examined the behaviors of such persons within therapeutic contexts. Moreover, there has been little effort to integrate these adult observations with specific developmental failures. Paradoxically, the efforts to formulate a theory for borderline patients that encompass all midlevel forms of character pathology have often been tied to some specific and narrow developmental stages, whereas this theory is intended to apply to a narrower adult syndrome but requires a broader developmental base. The broader developmental base includes a likely role for constitutional factors as they interact with early parenting and for the important effects of the ongoing patterns of family interaction throughout development. The price of such broadness is that it offers little hope for finding specific origins to the borderline patient's dynamics.

This formulation remains incomplete and obscure about several major issues. The narcissistic issues of borderline patients require clearer elucidation. Although the concept of a transitional object seems more compatible with the observations on the dependency and separation sensitivity of borderline patients than does the concept of a self-object, the distinction between these two concepts is murky. It is especially confusing to sort out those aspects of the borderline's functioning that are reactive to narcissistic injury from those that reflect compensatory efforts to prevent object loss. Although the concepts of instincts and pathological splitting have been deemphasized, this formulation is not intended to dismiss their importance—only to suggest the need for a reevaluation of their role. For example, it remains unclear whether such phenomena of borderline patients as dissociative reactions or all-or-none thinking (Schulz 1980) can best be understood by invoking the concept of splitting.

Further work is necessary to help recognize psychotic vulnerability in borderline patients who do not present with a clear history of brief psychoses. Finally, this formulation has not attended to the variable forms of ego defect involved in impulse discharge and affect tolerance.

The major impetus of this formulation is the concept of ego as an active, resourceful, and responsive agency that is consistently and vigilantly helping the borderline person to maintain connection with and control over the objects considered to be essential. At its best, the ego can accept and work toward greater autonomy while, at its worst, it permits psychotic means of restoring objects that are lost. It is not a defective ego overwhelmed by hypertrophied aggression expressed in unrealistic demands that are in need of taming so much as it is a deformed ego that maladaptively but purposively directs behavior and organizes perceptions. Major defensive patterns of the ego include the regressive use of grandiose and omnipotent fantasy, impulsive actions, and the loss of reality testing. The mechanics by which the regressive loss of reality testing occur include the invocation of more primitive defenses such as splitting, denial, projection, and dissociation.

Although schematic, this formulation describes patterns in the relationships among the descriptive characteristics, object relations, and levels of psychological function of borderline patients. It is hoped that this contribution offers a step toward the development of a more specific theory for the psychological functioning of those persons having a borderline syndrome. The development of such a theory offers an important source of validating evidence for the establishment of this syndrome as a specific personality disorder.

3

Psychotherapy:
Clinical Considerations

COUNTERTRANSFERENCE

The subject of countertransference rightly belongs at the start of a discussion on psychotherapeutic principles and practices with borderline patients. Much of the literature on psychotherapy with borderline patients has been permeated with discussions of countertransference issues and the subject will be returned to throughout this book in discussing specific clinical dilemmas. Its prominence is deserved in view of the inevitably strong emotional responses in therapists that borderline patients evoke.

The term *countertransference* is used here to encompass the broad variety of emotional and attitudinal responses by therapists. Its narrower definition emphasizing only the unconscious reactions to the transference are relevant to borderline patients, but account for only a rather minor portion of the characteristically intense reactions evoked. These intense emotional reactions are often to fully conscious aspects of the therapeutic situation (e.g., interactions involving dangers to the patient or the therapist's safety, self-esteem, or sense of control). With more disturbed patients, leading clinicians like Fromm-Reichmann (1950), Will (1959), Kernberg (1965), Giovacchini (1979), and Searles (1979a), have accepted the fact that emotional neutrality is not only unlikely, but if present probably reflects a serious countertransference problem. There remains, however, little consensus on whether or how such emotional reactions should be introduced or made an explicit aspect of the therapist's communications.

Therapists working with borderline patients must adapt ways of responding to the intense and immediate transference demands. These adaptations are complex products of their personality style, of their training and level of experience, and of the more discrete vulnerabilities of their unconscious conflicts about such issues as dependency, sadism, or authority. The relatively stable but quite diverse styles that experienced therapists evolve for working with borderline patients involve some unique balance between these forces. Psychoanalytic theory has helpfully identified how departures from technical or emotional neutrality often reflect countertransference problems in working with healthier patients. However, no such guideline is available in working with borderline patients where the range of emotional reactions and needed techniques are broader. That this is the case makes it confusing and hazardous to point with much certainty at what behaviors constitute evidence of countertransference problems. Indeed, the whole style under which one or another expert psychotherapist carries out his or her work may be viewed as evidence of countertransferential problems by other experts. A therapist advocating more supportive techniques may be viewed as evidencing countertransferential fear of anger and, conversely, therapists advocating more confrontative techniques may be viewed as evidencing countertransferential anger or sadism. Because of this, I believe it is more useful to frame a discussion of countertransference with borderline patients in terms of a model by which countertransference problems exist on a continuum with normal and even helpful aspects of therapy, and to lean more heavily on a model of psychotherapy that puts greater emphasis on the "fit" between patient need and therapist style.

One set of countertransference problems involves extreme manifestations of usual and positive ingredients within psychotherapy rather than qualitatively separate types of reactions. In this framework, there are two major types of sustained countertransference reactions that I frequently observe within myself and others. For purposes of simplicity, I will refer to these as the "good mother"/ "strong father" paradigms. In the good mother paradigm, which parallels Kernberg's "withdrawal from reality" type (Kernberg 1965), there is a denial of the patient's aggression and a joining with the patient in externalizing the sources of the problem. In a supposedly empathic way, the therapist may be joining the patient's view of reality and wittingly or unwittingly fueling a fused or idealized transference. In this instance, the resulting relationship gratifies the therapist's wish to be seen as especially good. This counter-transferential style runs the risk of accepting impossible situations and ignoring self-destructiveness. In the strong father paradigm, there is denial of the patient's illness and an undue sense of optimism about the prospects for change. The therapeutic atmosphere is likely to be marked by confrontation and limits that may be presented with such enthusiasm or intensity that they are experienced as intolerance. Here the therapist's intolerance of impotence and wish for special therapeutic prowess may be salved. This paradigm may be costly when there is a failure of empathic appreciation for the value of emotional expression as well as an appreciation of the patient's long-term and presently unchangeable limitations.

A model of countertransference that emphasizes the fit between patient and therapist is less perjorative about therapist reactions and gives more appropriate recognition to the nontransferential corrective processes within psychotherapy that are especially important with sicker patients (Gunderson et al. 1975b). Certain therapist personality traits seem especially important for work with borderline patients: a comfort with aggression, sensitivity to separation experiences, a sense of adventuresomeness, and clarity of conceptual orientation. Less clear is the role of the therapist's wish to be needed and important. This appears to cut both ways—it has seemed very helpful in some matches by allowing the patient to depend on and feel special to such a therapist comfortably. In other instances, this quality in a therapist has posed problems by expecting more recognition of the therapist's importance than a patient could provide. This area of matching between patient and therapist deserves much more systematic attention.

An overly broad use of the borderline diagnosis has drawn attention to the profound transference/countertransference issues in treatment, but has left it unclear as to whether there is any specificity in these phenomena. Narrowing of the diagnostic boundaries for the borderline diagnosis offers new hope that more specific countertransference dilemmas may be delineated and that borderline subgroups may yet be sorted out who do well or poorly with therapists having different styles.

GENERAL PRINCIPLES: GOALS, TYPES, AND STRUCTURES

Many authors in the psychotherapy literature have utilized a division of supportive versus so-called exploratory, expressive, or insight-oriented approaches to psychotherapy. Supportive is generally meant to reflect a preponderance of techniques designed to help the patients feel better, such techniques as advice, education, reassurance, and self-disclosure. The predominantly exploratory therapies are thought to contain techniques directed toward self-understanding, especially utilizing the devices of dream and transference interpretations.

   In the section that follows, I also utilize this division despite the fact that it is now well established that the division between insight-oriented and supportive techniques is either a very weak or invalid paradigm for typing psychotherapies. From a study utilizing experienced therapists with an expressed commitment to either supportive or to insight-oriented modalities, we, nevertheless, found considerable crossover between the techniques employed to the extent that a more continuous model of exploratory and supportive techniques was needed to characterize the treatments adequately (Stanton et al. 1984). Moreover, the Menninger Psychotherapy Study, which was designed on the basis of the presumed differentiation between supportive and expressive psychotherapies, also showed that they, in fact, could only be characterized by admixtures of the two techniques (Wallerstein 1983). Both studies indicated that supportive techniques and processes were much more common within the so-called insight-oriented or expressive psychotherapies than psychoanalytic theory and the research designs had recognized.

   Despite the inadequacy of the supportive versus exploratory typology for therapies, it does have some value in discussing techniques as long as it is recognized that they exist on dimensions (i.e., either more or less present within any psychotherapy). I prefer the term *exploratory* to either *expressive* or *insight-oriented*. The term *expressive* is too content oriented and suggests that other therapies are suppressive. The term *insight-oriented* tends to connote uncovering the unconscious disproportionately to its actual role in therapeutic processes. In any event, supportive and exploratory therapies have already become well-established paradigms in the clinical literature on psychotherapy with borderlines (for example, see Friedman 1975).

Nonintensive/Supportive

Individual psychotherapy remains the backbone of treatment for the majority of borderline patients. Most frequently, it is conducted on a once-weekly basis and contains considerable supportive elements. This approach is aimed at bolstering defenses and focusing on practical issues—an approach first suggested by Knight (1953) and later advocated by Grinker et al. (1968) and Zetzel (1971). All felt it was the treatment of choice because borderline patients cannot establish workable transferences. For most borderline patients, this approach provides a stabilizing relationship that considerably diminishes the likelihood of self-destructive acts, and is sufficient to diminish time within hospitals greatly. Because of the latter, it is a very cost-effective form of treatment. In any event, the goals for a nonintensive treatment are to decrease the chances of suicide, to support more adaptive role performance, and to diminish the chaotic interpersonal relationships. Wallerstein (1983) indicates that supportive treatments may, in fact, do more than these goals; they may, like their insight-oriented brethren, bring about desirable structural changes.

Just as with more frequent schedules, an immediate intense relationship develops in which the therapist is assumed to have powerful healing and nurturant qualities that can beget compliant transferences. These in turn can be very helpful. Still, a low frequency of visits is believed to diminish the likelihood of intense transference distortions.

Such treatment can be expected to last indefinitely with progressive tapering of frequency of visits. Unless unusual circumstances (e.g., marriage or financial crisis) intervene, the frequency of visits usually remains once a week for four or five years of treatment, at which time it may switch to an as-needed basis. No formal termination should be anticipated, and ongoing availability should be offered. Still, gradual discontinuance frequently occurs when substitutive relationships have developed.

Kernberg et al. (1972) concluded after the Menninger Psychotherapy Study that supportive treatment of borderline patients had toxic effects. More recently, he has recognized the important and common value that this form of therapy has (Kernberg, in press). Although his descriptions of what supportive psychotherapy entails overlaps heavily with what I would consider to be usual exploratory psychotherapy, and although he still maintains that supportive and expressive techniques should not be combined, it is nonetheless a departure from his earlier position, which stood apart for its exclusion of supportive techniques. Although Masterson (1976) joins Kernberg in seeing supportive therapy as only modestly effective, he has recognized the role of supportive treatment as an initial form of treatment as a usual and practical matter preliminary to more intensive work. Still others have recently indicated that interpretation and confrontation are either useless or even harmful for extended periods early in treatment (Adler 1981; Chessick 1982).

Intensive/Exploratory

The goals of exploratory—equated here with expressive, psychoanalytic, or reconstructive—psychotherapy are more ambitious. A restructuring of the basic personality is attempted with the idea of allowing a self-sufficient, reasonably stable, and enriched quality of life to result. The aforementioned report by Wallerstein (1983) indicates that while such goals may be achieved in psychoanalytic psychotherapy, it is frequently accomplished by processes other than acquisition of insight.

The literature and my own experience on the intensive psychotherapy of borderline patients (meaning three or more times a week of psychoanalytically oriented psychotherapy) suggests that there is a minimum of approximately four years before termination could be considered and that most frequently the duration of therapy is between 6 and 10 years. Even here, where termination is sometimes possible, many of the experts favor a tapered pattern of visits with PRN return visits for the indefinite future (Waldinger and Gunderson 1984).

The decision to undertake an exploratory approach with a borderline patient must take many factors into consideration. By no means should it be undertaken routinely or easily. In this regard, I disagree with both Masterson (1972, 1976) and Kernberg (1968, 1975, 1979b), who feel it is the treatment of choice for any borderline with adequate motivation and resources. Some of the most important selection factors lie within the available therapist. The therapist's motivation, talent, and experience for doing this sort of work are all important. The inexperienced therapist, no matter how talented or interested, should not undertake an exploratory intensive therapy with a borderline patient without having good quality ongoing supervision. Also, the feasibility of exploratory therapy is tied to the frequency of visits. It is difficult to conduct an exploratory, insight-oriented psychotherapy on a once-weekly basis with borderline patients. This is both because of the time needed to work through deeper issues (evoking transference is seldom a problem) and because of the flight or other potentially harmful acting out that occurs when such issues are addressed without that (i.e., working through) possibility.

Another issue to be considered in undertaking exploratory psychotherapy with a borderline patient involves the patient's available support system. It is hardly coincidental that both Masterson and Kernberg were among the most outspoken advocates for early confrontations and interpretations with borderline patients and that their recommendations arose when their careers were enmeshed in long-term inpatient services (Menninger and Payne Whitney, respectively). Therapists such as Buie (1982), Adler (1982), and Chessick (1982) who have worked predominantly in outpatient services have opposed reliance on interpretive techniques in the treatment of borderline patients. After their practices moved into more exclusively outpatient settings, Masterson and Kernberg have also come to see the place for noninterpretive techniques. The general principle here is that in situations where borderline patients have considerable social supports, more confrontation and interpretation may be possible within their therapy. A borderline patient who leaves a therapy session in which he or she has been asked to look at painful experiences can go to a situation in which the therapist will be portrayed as sadistic or to another situation in which the need to look at and experience feelings is reinforced. Such differences will greatly affect the degree and way in which such psychotherapeutic experiences get digested.

There are other factors within the structure of psychotherapy that also determine the degree to which an exploratory approach makes sense. One is the use of the couch. Among others, Boyer (1982), Chessick (1977, 1983), Giovacchini (1979), and Volkan (1981) have argued for the advantages of using the couch in the treatment of borderline patients. All stress the comfort it allows the analyst. To a larger extent than has been recognized by these authors, I believe this utilization is dependent on having patients who, although internally very primitive, are sufficiently well functioning or obsessional to withstand the added frustrations this imposes. In some instances (e.g., Abend et al. 1983), the so-called borderline patients with whom the couch has been used are simply not impaired sufficiently to be given this diagnosis. In other instances where the patients really are borderline, I think the couch forces the therapist to adopt a less confrontational/interpretive style so as to allow the borderline patient a greater sense of control (see Gunderson 1983a for discussion).

PHASES AND PROCESSES OF EXPLORATORY PSYCHOTHERAPY

The four phases described next are derived from my clinical experience, the extensive examination of a series of five intensively treated successful cases by colleagues, and the experience of supervising and consulting on many other borderline patients in intensive psychotherapy. Only after preparing these descriptions did I review the descriptions of phases made by Masterson some years ago (1976). There are striking areas of overlap between his earlier report and the characteristics reported here, which should offer confidence that these descriptions are not simply products of one observer's prejudices or of one therapist's style. Areas of difference also appear, and these I will comment on.

Stage I: Boundaries

This is the phase of treatment with which therapists are most familiar simply because fewer than one in four patients who begin psychotherapy move through it with the same therapist. Most of the action in this phase of treatment takes place around the boundaries of the treatment setting; namely, the fees, the bills, nonappointment contacts, scheduling, and the use of the sessions to talk about subjects with meaning. When the time is not being spent attempting to establish some stable and reasonable therapeutic contract around these issues, it is likely to be spent on the issues of the patient's safety and whose responsibility that will be. The technical issues of dealing with many of these issues are addressed in the chapters on self-destruction (Chapter 5), aggression (Chapter 6), and psychotic regression (Chapter 7).

It is a major task of the therapist in this period to remain stably available and to avoid the pitfalls of offering unrealistic promises or failing to address such things as bills and appointments. The management and use of such parameters as between-appointment phone calls, extra appointments, and phone contacts during absences are variable; once again, the general principle can be offered that for most borderline patients a therapist's commitment to that patient's welfare will be tested by actions and must be conveyed in action. This will as frequently involve setting reasonable limits as it will involve making exceptions to rules. From the therapist's point of view, there is a continuous tension during this period between the dangers of too much frustration and being overly seductive. The patient too will experience this tension as demands for the therapist's support and availability are frustrated while at the same time the therapist's expectation of self-disclosure and trust seem impossibly self-destructive.

As noted already, opinions are divided about the role of interpretive and confrontative techniques in the early phase of treatment. It has seemed to me inevitable that this phase of treatment includes strongly supportive elements. The repetitious and concerned indications that the patient's actions are destructive to the patient's self-interest are highly supportive—whether described as confrontations (a la Masterson) or interpretations (a la Kernberg). The effect is not simply in the content and hence descriptions of proper techniques can be very misleading. It seems possible that a process of beneficial change occurs as the result of the relatively nonspecific process of progressive disappointment and disillusionment of a borderline patient's more grandiose and unspoken transference demands. However, it is my impression that such a process is facilitated by the therapist's consistent interpretation of the patient's implicit and indirect, usually acted-out demands for indications of love, and by the active clarification of the angry feelings that lie behind the withdrawals, silences, and manipulations following frustrations of these felt needs. The identification of such angry feeling is the first task and will often depend on the patient's willingness to delay acting on them first. A cognitive learning process may be a part of this process (see Chapter 6).

A major achievement of this period of the treatment is for sufficient stability to be established in the areas of these tensions, that the patient's life is less often endangered by acting out the demands for help, and by the abrogation of personal responsibility for their actions. The progressive diminution of self-destructive acts is in fact the most graphic measure of whether progress is occurring during this phase. Such acts may continue but there should be observable or measurable decreases in their frequency or severity. The failure for this to occur within the first year should be cause for concern, and a review with a consultant would probably be indicated. If it has not occurred by two years, a basic change in the treatment is probably necessary. This may involve the addition of medication, the introduction of greater family involvement, a shift into a residential setting, or, most probably, a change in psychotherapist.

Masterson's (1976) description of the first "testing" phase of psychotherapy has many parallels with this phase. It too emphasizes the struggles around the boundaries of treatment. He believes that patients' behaviors are designed to test the therapist's effectiveness and reliability before establishing a parental transference and alliance. He also emphasizes the role of confrontation during this phase for the purpose of making destructive, harmful actions dystonic. Without differing on the central role of identifying self-destructive effects, as noted, I place more emphasis on the role for supportive processes during this phase than did Masterson. Also, I prefer the term *boundaries* because the patient is not just testing the therapist's resilience before being willing to establish a therapeutic relationship. The borderline patient during this phase is expressing deeply felt, but unrealistic, interpersonal expectations in the therapy. There is a progressive self-disclosing aspect to this phase. They are actively establishing and creating a more realistic relationship during this period. Thus the testing reflects an internal problem in establishing some realistically limited and separate sense of self and not a regression in which reassurance is sought via limits. The term *boundaries* is thus associated with both the internal process of change occurring in this phase as well as the external problem in the interpersonal management of this process.

Stage II: Negativity and Control

During this phase of treatment, the activity that previously took place around and outside the therapy now has moved much more directly into the here-and-now interaction with the therapist. The patient at this point is much more aware of and object-directed in expressions of anger at the therapist for failing to know and gratify what are experienced as needs. Much of what has been acted out is now acted in by virtue of silences, threats, seductiveness, and so on. Testing of limits can be expected to continue around appointments and bills, but the aggressive motivations are now much more clearly a subject for exploration. If availability and commitment

were the hallmarks of the good therapist in the first stage of treatment, during this phase it is the steadfastness and nonretaliatory
aspects of the therapist's personality that are needed and tested.
The major task of the therapeutic work—which now clearly rely
heavily on confrontation and interpretation—is the analysis of the
controlling motives behind the patient's dependency, masochism,
devaluation, envy, and manipulation as they are openly part of the
here-and-now relationship to the therapist. These issues require
repetitious interpretation in the manner of character analysis first
described by Reich (1949), which attempts to make dystonic those
parts of the usual self that have been ego-syntonic.

This is also the phase of treatment where the patient can be
expected to begin to make meaningful use of past memories. In
fact, many borderline patients who have been previously amnesic
for most of their childhood will begin to recall and fill in their
past—a sequence first identified by Searles (1982). Attaining an
historical perspective on the current reactions, and with this a sense
of how the past has helped create the present, is clearly an important part of this phase and signals the evolution and identification
of a more coherent transference. The need to control relationships
as a price for attachment is eventually seen as an adaptation made
in early life to experiences in which the patients felt powerless and
helpless.

I believe that concurrently with the development of these insights—
and equally meaningful for change during this phase—is the
corrective experience that occurs from the therapist's failure to
retaliate as the patient more directly expresses anger. This experience is not only critical in the further consolidation of boundaries
for the self (Winnicott 1975), but it leads to increases in the capacity
to tolerate frustrations and limitations in others. Finally, it activates
the emergence of separation anxiety. These changes represent a
fundamental shift in object relations and cognitions. The tendencies
toward all-or-nothing and now-or-never thinking become dystonic.
Thus the phase that began with efforts to make behaviors dystonic
ends with being able to be aware of alternating feelings toward
objects—an initial step towards ambivalence.

This description echoes in many important ways Masterson's
(1976) description of his second, "working through" phase. The
descriptions are parallel insofar as both see the emergence of a
coherent transference during this period and emphasize the ongoing needs for limits and confrontation to manage the acting out

within the transference. Both identify this phase as a period where memories begin to emerge and where a major task is the shift from action to verbalization. In other respects, the descriptions diverge. Masterson emphasizes the emergence of depression during this period as part of his larger conceptual scheme whereby during this phase the patient is working through the core rapprochement issues. As part of this scheme, he also sees this as a period in which new feelings and interests emerge, which require techniques of "communicative matching" that seem to involve techniques of counseling and self-disclosure. These are a set of phenomena that I have not observed in this second stage as described above. Rather, I give much more emphasis to the aggressive, controlling, characterological defenses during this stage and the need to identify and make these dystonic. Hence, like Kernberg (1968, 1979b) there is more ongoing attention and vigilance to the negative transference issues during this phase in my scheme. Moreover, as noted earlier, I did not see the phenomena in the first phase of treatment as a regression from core rapprochement issues, and likewise I do not see the second phase as primarily a working through phase. Both phases involve working through by patterns of contact, testing, affective expressions, and containment of hostility, and so on. The "holding" aspects of the treatment situation (Modell 1976; Shapiro et al. 1982) continue to be important during this period, more than is suggested by Masterson's description.

Stage III: Separation and Identity

As noted, the patient's intensely ambivalent view of the therapist predominates at this time. This progressively gives way during the third phase, and the alternating feelings become sufficiently mixed up to override the rageful feelings and acting out reactions to separation and frustration. The patient now is more consciously aware of anger at separations and also concurrently more aware of the anxieties over loss associated with them. Relationships more generally take on more complexity as the issues of entitlement and vengeance recede and are replaced by self-consciousness about readily available conscious feelings of anger, envy, and sadistic fantasies. There has been a decrease in expression of anger and an increase of anxiety and confusion.

At this point, patients begin to show increasing evidence of improvement in their role functioning and social relationships.

Whereas during the first phase of treatment the patient was almost exclusively invested in the enactment of a transference demand, and in the second phase that demand became focused and was altered, at this point the patient now has sufficient perspective on the unrealistic parent–child nature of this demand that some energy is available to spend experimenting with realistic peer relationships.

Also during this stage, and perhaps as a result of the failure of the angry expressions of earlier phases to have had destructive effects, the previously unconscious magical, omnipotent, and grandiose views of the self emerge from their shrouds. One patient, for example, began to speak of her sense of superiority from not having had to "march to the same drummer" as other kids. Her longstanding sense of alienation was now revealed to reflect her contempt for "normals." Another patient began to reveal and give up her beliefs that she could kill by her rejection of her suitors. This, I expect, is the type of issue that led Adler (1981) to theorize that borderline patients who were getting better became narcissistic. However, this does not emerge as a grandiose self with the narcissistic person's behavioral signals (i.e., social arrogance and entitlement); rather, it emerges concurrently with the corrective disillusionment noted above that allows such patients actually to become more tolerant and humble socially. It is a process of uncovering another deeper level of meaning to the borderline's psychopathology rather than signaling a movement to a more developmentally advanced level of ego function. Another of Adler and Buie's (1979a) conceptions fits more comfortably with my own observations during this period. It does seem that, with the emergence of separation anxiety and the cleaner expression of affects around separations, a process of internalization takes place that may involve object constancy. This process is marked by the emergence of a more organized separation response—a response that had been missing altogether during stage I and that was frequently enacted during stage II when phone calls, pictures, letters, hospitalizations, and interim therapists often are felt to be needed during separations. In stage III, the therapist can rely almost entirely on interpretations in managing this and other therapeutic issues.

It is also during this stage that the borderline's identity failures become evident. What had been marked by negativity now is evident as a vulnerability (e.g., "to be whatever someone else wants," to have no sense of purpose, to lack a coherent self-image). This failure to have a stable sense of self is modified best by noninterpretive techniques within the psychotherapy. The therapist should adopt an inquiring and curious attitude that invites the patients to explore themselves and that expresses interest in the complexity of the patient's personality. Here the identification of new ideas and feelings and the support for their importance are important parts of the therapeutic process. The patient's self-integrity is encouraged by noting the value and importance of voicing displeasure, concerns, and wishes. Also useful during this phase is the anchoring of feelings as psychological experiences with the body, as described by Mann and Semrad (1959). Although the patient now is presenting fewer problems of transference management, the basic disorder in self continues to require therapeutic techniques that encourage corrective experiences to ensue.

Thus stage III is marked by the transition from a relationship that has been experienced as intensely needy to one in which it has assumed a place of recognized importance but increasingly as optional. The evolution and continuation of this third stage may depend on factors within the patient's life outside the therapy. Many patients, successfully treated, will leave when a suitable substitute object or work opportunity permits it. The Waldinger study (1984) identified the tendency of the borderline patients—even those who might otherwise have quite reasonable cause for terminating—to prefer doing so from a negativistic and devaluative posture. This does not contraindicate the completion of the treatment but clearly reflects the failure for the positive transference to have gained a stable ascendency over the negative in periods of loss. It also signifies ongoing problems with giving up interpersonal controls.

This description of stage III contains some elements found in Masterson's phase 2; namely, the emergence of new feelings and interests and the role for a more paternalistic response by a therapist. In other more important ways, however, the descriptions of this style are similar to Masterson's third phase. Both emphasize the emergence of good social adaptation and separation anxiety during this period and the considerable diminution of rage. The descriptions differ insofar as I have pointed toward the importance of the acquisition of object constancy and the capacity for ambivalence during this period. When this stage is completed, major problems still remain in identity formation, initiative, and the tolerance of helplessness. These require a fourth stage not part of Masterson's scheme.

Stage IV: Termination, Initiative, and Letting Go

Consideration of termination is indicated any time after the patient has entered stage III, believes that treatment is optional, and has stated a wish to leave. Once the issue of therapy as a potential source of need gratification is not felt to be at stake, borderline patients will vary considerably in their interest in the therapeutic process as more purely a vehicle for self-knowledge and expansion of adequate adaptive cognition. Here the therapist's interest in depth psychology and comfort with positive transference—including the patient's sexuality—may also be important determinants of continuation. This does not mean that the patient will necessarily be able to terminate but that the patient has permission to do so. As a result, this begins a struggle with that issue which is inevitably productive. In this period, the therapist may function as a "good mother of separation" in the way that Masterson and Rinsley (1975) postulated had failed during the borderline patient's childhood.

The termination process itself can be expected to bring with it a regression back to the earlier issues of treatment, but should not be expected to include a full behavioral regression. Volkan (1981) notes that "even after the borderline patient develops a transference neurosis, the background situation [splitting] so turbulent at first, must continue to have attention. . . . Primitive splitting returns in the termination phase as though for review." An important process in the termination will be the patient's growing distance from and comfort with the previously unconscious wishes for passive gratification that had been a major part of the patient's psychology. The fact that leaving involves taking initiative brings into focus guilts about individuation but also other more clearly phallic activities. The guilt is often responded to by a regressive retreat into explanations of being pushed out of therapy and otherwise not being responsible for the steps forward being taken. In any event, the process of termination is best prompted (and greatly facilitated) by the patient having a life outside the treatment, which at this point is sufficiently rich that it competes for the patient's time, energy, and money.

Opinion is divided about the proper method for terminating treatment. Some favor gradually tapering the frequency of sessions (e.g., Giovacchini 1979; Masterson 1976). Others continue frequent sessions until the termination date and then stop abruptly. I favor the latter whenever possible. Too often, the process of tapering can be employed because of the therapist's conviction of a patient's inability to complete a termination—a conviction which has been untested and which may unduly handicap the patient's confidence. With respect to returning, this option should be left open but should require some lapse of time and should also require clear initiative from the patient.

OUTCOME

What then is the result of a successful treatment? The results of a survey conducted by Waldinger and myself (see Chapter 4) largely reinforced the clinical impressions gained through the treatment of patients in my practice and those of colleagues. These observations are at distinct variance with those that explain therapeutic changes in terms of an evolution toward less severe, even neurotic, forms of psychopathology consistent with a developmental model (e.g., Adler 1981; Kernberg 1968, 1980; Volkan 1976, 1981). Successfully treated borderline patients are not healthy, and they do not develop into typical forms of psychoneurosis. They are much more socially adaptive, but they are still vulnerable persons. Therefore, as noted earlier by Giovacchini (1979), a model of successful treatment that requires a resolution of conflict and a consequent developmental step forward does not appear accurate.

Rather than a resolution of old conflicts and defenses, successful treatment of borderline patients opens up new and more adaptive possibilities for action. Action patterns such as the defensive use of manipulation and dependency are no longer used reflexively, but remain available for selective employment. Although such patients have a clearer insight into themselves, they often do not have a stable and fixed sense of their own identity—this is so even in the presence of much more adaptive social role performance and more stable relationships. Difficulties in boundaries are frequently evident in feeling either overly responsible or being overly passive, thereby betraying the residues of both their grandiosity and their externalizations. Successfully treated borderline patients are obviously capable of being more open, self-revelatory, and more trusting. However, these characteristics may be selective and discontinuous. The borderline patient is frequently troubled by recurrent feelings of bitterness or by feelings of inner inadequacy or incompleteness.

These are intermittent concerns, however, and likely to be managed through the reassurances offered by supportive relationships.

DROPOUTS

The high frequency with which borderline patients drop out of treatment needs to be underscored. Several perspectives on this have proven useful to me. One I discuss elsewhere (Chapter 6) is that the abrupt or even angry discontinuation of treatment cannot be assumed to be the equivalent of failure. Far worse to continue in a psychotherapy that is unproductive or involves actual support for the patient's psychopathology. Second is the observation that many patients who prematurely discontinue treatment nevertheless may learn from it. This learning may involve things which set the stage for them to begin therapy again with someone else and which may make them more likely to accept the required frustrations and tasks of therapy. This acceptance/compliance with the boundaries of psychotherapy becomes more probable with each shift that takes place. This observation was made in a study on psychotherapy of schizophrenia (Gunderson, in press) and seems equally true with respect to borderline patients. It is unclear whether this reflects attrition of will or a progressive reconciliation to the limits of treatment, but it is an important process for clinicians to be aware of. Borderline patients commonly work through the stage I part of treatment by using many therapists and then move into more durable therapies where they continue already as stage II patients. Senior therapists are more apt to get such referrals. At the very least, the failures of a borderline patient to have remained in previous treatments should not be seen as a relative contraindication for them to begin again with someone new.

Another perspective comes from Searles (1982, p 155): "One of the most stressful aspects of work with borderline patients is premature termination of treatment. . . . The cumulative effect of such experiences progressively undermines the analyst's confidence in their ability to feel loving feelings and to be capable of grieving." Searles seems to refer here to the borderline patients' usual pattern of exiting because they believe the therapist has failed in the delivery of basic caregiving. Just as important as these reactions in my experience have been the feelings of betrayal and disappointment which accompany the often sudden and spiteful departures of patients toward whom I or other therapists have often invested a commitment surpassing that with other patients, a commitment that clearly seems to be unreciprocated. Making the investment required to work with borderline patients may require some object hunger. Buie (1982) alludes to this by describing the countertransference problems of therapists who hold onto such needy patients to diminish feelings of aloneness/abandonment. The following case example illustrates some of the issues involved in dropping out:

> Joan was a 23-year-old office worker who began twice weekly psychotherapy with me while an inpatient and then continued with this as her primary form of aftercare. Her sessions with me were soon dominated by elaborations on the twin themes of her bitterness at her parents for their failures to nurture her and her inability to become independent from them. Increasingly, she directed both of these complaints at me whom she experienced as uncaring and withholding and who she felt had made her dependent. I repeatedly pointed out the transferential aspects of this but also inquired what expressions of care did she feel were lacking and what evidence of withholding did she perceive. What was discernible in these discussions was only that she wished me to tell her what to talk about and that she wished to be seen at a reduced fee on a more convenient schedule. Since I had already changed appointment times at her request several times, and since her fee was largely paid by insurance so that the remaining sum was not substantial, there seemed little more I could do to mollify her on these counts. Moreover, she refused my suggestions of topics because they made her "feel worse."
>
> She so repeatedly expressed her intent to leave treatment that it was almost a surprise to me when she finally did so. I was left feeling that perhaps beyond the particulars of her unrealistic demands she had correctly perceived in me a coldness or aloofness and that perhaps someone else might better be able to diminish her feelings of deprivation. She next sought out a social worker whom she (and I) believed to be of a kinder temperament. However, the therapy lasted only six months before terminating abruptly for the same reasons. She then began with a third and somewhat more experienced therapist, Dr. L, with whom she remained in therapy. I reluctantly concluded that this was probably a tribute either to his greater warmth or his greater skill.
>
> Six years later—by which time I had moved to my position as Director of Psychotherapy—by sheer coincidence I once again heard from the patient. She called to ask my office for a referral. Since I was curious about what had happened and would, in any event, have been reluctant to make the referral if she were currently in treatment, I called her back. She was surprised but not partic-

ularly glad to hear from me. Neither, however, did she seem at all hesitant to describe her problem. She was leaving Dr. L because he overcharged her, wouldn't compromise about where to meet, and had said that she wanted "to be spoon fed." The latter was his exasperated response to her demand that he tell her what to talk about. In fact, he had been meeting her halfway between their offices on her lunch breaks! She wanted a more experienced therapist who would see her for an even lower fee and whose office was within a block radius of hers.

Certainly the patient's subsequent course of treatment showed that the price she exacted for continuance was to castrate the therapy's potential usefulness. Dr. L's heroic efforts to maintain this patient in treatment can only be understood in terms of an extreme countertransference problem. The countertransference problem may be one of dependency (object need) or submissiveness (intolerance of aggression) as suggested by Masterson (1976), but occasionally such extreme efforts to maintain patients in treatment may also be calculatedly avaricious.

It is rare for a therapist to get this kind of follow-up on patients who have dropped out. It is probably even more rare to get the kind of reassurance from a follow-up that was provided by this case. Most of the time, the follow-up information about patients who have dropped out only aggravate the persisting questions as to whether the discontinuation of treatment was due to the patient's pathology or the therapist's limitations. This then remains an unanswered question, a question that experienced therapists often resolve by simply becoming clearer about the limitations of what they have to offer. For all therapists, it is important and reassuring to know that there are instances, such as illustrated in the case of Joan, for whom dropping out may be the most reasonable outcome for the patient to take!

The attrition of morale that accompanies being dropped often leads to a reluctance to take on a new borderline patient. So common is this that virtually all borderline patients are dependent for their treatment on the naive enthusiasm of trainees or the energy and financial neediness of recent graduates. This loss of enthusiasm is aggravated by the therapist having few acceptable opportunities to express the feelings of anger or hurt associated with being left. Another reaction observed in myself is the trying to be "nicer" to the next patient. "Nicer" is such instances amounting to seductiveness or at least inconsistencies in technique and style. Hopefully, a clearer perspective on the, at best, partial degrees of expectable change and on the possible role of successive therapists in bringing about these changes can help make the experience of being dropped less discouraging.

GENERAL COMMENTS: THERAPEUTIC PROCESSES

There are parallels between the processes of intensive psychotherapy and the dynamic theoretical model I described earlier (Chapter 2). The first stage of treatment can be understood to address the underlying problem of objectlessness by providing a stable, consistent holding environment. Whether interpretative or confrontational techniques do more than facilitate passage through this period is unclear. Availability, limits, and good intentions seem to be more central features of interactions that determine passage through this stage. This process continues into the second stage in which, however, the patient is much more object-directed and consciously purposeful in efforts to force compliance and test the limits of their sense of omnipotent control.

In this regard, the phenomena I have described as reflecting the second level of borderline psychopathology with its rage, devaluations, paranoid accusations, and manipulations are central to the psychotherapeutic process. In this second stage, the patient's intentions and wishes are clearly related to and directed at the therapist. Here, central to improvement is the experiential correction that comes from the therapist's survival and nonpunitiveness in the face of the overt expressions of rage. Passage through this stage is clearly dependent on interpretive and confrontational techniques in treatment. Identifications (transmuting internalizations as per Kohut 1971) with the therapist's tolerance of affects and with the therapist's interest in their causes occurs in this period. Out of this stage, the patient emerges with both object constancy and with a more consolidated capacity for ambivalence—both reflective of an ability to retain soothing memories in the absence of some form of overtly supportive relationship (Buie and Adler 1982; Rinsley 1982). Nevertheless, much of the learning that has taken place is both behavioral and cognitive rather than involving closure or resolution of the problems of either object inconstancy and the problems in owning affects rather than their projection (a process often called splitting). As noted here, the successful treatment of a borderline patient does not result in a primarily oedipally oriented neurotic person.

In psychoanalytic theories of therapy, one would not expect that nonintensive supportive therapy by itself would do more than help borderline patients through stage I issues. Nevertheless, as indicated by Wallerstein's report (1983) and as suggested by the above understanding of therapeutic processes, I believe it can. A supportive treatment may allow important identification processes to take place. In fact, supportive treatment may actually bring about more rapid improvement in areas of role performance and social skills, which are inadvertently delayed by the pressures within a regressive transference or by the frustrations of negative transference work. The price paid for failures to identify and work through negative transferences (i.e., the vicissitudes of the patient's aggression) are not so much in the possibilities of sustained improvement in ego factors like delay, adaptive regression, or mood regulation. The price is more apt to be seen in areas of interpersonal relationships. Here the development of capacities to see and accept the necessity of conflict and anger within relationships allows patients to leave and be left more reasonably, to manage the tasks of early child rearing more ably, and to compete more openly. I believe that negative transference work also leads to a more coherent identity insofar as patients acquire more specificity and definition in their self-knowledge.

4

Psychotherapy:
Empirical Considerations

In this chapter, the present status and future prospects of translating the clinical descriptions of psychotherapy into controlled quantitative examinations will be discussed. This chapter begins with a critical review of the existing efforts to evaluate empirically the effects of psychotherapy with borderline patients. It continues with a look at problems that confront future psychotherapy research efforts. The prerequisites for more definitive evaluations of psychotherapeutic process and outcome with borderline patients are described along with a set of recommendations about a selected set of studies that are needed before issues of psychotherapeutic efficacy can be addressed.

EXISTING EMPIRICAL STUDIES OF PSYCHOTHERAPY WITH BORDERLINE PATIENTS

The Menninger Psychotherapy Research Study

There have been very few efforts to assess systematically the effects of psychotherapy with borderline patients. The first study that can be considered to bear on this question, the Menninger Psychotherapy Research Study (Robbins 1956; Sargent 1956a, 1956b), intensively examined the courses and outcomes of 42 patients at the Menninger Clinic. Patients in this study subsequently received between 6 months and 12 years of various forms of psychotherapy (Wallerstein 1983). The sample was made up of patients with char-

69

acter disorders, borderline patients, neurotics, and a few patients with latent psychoses. Subsequently, the subgroup with low initial ego strength was generally equated with the diagnosis of borderline personality organization (Burstein 1972; Kernberg et al. 1972). The initial diagnosis and ego strength assessments done at baseline were largely derived from the case records and psychological tests routinely done as part of the clinical record. At the conclusion of the psychotherapy, a second battery of assessments, which employed the therapists' records and repeat psychological testing, was conducted. Two years later, there was a follow-up interview, which consisted of a third set of psychological tests and an interview with the patients.

Approximately half of the patients were assigned initially to psychoanalysis and the other half to psychotherapy with the intention of further subdividing the latter group into those who would receive either extensive or supportive forms of psychotherapy. Assignments to these various forms of therapy were based on clinical judgment. Of 22 patients initially assigned to psychoanalysis, 10 remained; the other 12 had a treatment drastically modified, 6 in terms of low frequency of visits and 6 actually converting to some form of psychotherapy. The treatment plan for the other 20 patients who had initially been assigned to psychotherapy was likewise modified. In practice, virtually all of the psychotherapy patients received some admixture of supportive-expressive techniques rather than pure forms of one or the other treatment.

In the first and most comprehensive summary of this study, Kernberg et al. (1972) reported that the borderline patients (i.e., those with low initial ego strength) improved "little or not at all" with psychoanalysis and improved "least" with supportive psychotherapy. Of the borderline patients who received the mixed supportive-expressive psychotherapy, some improved and some did not. Some analyses indicated that the good outcomes of patients in this group correlated positively with the therapists' skill, a focus on the here-and-now in sessions, and the lack of a "tense climate" (the authors attributed the latter to the therapists' disregard for external realities). The outcomes did not correlate with the type of therapy to which patients were initially assigned. In any event, none of the low ego strength patients actually received an expressive psychotherapy. Nevertheless, the investigators concluded on the basis of "clinical studies derived from this project" that borderline patients "do indeed require a special modality of treatment, a modality which can best be described as an expressive approach" (p 173). In view of the above findings, this conclusion can have little relationship to the reported data. Kernberg has written extensively about the characteristics of the "expressive" psychotherapy, which he believes is specifically indicated for borderline patients (Kernberg 1968, 1979b; Kernberg et al. 1972). The description of this treatment has concurred with observations about the preferred treatment of this patient group made by myself and many other therapists. Nevertheless, its virtues cannot be thought to have been tested or demonstrated by the Menninger Psychotherapy Research Study.

In a more recent summary of this study, Wallerstein (1983) also noted that there were enough good outcomes among low ego strength patients who received supportive-expressive psychotherapy to support the use of this therapy "if the ingredients are put together skillfully and imaginatively enough, and if one can insure truly sufficient concomitant life management." He went on to state that such extra-therapeutic supports as hospitalization or psychoactive drug management are central to the success of a supportive-expressive psychotherapy. This suggests that, in those cases where successes occurred in the borderline patients, the supportive-expressive psychotherapy was accompanied by considerable admixtures of such other treatments. If this is so, firm conclusions about the value of the supportive-expressive psychotherapy per se cannot be drawn from this study.

In a third report on this study, Horwitz attempted to draw more specific conclusions about the borderline subsample (Horwitz 1982). He identified a subgroup of 16 patients of the original 42 who might qualify for a diagnosis of borderline personality. This subgroup was identified by the presence of a poorly formed identity, nonspecific evidence of ego weakness, and intrusion of primary-process thinking on their psychological tests. Of these 16 patients, 5 were considered successes, 5 were considered unchanged, and 6 were thought to have become worse. The type of treatment the sample received was divided equally between psychoanalysis and psychotherapy. All 6 borderline patients who got worse had received psychoanalysis. The 2 others who received psychoanalysis did well, but they were considered to have higher initial levels of ego strength. All 5 of the successful outcomes occurred in patients who had received psychotherapy (presumably supportive-expressive). Nevertheless, 4 of these 5 still had evidence of primary-process thinking on psychological tests conducted at the follow-up evaluation.

These reports from the Menninger Psychotherapy Research Study suggest that (1) psychoanalysis is probably contraindicated for borderline patients; (2) a significant minority of borderline patients do improve over time, although the nature of their improvement rarely extends into the area of primary-process thinking; and (3) a supportive-expressive psychotherapy may be beneficial if provided in conjunction with adequate extra-therapeutic supports. Unfortunately the design of this study does not permit a high level of confidence in these impressions. Several aspects of this study prevent any conclusions about the efficacy of psychotherapy for borderline patients and the relative advantages of various forms of psychotherapy: (1) no untreated comparison group, (2) patients not randomly assigned to treatments, (3) no blind assessments, (4) questionable diagnoses, (5) no quality control over therapy, and (6) probable confounding effects by other treatments.

Michael Stone's Review of His Psychotherapy Practice

The second empirical study on the psychotherapy of borderline patients comes from Stone (Stone 1983a, 1983b). Earlier, Stone had looked at the family prevalence of mental illness in the borderline patients from his psychotherapy practice and discerned a relationship to affective disorders which has proven to be a fruitful observation (Gunderson and Elliott 1984). He subsequently returned to the clinical records of his practice with an eye toward evaluating the effects of treatment. In several reports, he compared 21 patients with broadly defined borderline personality to 23 patients with schizotypal personality. Each of these patients presumably received some similar form of psychoanalytically oriented psychotherapy, although patients in both groups also frequently received pharmacotherapy—usually antidepressants in the borderline group and phenothiazines in the schizotypal group. Stone assessed the change in psychopathology according to the Global Assessment Scale (GAS) both at the time the therapy was initiated and later when therapy was terminated. Virtually all of the borderline patients improved, and two-thirds of them improved quite significantly (greater than 10-point improvement in their GAS ratings at the end of treatment). In contrast, less than one-fourth of the schizotypal sample had a similar level of improvement, and one-third of them actually appeared to have gotten worse.

Stone's reports do not allow for examination of whether the changes were related to the duration of the treatment or initial scores on the GAS. However, the report is generally quite positive about the effects of psychotherapy, at least as Stone practices and evaluates it. Descriptions of the psychotherapy approach employed are presented elsewhere (Stone 1980, 1983a, 1983b). The approach seems to fit comfortably with a description of the supportive-expressive modality from the Menninger Psychotherapy Research Study. Although Stone's approach seems to be more openly supportive than the approach described in Kernberg's writings, Stone nevertheless includes consistent and sophisticated attention to the understanding of transference and acquisition of insight as major therapeutic processes. In contrast to Kernberg, however, he does not utilize early interpretations, focus on negative transference, or hesitate to provide supportive structures within the hours.

Obviously, this study has the same limitations of the Menninger study in terms of lack of an integrated comparison group and the absent controls in the therapy provided. The issue of unblind assessment is even more problematic here due to the author's inevitable investment in demonstrating efficacy and in confirming his more specific hypotheses.

Survey of Experts

More recently, another attempt to bring some systematic examination into this area has been reported (Waldinger and Gunderson in press). In this study, 30 experienced expert therapists were asked to describe the borderline patients they had in their practice and to provide retrospective assessments of the outcome of therapy. Special attention was given to those patients who the therapists felt had a successful outcome as scored in four areas: ego function, behavior, object relations, and sense of self (see Table 3). The 11 therapists who responded averaged 24 years of practice, and most had treated 40 or more borderline patients (total $N = 790$). Of the borderline patients who began treatment, 54 percent continued beyond six months, and only about 33 percent went on to complete treatment. From this latter group, 78 (10 percent) were considered by the therapists to be treated successfully.

Examination of the effects of the psychotherapy in "successful" cases showed that consistent ratings of improvement paralleled the lengths of time that the patients remained in therapy. The longer they stayed in treatment and the more previous treatment they

TABLE 3. Levels of Functioning Before and After Successful Treatment of 54 Patients with Borderline Personality Disorder

	High	Medium	Low
Ego Function	Active pursuit of stable goals. Tolerates frustration and maintains motivation in pursuit of goals. Defenses primarily obsessional, subliminative, repressive.	Sets stable goals but pursuit deflected by moderate degree of frustration. Undermines positive pursuits and assumes passive stance under stress. Lapses into use of primitive defenses.	Intolerant of frustration, unable to pursue stable goals. Passive, entitled stance; refuses responsibility for own welfare. Reliance on denial, projection, splitting.
Behavior	Absence of purposeful self-destructive behavior. Productive in vocational role, stable social ties. Affects appropriate intensity and to situation; range includes guilt and humor.	Self-destructive behavior ego-dystonic but persists sporadically. Impulsive disruption of social and vocational roles under stress. Lapses into inappropriate anger, disabling depression.	Actively self-destructive. Unable to maintain stable institutional ties; poor work history. Affects inappropriate in social context and intensity: rage and depression predominate.
Object Relations	Durable, stable intimate relations. Tolerant and sensitive to needs of others. Not particularly exploitative or controlling.	Limited capacity for intimacy. Some ability to sense and tolerate needs of others. Continued reliance on manipulation to control important others.	Chaotic and short-lived relationships. Hostile-dependent and superficial object ties. Requires absolute control to sustain relationships.
Sense of Self	Clear and stable sense of identity which does not vacillate with circumstance. Appropriate sense of own strengths and limitations. Able to comfortably be alone.	Fragile sense of self; moderate suggestibility. Stress prompts flight into grandiosity or self-hatred. Ability to tolerate being alone for limited periods of time.	Little sense of identity; beliefs and self-concept vacillate widely with circumstance. Grandiosity coexists/alternates with low self-esteem and self-denigration. Cannot tolerate being alone.

Note: Adapted from Waldinger and Gunderson 1984.

had, the better their outcomes. Consistently, the movement on the four outcome scales was from moderately severe impairment to modest impairment. To illustrate what this meant in the area of behavioral change, the modal patient went from being actively self-destructive, with disruptive social roles and inappropriate intense affects, to having few self-destructive acts, some but still unstable levels of productivity, and some increase in their available range of affect accompanied by diminished rage and depression.

Bearing the limitations of such surveys in mind (e.g., retrospective judgments by nonblind and invested raters who cannot be assumed to represent the larger community of experts), this study nevertheless confirms the widely held impression that psychotherapy of patients with borderline disorder is extremely difficult. It was also instructive that so many patients who improved left treatment against advice.

PROBLEMS IN ISOLATING THE EFFECTS OF PSYCHOTHERAPY

To understand the effects of psychotherapy on borderline patients, it is necessary to know something about the natural course of this disorder and how the effects of psychotherapy may superimpose on this. Virtually all the follow-up studies completed on borderline samples have documented the serious morbidity associated with this diagnosis (Gunderson et al. 1975; McGlashan 1983a, 1983b; Pope et al. 1983; Werble 1970). These studies have shown that, in the 5-year period after the borderline diagnosis has been made, such patients remain dysfunctional with respect to major role performance and symptomatic behavior. Diagnostically, they remain identifiable as having a borderline disorder. The fact that the McGlashan study (1983b, 1984) indicates a picture of better functioning after a mean duration of 15 years from index hospitalization suggests that some of the acting-out behaviors and help-seeking efforts may eventually diminish. Although this apparent improvement in functioning found in McGlashan's sample may be due to natural course (i.e., the lives of borderline patients between 5 and 15 years take a more benign turn), it may equally be due to the extensive hospitalization and psychotherapy received at the time of their index hospitalization. Nevertheless, if the former is true (i.e., natural course), it means that reports of positive outcome occurring between 5 and 15 years after the onset of psychotherapy cannot be assumed to reflect the benefits from psychotherapy. On the other hand, these studies would suggest that any reports of marked improvement within the first 5 years of treatment are more likely to reflect positive effects from the treatment itself. As a next step, it would be informative to compare the course of a sample of treatment remainers with a matched sample of therapy dropouts or with some no-therapy control group.

Another strategy for isolating the effects of psychotherapy is to assign a comparable group of borderline patients to an alternative treatment randomly. It is difficult in practice to do such a randomization because patients who appear for help need to receive the best available treatment for obvious ethical and legal reasons. As described in the previous chapter, a logical comparison would seem to be exploratory, insight-oriented treatment versus nonintensive, supportive treatment. Such a design was utilized in both the empirical study conducted at the Menninger Clinic and more recently in the McLean/Boston University Collaborative Outcome Study with Schizophrenics (Stanton et al. 1984). In both instances, the distinctions between supportive or exploratory treatments in practice were found to be blurred. It is no longer reasonable to expect any psychotherapeutic strategy with such patients to conform to either a supportive or exploratory model. Thus future comparative outcome studies should consider other types of comparison treatment.

The third issue confronting the psychotherapy researcher in isolating the effects of the psychotherapy concerns the potentially confounding effects on course and outcome that concurrent or adjunctive treatments may be expected to have. As is described elsewhere (Chapter 9), family interventions, psychotherapy, pharmacotherapy, and group therapy can each be expected to exert their effects. As noted earlier, Wallerstein (1983) indicates that such treatments were present in the borderline patients from the Menninger study who did well. Moreover, both Masterson and Costello (1980) and McGlashan (1984) have interpreted their follow-up studies as indicative of powerfully beneficial effects from long-term residential treatments. Control over the inclusion, quantity, and quality of all such interventions is impractical for a long-term study; at best, what may be hoped for is to identify and monitor the presence of such treatments. These observations mean that it would be desirable to conduct the study in a treatment setting where resources available to patients are highly restricted a priori. In a treatment setting where such alternative and adjunctive treatments are common, it would be unlikely that the effects of the psychotherapy could be isolated unless it is extremely powerful or unless a very large number of patients are followed.

In the literature on schizophrenia, documentation of the impact of social contextual factors on relapse of discharged patients (Falloon et al. 1982; Gunderson and Carroll 1983; Leff 1979) underscores the need to provide control over these variables as well, if the effects of the psychotherapy are to be isolated.

ISSUES IN PATIENT AND THERAPIST SAMPLING

Given that there are a large number of borderline patients to select from for inclusion in a psychotherapy study, it is incumbent on an investigator to select a sample that is unequivocal in diagnostic clarity. Patients with concurrent conditions that might influence the response to treatment should be excluded. Drug abuse, antisocial behaviors, schizotypal characteristics, neurocognitive deficits, pharmocologically responsive affective disorders, and childhood learning deficits are conditions that might influence treatment response. Whether all such patients should be removed or whether only some of these conditions should be considered contraindications will depend on an investigator's aims and on other aspects of a study's design. In any case, there is an important need to describe the chosen sample carefully and to determine what baseline patient characteristics have prognostic significance.

Obviously, the issue of obtaining a patient sample is further complicated by the frequency with which borderline patients can be expected to drop out of psychotherapy. Reasonable estimates from available studies are that half will drop out by six months, three-fourths within the first year of treatment; only 1 out of 10 patients will continue on into a completed course of psychotherapy (Skodol et al. 1983; Waldinger and Gunderson 1984). Although these estimates are rough, they probably err on the side of underestimating the frequency of dropouts from assigned hospital or clinic psychotherapy. Further study is needed in the psychotherapy of borderline patients to document drop-out rates and to examine the influencing factors (e.g., therapist's experience, intensity of visits, previous exposures to treatment, the nature of the psychotherapy itself, familial supports, and the patient's motivation). All of these factors have been documented to affect drop-out rates with schizophrenic populations (Gunderson, in press) and could also be expected to influence engagement and continuance with a population of borderline patients.

The issues in selecting a proper sample of therapists to study psychotherapy of borderline patients are not unlike those discussed above with respect to the patients themselves. Studies of the relationship between process and outcome might be facilitated by employing a heterogeneous group of therapists who use a broad range of therapeutic techniques. On the other hand, an outcome study testing the effects of a particular type of psychotherapy would require as much homogeneity in the experience, background, and orientation of the therapists as possible. In either event, it is highly unlikely that a study on psychotherapy with borderline patients should employ inexperienced therapists. Both the difficulties of such treatment and the duration of it require some seasoning and stability within the therapist's personal and professional development. Even among experienced therapists, few have successfully completed psychotherapy with a borderline patient. In a study employing therapists without such prior successes, the results may not be credible or generalizable to questions of effectiveness in the practices of those who have claimed or demonstrated some competence in this area. This observation presents logistical problems insofar as finding an adequate sample of qualified therapists to assess the effectiveness of treatment is inherently difficult and perhaps only possible under circumstances where the confounding effects of other competing or adjunctive treatments are also most likely to occur.

ASSESSMENTS

Outcome Measures

A central task for a study of psychotherapy of borderline patients is to develop measures that reliably identify the aspects of the borderline patient's psychology considered to be modifiable by the given treatment. Psychotherapies directed toward reconstruction of the borderline patient's personality (i.e., those purporting to make a borderline person nonborderline), can be assessed only when measures of core borderline psychopathology are available. At present, there is no single pathognomonic feature for the borderline personality; definitions of what makes a person borderline involve the concurrent presence of two or more characteristics, that is, a syndrome. From such a perspective, the effect of a psychotherapy can be measured by its ability to alter one or more of these syndromal components. It cannot be assumed, certainly, that psychotherapy will affect all components equally or equally preferentially when compared with another treatment. For example, it is conceivable that a borderline patient's self-destructiveness might be modified by limit-setting interventions, unemployment history by a rehabilitation program, problems in self-esteem by supportive treatment, and problems in self-identity by insight-oriented psychotherapy. It is certainly no longer reasonable to assume that any internal change occurs only from treatments directed at understanding a person's internal life (Gunderson and Carroll 1983; Malan 1979; Wallerstein 1983).

There are a variety of instruments and interviews that purport to identify the syndromal characteristics of borderline patients. More extensive discussion of these instruments is available elsewhere (Gunderson 1982). For our present purposes, a selected review can focus on options available to the prospective researcher.

Conceptually and operationally, the tightest design would utilize the same instruments to identify the patient's psychopathology at baseline as are later used to assess whether that psychopathology has been altered. The Diagnostic Interview for Borderlines (DIB) has been widely employed and has well-established reliability. Its test–retest reliability has been documented (Cornell et al. 1983), and it appears to be well suited for measurements of change over time. Its principal liabilities are twofold. First, it has used a rather lengthy time framework for some of its components (e.g., questions on interpersonal relations cover a period of two years prior to the assessments). A new edition of the DIB utilizes a more uniform and limited time framework that does not exceed one year (Zanarini and Gunderson, in preparation). Even this time framework, however, would mean that intervals for assessing change could not be less than for a one-year period. The second liability of the DIB is that it views a relatively broad section of symptoms and functioning, some of which bear only an indirect relation to the areas in which psychotherapy is intended to bring about change. Hence, while work functioning can be expected to improve as a result of successful psychotherapy, it is not necessarily an area the psychotherapy can be expected to address directly and it is clearly an area affected by factors outside the psychotherapy. This contrasts, for example, with some other sections of the DIB (e.g., devaluation in relationships) that could be a central part of the psychotherapeutic process and that seem less likely to change due to life circumstances beyond the treatment.

Because psychotherapy outcome measures should be tightly linked to the psychotherapeutic process, researchers may prefer to use additional assessments in areas that are more purely intrapsychic. Along these lines, Kernberg (1977, 1981b) has developed a "structural interview" designed to assess instances of primitive defensive operations, identity diffusion, and reality testing. Because intact reality testing is generally considered to be characteristic of borderline patients, a change on this measure would not be expected from therapeutic intervention. However, reliability on assessing defenses and identity diffusion has not been obtained using the structural interview (Kernberg 1981b). Other investigators have also found the borderline patients' identity problems to be an elusive feature for reliable assessment (Frances et al. 1984; Sheehy et al. 1980).

Other investigators have attempted to take up the challenge of developing reliable measures in intrapsychic arenas. Perry and Cooper (1983) have made scales for rating a variety of defense mechanisms from videotaped interviews. The putative borderline defenses (splitting of self, splitting of others' images, and projective identification) correlated positively with a diagnostic assessment of borderline personality but not with diagnoses of cyclothymic or antisocial personalities. The reliability of the assessments on these defenses is not yet clear. In other assessments examining "major areas of conflict," Perry and Cooper reported that a sample of borderline patients had much more separation/abandonment anxiety, object hunger, and intolerant responses to feeling needy or angry. The ratings on these conflicts were based on descriptions abstracted from the same videotapes used to assess defenses. These ratings utilized the consensus of three raters whose reliability is not described. Hence, these promising new scales on conflict or defenses cannot yet be judged for their potential applicability in psychotherapy research.

In addition to these newly developed assessment techniques already noted, there is a considerable and still growing literature having to do with the performance of borderline patients on previously standardized psychological tests (Gordon and Gunderson, manuscript in preparation). Nearly all of these studies provide teasing suggestions of a discriminable profile for borderline patients.

However, all the studies are beset with major methodologic problems (most commonly very broad or unclear diagnostic procedures, small sample sizes, and inadequate comparison groups), and their ability to provide a useful basis for assessing change in psychotherapy is suspect. Most of these studies have focused on the issue of the reality testing of borderline patients—evaluating Rorschach's original suggestion that the otherwise intact reality-testing function in borderline patients fails when given unstructured psychological tests (Gunderson and Singer 1975; Singer 1977; Singer and Larson 1981). Findings from recent studies are inconsistent on this point (Gordon and Gunderson, manuscript in preparation). Other studies have attempted to identify a characteristic Rorschach pattern in borderline patients in terms of types of defense (Lerner and Lerner 1980), level of object relations (Krohn and Mayman 1974), or oral aggression (Frieswyk and Colson 1980). Again, the results of such reports are promising, but difficult to interpret in view of the major methodologic problems noted above, the questions of validity, and, of course, the problem of reliability. The issue of reliability is even more important and stringent with respect to outcome measures than it is for diagnosis. The reason for this is that the amount of variance from rater to rater or from judgment to judgment by the same rater must be less than the amount of variance introduced by change in order for a measure to be able to provide information about the change. Because the effects of psychotherapy are generally expected to occur gradually over long periods of time with borderline patients, the reliability requirements become very stringent indeed.

Even the development of a highly reliable outcome measure in core borderline problems specific to psychotherapeutic effects cannot replace the need for a broader network of measures by which to assess treatment effects. Traditional areas of outcome assessment in social relations, instrumental performance, signs and symptoms, and recidivism are also critically important. Special note should be made of the need to examine cost effectiveness with respect to borderline patients. The descriptive accounts of both supportive and exploratory forms of psychotherapy describe many similar changes. Both are expected to last at least four or five years before tapering off in those cases which are successful. Moreover, Wallerstein's report (1983) indicates that structural changes may occur with supportive treatment. With schizophrenic patients, a recent study indicated a less intensive, more supportive psychotherapy could be preferential in terms of subsequent work performance of the patients (Gunderson et al., in press). All of these observations raise questions as to whether the additional costs associated with intensive, exploratory therapy reap more or different benefits for borderline patients than will a supportive type of psychotherapy.

Schedule

Another major consideration in designing assessments for a psychotherapy study with borderline patients involves the times at which the assessments should be done. Although there has been general agreement that short-term therapy is not indicated with borderline patients (Mann 1973; Sifneos 1972), this does not preclude evaluating short-term changes within ongoing therapies. As indicated in the previous chapter, successful psychotherapy can be expected to undertake a series of more or less discriminable stages or phases. A more detailed delineation of these phases and stages would greatly assist the researcher who is planning to measure the effects of psychotherapy. The appropriate measures for change during the early period in psychotherapy may well be primarily behavioral, that is, the diminution of self-destructive acts in contrast to, for example, the resolution of splitting mechanisms. The latter might not be expected to occur during this phase but might, in turn, be expected to precede the capacity to maintain a stable or intimate relationship, and so on. A study assessing outcome at six months would utilize very different outcome measures than one assessing outcome at five years. A more definitive description of the different processes of interaction and change within psychotherapy and their external manifestations could greatly assist the researcher. They represent the first step toward the development of manuals that prospectively define the treatment and help monitor and guide homogeneity of techniques. The delineation of phases will also help to select outcome measures and to determine the relative emphasis which the measures should receive over the course of a long-term treatment.

Beyond this, the study of the phases of psychotherapy with borderline patients provides a unique opportunity to understand critical issues of psychotherapeutic process. Horwitz (1974), Langs (1977), and Moras and Strupp (1982) have all pointed to the need to study alliance formation and its relation to therapeutic outcome with seriously disturbed, nonpsychotic patients. Borderline patients are ideally suited for such studies because they cannot be expected to have an alliance initially, but are thought to develop it in cases that eventually have good outcomes (Adler 1979; Frank, manuscript in preparation). The high frequency of dropouts makes study of early interactions of particular importance. Aside from research use, the documentation of such sequences of changes in psychotherapies can obviously provide a framework for clinicians to measure progress and to adjust to the development of therapeutic impasses more responsibly.

Statistical Techniques

Although the data analytic techniques are determined largely by the design, there are several aspects of studying borderline patients that point toward special needs. One of these aspects is that the borderline syndrome is composed of patterns of behavior rather than discrete symptoms. A second aspect is that therapeutic processes occur in stages, and that discrete interactions or techniques may overlook ongoing patterns in interaction that are more critical. This complexity of the psychopathology and of the therapeutic process calls for statistical techniques that assess patterns and sequences of behavior rather than cross-sectional behaviors. Guttman's facet analytic techniques are a constructive effort to develop such techniques, but more experience is needed with them to understand their potential (Shye 1978).

SUMMARY

This chapter has attempted to introduce the formidable array of difficulties that confront the researcher who would like to evaluate the effects of psychotherapy on borderline patients. In the course of this discussion, a number of preliminary studies have been identified as prerequisite before the larger questions of psychotherapy's effectiveness in this patient group can be answered. Among these are the need to identify important prognostic factors or subgroups within the borderline population so as to assure homogeneity or comparability within borderline samples. Current follow-up studies can provide much help by identifying prognostically significant baseline behavior. There is a need to test out the feasibility of gathering an adequate number of willing and qualified therapists to provide treatment and to find a treatment setting in which some control can be exercised over other factors that can be expected to influence treatment outcome (e.g., family, social supports, drugs). Further studies are required on the frequency and causes of dropouts to determine how large an entry sample is needed and what biases exist within samples of remainers. This area has been largely neglected. In addition, reliable assessments on the intrapsychic characteristics which are central to borderline patients and which psychotherapy is specifically intended to modify still need to be developed. There are many hopeful starts in this area but more work is needed. Finally, specific hypotheses regarding the phase-specific techniques and changes that occur in psychotherapy need to be formulated. The accumulative and converging reports from various therapists are helping to fill this need.

Having stated the problems of doing evaluations on the effect of psychotherapy and having listed some of the projects that first need to be done, it should nevertheless be underscored that such investigations are a necessary and inevitable frontier into which the psychotherapy of borderline patients must move. Borderline patients represent a substantial portion of patients seeking treatment. Moreover, both their frequent utilization of hospitals and their substantial long-term problem in work functioning target them as extremely expensive consumers. At this time, the types of treatment for borderline patients are rapidly proliferating, yet most revolve around the central axis of a good and sustained long-term, patient–therapist relationship. The ways in which this backbone to the treatment system operates effectively or ineffectively with borderline patients and the problems in its "taking hold" with many borderline patients demand and await systematic, prospective, empirical inquiry.

5

Self-Destructiveness in
Borderline Patients

Self-destructiveness is the characteristic of the borderline patient's psychopathology that generates the most discomfort in those who attempt to help them. Perhaps nothing enthuses young therapists more than the chance to fulfill the literal promise of their profession and, more generally, one of life's most valued enterprises—saving an endangered life. For therapists who adopt such a clinical mission there are very few experiences that will be as painful as the seemingly spiteful efforts of borderline patients alternately to extend and then to deny the hope that this ambition will be fulfilled. This chapter addresses the nature and extent of this self-destructive activity by borderline patients, the contexts in which these behaviors occur, and what constitutes a useful therapeutic approach to this problem.

DESCRIPTION

Self-destructive behaviors were one of the characteristics of borderline patients which emerged from a review of the descriptive literature (Gunderson and Singer 1975), and which subsequently were found to discriminate clinical samples of borderline patients (Gunderson and Kolb 1978; Perry and Klerman 1980; Spitzer et al. 1979). In work done at McLean Hospital, not only did manipulative suicide gestures emerge as one of the major discriminating characteristics of borderline patients, but several aspects of their personal relationships that were particularly discriminating (i.e., their

85

manipulativeness and masochism) were highly related to this (Gunderson 1977; Gunderson and Kolb 1978). The study by Conte et al. (1980) showed that the depressions of borderline patients differed from other patients with depression by their impulses to hurt themselves. Others who have worked primarily to identify the characteristics of either self-mutilative patients (Graff and Mallin 1967; Grunebaum and Klerman 1967) or adolescents who attempt suicide (Crumley 1979) have shown that a diagnosis of borderline personality is most frequent in such samples.

The summary of admission data collected from 57 patients with a diagnosis of borderline personality disorder who were systematically interviewed further illustrates the extent of the self-destructiveness (Table 4). It also points out that such behaviors are very common prior to hospitalizations or other forms of psychiatric treatment; they are not iatrogenic phenomenon as some have cynically hinted. Almost all of the patients were involved in suicide threats, overdosing, or self-mutilation. Virtually every form of self-mutilation catalogued by Ross and McKay (1979) was represented within this sample.

It is my impression that wrist slashing, the most common form of self-mutilation, is proportionately more common in females than males, whereas no such sex pattern is evident with respect to overdoses. Although there was no usual type of drug used in overdoses, it was noteworthy that none of the hallucinogens that otherwise

TABLE 4. Self-Destructive Acts $(N = 57)$

Variable[a]	N	Noteworthy Patterns
Suicide threats	42	To get attention To cause trouble In rage
Overdose	40	No usual pattern Barbiturates most frequent
Self-mutilation	36	Wrist slashing > body banging >> burning, puncturing, hair removal
Drug abuse	38	Polydrug abuse >> amphetamines, alcohol binges > marijuana
Promiscuity	36	Usually under the influence of drugs or alcohol
Accidents	14	Reckless driving

[a]From the Diagnostic Interview for Borderlines, items 23–28 (Gunderson et al. 1981).

were often used by this group had been employed for this purpose. It is more difficult to generalize about the self-destructive intent of promiscuity, drug abuse, and accidents. Often the interviewer considered these acts more self-destructive than did the patients—a characteristic of borderline patients which is itself familiar to therapists. Overall, 43 of the 57 patients were considered to have made at least one manipulative suicide attempt. These attempts were considered manipulative on the basis of their having been carried out, usually repetitiously, under circumstances where their rescue would be likely and under circumstances that seemed designed to exact some saving response from a specific other person. The three most common explanations given by borderline patients for these attempts were rage at another person, a wish to punish oneself, and a state of panic. The degree to which we found that the variables on Table 2 could distinguish borderline patients from other groups was also found in the work by Perry and Klerman (1980), who were studying an outpatient sample. Sheehy et al. (1980) did not evaluate their sample for the more explicit forms of self-destructiveness but did find that promiscuity and drug abuse were common in their outpatient sample. The high frequency of such self-destructive behavior found in these studies accounts for its inclusion as one of the criteria for borderline personality disorder in DSM-III and, as noted earlier (Chapter 1), it may come closest to representing the "behavioral specialty" which Mack (1975) felt was needed to help define this particular form of character disorder.

The actual extent of the self-destructiveness among borderline patients is grossly underestimated by the gross indices that have been employed in the empirical studies noted above. In more subtle and recurrent ways, therapists recognize the ubiquitous, albeit less dangerous, evidences of self-destructiveness in the everyday life of borderline patients. Characteristic of many of these instances is that the patients themselves ignore the potential dangers or deny any self-destructive intention despite its obviousness to those around them.

PSYCHODYNAMICS:
THE INTERPERSONAL CONTEXT AND PURPOSES

The appearance of self-destructive behavior in borderline patients can often be understood in terms of relationships to primary objects (see Chapter 2). When primary objects are present and supportive, the depressive and masochistic features will be evident, but purposeful self-destructive behaviors of a serious nature do not occur. When a primary object is frustrating to the borderline person or the specter of their loss is raised, then the angry, devaluative, and manipulative features predominate. These are the circumstances under which manipulative suicide gestures and threats are frequent. These suicidal gestures are accompanied by angry and/or despairing affect. They represent efforts to keep the object from leaving and, from an intrapsychic point of view, these acts are used to sustain a belief in the ability to exert omnipotent control over an object as well as to prevent the consequences of object loss. Self-destructive acts here are more interpersonally directed. Interpersonal functions include expressions of (1) anger, designed to hurt a frustrating other (sadism); (2) desperation, designed to gain the attention and protective intervention by others (a cry for help); and (3) anger and desperation, designed to coerce another into compliance with their felt needs (manipulation). In some instances, as Sifneos (1966) had noted, patients whose original self-destructive behavior was accompanied by rage or despair later learn to employ the same act in a more purely manipulative manner as a result of the unexpectedly gratifying response they had received earlier. As noted, these interpersonal functions are especially characteristic of self-destructive behaviors that occur when a primary object is frustrating or a separation is imminent; they can be understood as efforts to reassert a sense of power and control over that object.

When a borderline patient feels an absence or lack of any primary object, then psychotic phenomena (Chapter 7) or intolerable states of "objectlessness" or aloneness (Adler and Buie 1979b) may occur. The central affective experience here is no longer depression or rage; it is one of fear or panic. To avoid these states, several forms of self-destructive activity can be precipitated. These may appear the same as those described above, which are interpersonal and manipulative in nature, but which now occur with different functions and require different therapeutic interventions. To stave off the panic associated with the absence of a primary object, borderline patients frequently will impulsively engage in behaviors that numb the panic and establish contact with and control over some new object. Fights and promiscuity, often assisted by the disinhibiting influence of drugs or alcohol, are common and potentially quite dangerous even though their intent is not self-injurious. If such activities are unavailable, or fail, then dissociative phenomena may occur, and another type of self-destructive action may ensue. Dissociative experiences accompanied by nihilistic fears (e.g., "Am I dead?") may give rise to self-mutilation in order to confirm being alive by feeling pain. Under such circumstances, the self-mutilation is accompanied by restitutive fantasies in which the absent object is either believed to be performing the act or is being punished by the act.

The dynamics of self-destructive behaviors of borderline patients who are reacting to the absence of an object are always complex and almost certainly involve several components. The components, however, are more purely intrapsychic than the interpersonal dynamics prevalent in the second level of function when object loss has not yet occurred. In the absence of a primary object, latent convictions of innate badness may become overwhelming to some borderline patients. The intrapsychic dynamics include: (1) efforts to remove or expel "badness" literally from one's body or self; (2) efforts to punish or hurt an introjected and "hated parent-image" other (Searles 1980), who is experienced as overwhelming; or (3) an act of expiation for sins believed to be committed toward a needed other. In this regard, patients may have borne a guilt for being alive or the guilt may be related to having failed to cure the parent–therapist of some illness they feel responsible for causing. Finally, the behaviors can represent an altruistic retreat from externally directed anger, which serves as a private protest of one's innocence ("I wouldn't hurt anyone"). The degree to which these dynamics get concretized and internalized in bizarre forms reflects the degree to which the breakdown in reality testing has occurred and the degree to which the patient is attempting to deal with a state of objectlessness. One patient, for example, believed that her slashing was "releasing the devil from my body." Another patient, in conscious emulation of his dead diabetic father, would slash himself "to feel as if I am with my father again." More typically, these dynamics do not take on such a concretized or explicitly distorted meaning, but are separated out into their various components only very gradually as part of an analysis of unconscious processes.

These observations provide a grid that can be used for evaluating the self-destructiveness of borderline patients. First is the affect, whether depressed, angry, or desperately frightened; second is the nature of the patient's current relationship to some sustaining or primary object, whether present, frustrating, or absent; and third are the particular dynamics, both interpersonal and intrapsychic, associated with the act. It is critical to know who has been functioning as a primary object for a patient and thus who is necessary for the patient to experience a sense of control over. Finally, although not specific to borderline patients, the context and seriousness of previous self-destructive acts has obvious prognostic significance. Evaluation of these variables can help understand the borderline patient's self-destructive activity; this, in turn, helps to determine which treatment response should be made.

Clinical Management

There is a subgroup among the borderline patient group whose self-destructiveness represents a more malignant pattern. Self-destructiveness among this subgroup is identifiable by its relentlessness, urgency, and indiscriminant quality. When identified, the histories of such patients will often include extreme trauma, such as murders and suicides among close relatives during development. The self-destructiveness is often a reaction to the permanent loss, usually by death, of a primary object. Such patients generally require institutionalization, with sustained preventive restrictions. They usually need to form a strong institutional transference before they can respond to verbal psychotherapeutic limits or interpretive efforts. Such patients are the exception. Most borderline patients undertake psychotherapy with only intermittent and adjunctive use of psychiatric hospitals, and the issue of a patient's ability to control self-destructive behavior or the degree of dangerousness involved will be in an intermediate area where one's clinical judgment is bound to be indecisive because of the intrinsic uncertainties of the situation.

Borderline patients will frequently reveal their self-destructiveness in ways necessitating concern and encouraging active noninterpretative interventions by therapists. A common example is when a patient misses the following appointment after expressing suicidal impulses. Under such circumstances, a therapist is likely to feel that the patient is sadistically holding the "threat" of self-injury over the therapist's head. This is what Brenman (1952) aptly called "emotional blackmail." The therapist may refuse the manipulation and thereby risk the patient's physical welfare, or comply with the manipulation and risk the patient's psychological growth. The former has been advocated by Friedman (1969), Grunebaum and Klerman (1967), and Wishnie (1975). Grunebaum and Klerman concluded that despite "the hazards of suicide . . . response to the regressive and self-destructive symptoms are the greater hazard" (p 170). The latter position, to make the prevention of suicide a primary task of therapy, has been advocated by Shein and Stone (1969). They admonished therapists to make clear to suicidal patients that "the therapist, will do everything . . . to prevent it and that the potential for such an action arises from the patient's illness" (p 143). Neither of these approaches seems necessary or optimal. I believe there is little danger from being manipulated as long as the reason for the intervention is clarified, the meaning of the manipulation is interpreted, and its wisdom is explicitly questioned.

Early in treatment it may make sense to telephone to inquire about missed appointments. Likewise, it may be natural to respond to a patient who complains of an untreated illness by urging medical care, or who reports driving too rapidly by expressing concern. Such commonplace indications of concern may lead to unwanted consequences. The borderline patient may voluntarily give up other functions or may expand the self-endangering behaviors with a new motive: to invite and test a therapist's apparent willingness to look out for the patient's best interests instead of having the patient do so. The skill with which the therapist meets this problem will often determine whether and how quickly a safe and useful therapeutic process will occur.

A borderline patient who had entered treatment because of a depression, which led her to overdose, reports to her therapist that she has a shard of glass in her foot which is festering. The doctor inquires about its severity and then suggests that she should have it seen by a physician. The patient seems pleased by this unsolicited advice. She misses her next appointment. The therapist, worried, calls and she says she is unable to walk and no, she didn't go to see a doctor about her foot. The doctor says her wound could be quite dangerous and urges her to go to an emergency room and reminds her that their next appointment is in two days. She thanks him for calling and sadly adds that the wound and her fever have conspired to make attending her recently acquired job impossible. Lastly, she states that she feels increasingly hopeless and depressed. The therapist inquires whether she feels suicidal. She replies she "doesn't think so." He suggests an additional appointment. She agrees but doesn't come to her next appointment. After 20 minutes, her therapist overcomes an angry impulse not to call but then fears that she may have overdosed again—as she had the last time she'd described herself as "depressed." He calls. There is no answer. Now he is really frightened. As he frantically searches for a phone number of someone in the patient's family, she walks into his office looking very well.

By virtue of subtle but relentless evidence of self-destructiveness, a transition occurred in this therapy whereby the therapist gradually assumed increasing responsibility for the patient's well-being. The patient seemed to accept this passively. Because of the intense feelings generated in the therapist, such a sequence often is the forerunner to the angry disruptions that lead to breaking treatment, and that unreasonably has given borderline patients a "bad" name. This is unreasonable because therapists must share the responsibility for this sequence when it occurs. In fact, borderline patients rarely ask explicitly for the interventions that are made on their behalf, and therapists have little reason actually to be surprised when their unilateral efforts lead to regressions or accusatory flight rather than to the compliant gratitude they may expect. There is little reason for the therapist to withhold such interventions as long as the patient is held responsible for asking for them. Once this is clear, however, the desired sense of "magical control" is no longer at issue, and the patient will find little reason to continue the manipulation.

> Near the end of a psychotherapy session, a hospitalized patient told her therapist that she had lost her appetite and that, in the past, this symptom had preceded her self-inflicted burns. The therapist inquired whether she was concerned that this might occur again. She said she didn't know. He asked whether she had informed the nursing staff. She replied she hadn't and that she didn't feel she could. The therapist expressed skepticism about this but asked whether she wanted him to do this for her. She didn't respond. Since the time was up, the therapist said he would be willing to talk with the nursing staff but he wanted her to accompany him. As they approached the nursing office, the patient became embarrassed by what was an increasingly obvious charade. In the nurses' presence, the therapist again inquired whether the patient wished him to speak for her. She angrily stalked off. The therapist told the nurse of the patient's symptom, the nursing staff responded with concern, and the exchange became the subject of subsequent psychotherapy sessions. The patient said she felt like a "baby" and resented that the therapist didn't "just do it" without "including her." The episode proved a useful frame of reference to understand and circumvent acting on the recurrent

and highly charged passive controlling wishes by the patient and to illustrate the boundaries and functions of the psychotherapy.

When a therapist feels that a patient is "asking" indirectly for something, the therapist should point this out before intervening and inquire whether this perception is correct and what, if anything, the patient had in mind. When therapists feel they must undertake such supportive interventions without explicit solicitation, the patient's reaction to it should be explored immediately thereafter. Some borderline patients will be surprised by the intervention. Its main significance then may be to invest the therapist with a transference as a primary object. Often borderline patients will say they felt the interventions were unnecessary or undesirable. The therapist then can feel relieved of responsibility to continue what might otherwise become a progressive pattern. Having shown a willingness to act in response to what is felt to be indirect solicitations, it can then be safely discontinued only in response to a borderline patient's direct and explicit protest, or after sufficient exploration has occurred whereby the patient has come to recognize it is not in his or her best interest for the therapist to continue to respond in that way. This often means that the therapist must convey an inability to work as a therapist for the patient if he or she cannot work to understand the self-destructivity without acting it out.

If adequate investigation into the patient's reaction to a therapist's interventions is not undertaken, the provocative signals of impending self-destructive activity will recur, and the danger to the patient will be even greater should the therapist (or other object) fail to respond on cue.

A borderline patient periodically rented a motel room and, with a stockpile of pills nearby, would call her therapist's home with an urgent message. He would respond by engaging in long conversations in which he "talked her down." Even as he told her that she could not count on his always being available, he became more wary of going out evenings without detailed instructions about how he could be reached. One night the patient couldn't reach him due to a bad phone connection. She fatally overdosed from what was probably a miscalculated manipulation.

Problems arise when a therapist shows an unwillingness to offer such supportive interventions (to be "manipulated" as the therapist feels it, to indicate "concern" as the patient sees it) or, having offered them, fails to inquire about and respect the patient's reactions to such interventions (the therapist assumes or sees only that it gratifies the patient). In the previous example, a situation had developed whereby the therapist had come to feel increasingly responsible for the patient's life and was increasingly involved in activity outside the psychotherapeutic arena. It is too simple to say this is countertransference; it begins as a generally reasonable approach which will usually be useful with depressed patients. With borderline patients, however, the line between showing concern without inviting a regressive transference reaction is especially fragile. The efforts to be supportively available in the above examples led to a progressive shift of responsibility for the patients' welfare onto the therapists. The therapists saw this shift as manipulative but also as a shift warranted by the patients' neediness.

Supportive interventions bring about such loss of function or increasing self-destructiveness when they are unaccompanied by concurrent recognition and interpretation of the active, adaptive, and purposeful functions served by the patient's response. Therapists often are primarily aware only that such supportive work gratifies the patient's wish to be important to the therapist and to exercise control over the therapist. Less obvious but essential is that the borderline patient is also reacting to the frightening aspects of the therapist's growing invasiveness, that is, that the patient will be overwhelmed and lose control.

In both the first (the injured foot) and third (the pill taker) examples, the therapist's supportive efforts needn't have led to further acting out by the patient—nor to as much anxiety for himself— had the oppositional, sadistic, and controlling nature of the patients' responses been anticipated, accepted, and interpreted.

In the third example, an unworkable situation had developed. If a patient is unable to survive between appointments without repeated contacts with a therapist, hospitalization is indicated. In any event, such phone contacts should be focused on why the patient called and what is wanted: "I know you feel lousy, but what did you hope I could do for you?" This approach—without support or interpretation—will usually discourage the continuation of such phoning insofar as it requires that the patients act collaboratively and make explicit what they can only hope to preserve by its remaining covert.

Thus far I've focused on issues that arise when a therapist intervenes supportively to prevent self-destructive behaviors. Equally common and perhaps more counterproductive is to minimize or ignore the self-destructive dangers. This can be due to a determinedly "analytic" stance by the therapist, or because the behaviors do not seem sufficiently dangerous, or because of a refusal to be manipulated. Whatever the reason, this reaction will encourage the patient to feel neglected or disliked, and borderline patients will respond by "testing" this—usually by flagrantly repeating or expanding their self-destructive behaviors.

A patient who recently moved to a new city began outpatient therapy. After her second appointment, she called the therapist and reported that she had a knife and felt tempted to stab herself. In an ensuing session, she refused the therapist's recommendations to enter the hospital and noted that she was successfully finding an apartment and job. They agreed to meet more intensively for awhile. During the next week she became increasingly angry at the therapist for not giving her adequate direction and alluded again to recurrent impulses to stab herself. The therapist was determined to resist the unwanted burden of being responsible for the patient's life and to create a more "realistic" therapeutic climate. At the same time, he was increasingly concerned about the patient's safety. The issue reached a head when, after leaving the therapist's office, she drove her car into a tree on the hospital grounds—literally outside his office window. The therapist was shaken by the accident and angry at being forced to assume responsibility for her life. Her self-destructiveness had reached a point where it clearly was life-endangering and he decided he must insist on her admission. He recognized that she would respond angrily to this but his major concern was that she would also find it a gratifying precedent. In seeing her shortly after the car accident, he arranged for security people to assist in the hospitalization he was going to impose on her. He informed her of this intent but also informed her that it was not in her interest for him to decide how she should run her life and that she had forced him to do this. The patient responded by smashing his office and then curling up in a fetal position in the corner until she was bodily escorted to an inpatient service. The therapist later felt she had responded violently because she interpreted his statement as meaning that he didn't care about her. She later said she got enraged because he had security guards outside the office and that she would have entered the hospital cooperatively if he had "told" her to. In the course of the hospitalization, the patient decided to move back to a more familiar environment.

One of the important issues illustrated in this fourth example is that therapists need to create situations in which their own anxiety can be sufficiently limited to help patients understand their own behavior. In the first visit after she had called him about her suicidal impulses, the therapist should have stated that even if she opposed hospitalization, his own anxiety about her welfare was sufficient that it endangered his ability to function as a therapist for her. In this instance, both the immediate danger to the patient's safety and the dangers to the therapist's own well-being (legal, professional, and level of anxiety) necessitated the hospitalization. The therapist dangerously underestimated the first issue (the danger to the patient) largely because he was fearful of overestimating the second issue; that is, he felt he shouldn't "give in" to the patient for reasons of his own well-being. Although it is clear, in retrospect, that his efforts to maintain his therapeutic neutrality in the course of hospitalizing her may have been ill timed, it is important in working with self-destructive borderline patients to convey convincingly that you are, in the long run, not able to take responsibility for their lives, that you are motivated by self-interest as well as their interests, and that if they wished to know whether you or anyone cares about them, it cannot be learned by eliciting preventive responses to their self-destructiveness. In this area in particular, therapists are governed by rules of conduct as professionals with legal responsibilities and by rules of society that require them to respond and that clearly complicate any interpretation of such "saving" responses as being motivated only by concern for a patient's welfare. The failure to clarify this aspect of one's interventions will foster the repetition of the self-destructiveness.

Defining the boundaries of the therapist's responsibilities and willingness to accept self-destructive behaviors emerges as a critical issue in the early phases of treatment in the course of any intensive therapy with borderline patients. The pace was accelerated in this instance by the absence of any other objects in this patient's life. Within this example, we see the therapist vacillating between the two reactions commonly prescribed for borderline patients: "set limits, don't be manipulated"; or "be available, prevent suicide." They are basically flip sides of the same coin in which the patient is being seen, unreasonably, either as an angry and greedy child or as a despairing waif. Therapists easily overlook and fail to address that aspect of most borderline patients that genuinely wishes to use the therapist for constructive change. When patients desperately seem to be seeking some form of supportive gratification, it is not obvious that they will be able to address the question as to whether it is in their interest for you to deliver it—even if you could. The therapist in the fourth example was understandably discomforted by accepting a referral whom he experienced as immediately trying to place numerous unrealistic responsibilities on him. In this case, it is probably unreasonable to assign too much conscious manipulative intent to the patient. She was desperate to find someone, anyone, to "hold onto," someone to feel in control of—an issue related to the third and lowest level of function, feeling objectless, as described in Chapter 2. Had the therapist recognized this, he would not have "personalized" her demands and perhaps would have been more appreciative of the need to help her arrange a more structured holding situation in her life—including the possibility of hospitalization—which would make psychotherapy possible. Because he felt that the patient was manipulating him into taking over responsibility by asking him for structure and thus deflecting them from psychotherapeutic work, he underestimated her realistic needs. Therapists commonly underestimate the degree to which borderline patients can later work themselves out of a transference relationship based on a view of the therapist as a "life saver." As long as this remains a transference issue not based on reality, it is subject to the usual processes of revision.

The use of hospitalization is a common problem for therapists intent on not gratifying borderline patients' regressive wishes. Such therapists often view hospitals as harmfully regressive and either openly resist their use or openly encourage rapid discharge. Such attitudes are likely to reinforce some borderline patients' paranoid fears of hospitals or to shame others who feel depressed into even more self-accusatory preoccupations. To outpatients, a reluctance to use hospitals may convey a commitment to be with the patient even though it involves a course that could be life endangering. The clear position that the therapist can be expected to have and exercise independent judgment about the patient's welfare needs to be explicit with borderline patients in order to provide a reassuring structure or boundary within which the therapy takes place. In itself, this position makes hospitalization far less likely. To take a "limit-setting" position with borderline patients about hospitalizations will encourage a regressive transference. Paradoxically, its effect is the same as to take the stance that the therapist is determined to prevent suicide. In the last example, the patient quickly recognized her therapist's countertransference concern about taking "too much" responsibility. It angered her that she was seen as "too much" and frightened her insofar as she had no one else to whom she could turn. She turned her car into the tree and eventually, on leaving the hospital, turned back to the object world from which she came with, I would guess, a deeper conviction of her inability to get something good from relationships. This result is frequent when an approach that is openly wary of the patient's infantile gratifications is taken. I believe that the advocacy of such an approach remains common only because the therapists who advise it only see those for whom such limits can be accommodated. Such patients usually do not form a deep transference relationship—which suits the therapist fine—and they are likely to use the therapist supportively even while they exercise their peculiar "behavioral specialty" or some object outside the therapeutic arena. In such cases, the therapist's task often involves anticipating or interpreting the patient's self-destructive reactions to the vicissitudes of those relationships.

DISCUSSION

This chapter has documented the varied forms of serious self-destructive behavior characteristic of borderline patients. It is important to identify whether such behaviors are primarily designed to: (1) reassert a sense of control over some already-established primary object, (2) locate and control a new object, or (3) delineate or destroy one's "bad" self. The first variation is the most common and the most problematic insofar as the other variations, once identified, may require active unilateral interventions whose gratifying aspects are less central to the reason behind the act itself and thus are less likely to exacerbate the self-destructiveness. When such interventions are employed for the borderline patient who lacks a primary object, it serves to make the therapist into that object. Thereafter the therapist may become the target for the first type of self-destructive behaviors, which are designed to illicit some saving response (i.e., manipulative). If such a saving response is again elicited, it will be likely to perpetuate the self-destructiveness. Recognition of this latter problem has been the usual rationale for a limit-setting approach. Such a limit-setting approach can also result in further and more dangerous self-destructiveness insofar as it heightens the borderline patient's sense of rejection and aloneness and thereby transforms what was originally an interpersonal manipulation into the more dangerous private act of self-delineation or self-destruction.

As Kernberg (1975) has described, the problem is how to provide sufficient support or structure so that a psychotherapy can take place without foregoing the therapist's essential neutrality in the process. The therapists who become intent on preserving their neutrality or who are highly resistant to taking responsibility away from a patient are likely to give inadequate support when it is needed and to exaggerate the power of transference interpretations directed toward manipulation at times when the patient's self-destructive behaviors are due to the absence of having a primary object.

The tensions surrounding self-endangering activity can be resolved by a therapist's readiness to be manipulated as long as it is accompanied by clarification and analysis of the meaning of the saving response. This includes, on the therapist's part, an early clarification of the limited ability to prevent suicide and the legal restraints under which any options not to act are limited. Moreover, it involves early clarification of the harmful and potentially irreconcilable effects that the need for any life-saving activity will have on the therapist's ability to function and on the patient's ability to have a useful therapeutic experience. The consistent, firm, clear, and sometimes repetitious description of these parameters provides a reassuring boundary that most borderline patients will recognize and even appreciate.

One of the major problems therapists have is when they provide supportive interventions without interpretation of the hostile and controlling motivations by patients (see Chapter 6), or when they fail to recognize and respect that such interventions have frightening as well as gratifying significance. A second major problem therapists have is that their concerns about preserving technical neutrality and insisting on collaboration will lead them to personalize too much and fail to intervene in self-destructive activity not primarily designed to manipulate them but reflecting the degree to which a patient's primary objects elsewhere in their life are failing them.

6

An Ego-Psychological Approach to Aggression

Psychoanalytic efforts to understand primitive types of psychopathology often center around the problems in managing aggression and the developmental processes whereby the child walls off, projects, or otherwise directs angry responses to disappointments with their parents. This chapter explores a series of clinical situations in which the expressions of aggression lead directly into the controversies from the literature about how to understand them. These clinical situations also clearly illustrate the limitations of following any simple prescriptive approach to their management. An ego-psychological approach to therapy is offered as a guide that has particular value for some of these situations. This approach will be contrasted with those of Kernberg (1975, 1976, 1979) and Kohut (1971, 1972; Kohut and Wolf 1978), and special attention is given to the concepts of aggressive drive and splitting.

The debate in the 1970s between Kernberg and Kohut clearly involved differences around the management of aggression. Kernberg's object-relations view saw the extreme anger of borderline patients as an expression of a poorly modulated aggressive instinct whose discharge needed to be limited and whose unrealistic basis should be confronted and interpreted. My views differ from this insofar as it includes a conscious effort not to assume that the patient's anger is invalid. In contrast, I support the importance of exploring the actual problems of self-interest, distraction, and personal idiosyncrasy that provoke the anger in the here and now as well as in the patient's past. On the other hand, Kernberg's views give special attention to the maladaptiveness of a child's reactions to early parenting problems and to the resultant pathological sensitivity to reasonable aspects of the therapeutic relationship. Here I find myself in agreement with his views and will illustrate the importance of this in a number of the examples.

Kohut's (1971, 1972) self-psychology has attempted to redress the balance by giving more attention to the secondary and reactive aspects of aggression. He thus emphasizes the real parental failures in development to which the child responded and the real failures within therapy to which patients react. Kohut suggests the experiences of rage be tolerated with implicit approval and that it not be interpreted as defensive, maladaptive, or otherwise pathological. My views differ from this insofar as I would not accept the patient's reconstruction as valid and I would vigorously set limits on the expression of anger directed toward past parental failures. Still the emphasis on anger as reactive to actual limitations and failures is very helpful in both understanding and managing rage. By seeing anger as reactive, the more positive, object-valuing aspects of the borderline patient's pathology are recognizable.

SYMPTOMATIC BEHAVIORS AND THE IDENTIFICATION OF ANGER

Many of the common behavioral problems in the early treatment of borderlines should be actively explored by a therapist from the viewpoint of illuminating their aggressive meaning. The following case vignette illustrates this.

> A recently admitted female patient called her therapist at his home late at night. She was clearly upset. In response to his inquiry, she explained that she did not feel well, her stomach ached, and there was no one on the hall that she felt she could talk to. The therapist inquired carefully and sympathetically about the nature of her symptoms. He then volunteered to call the staff to talk with them about some medication. The patient seemed pleased by his responsiveness.
>
> Earlier that day, she had described to the therapist how she had slept with her mother until the age of 12 and how bitterly angry she was at her mother for having encouraged and supported her handicapping dependency.

Clearly it was not realistically necessary for her to bypass the usual structures by which physical complaints are managed on an inpatient service. The therapist's response implicitly accepted the patient's spiteful and devaluative statement about the hospital staff's lack of concern or competence. That this response lent itself to a subsequent split by which the staff came to be seen as cruel and withholding while the therapist was seen as powerful and kind will hardly surprise the experienced clinician, but is not really the issue here. The therapist's acceptance of the patient's call overlooked its obvious inappropriateness and intrusiveness. Surely she expected him to be asleep when she made the call, and perhaps she even considered he might not wish to be awakened. His response actualized the maternal transference, which in the patient's own reporting of her past experience was harmful. It ignored both the current and historical reality of how the patient's getting into her therapist's, and previously her mother's, bedroom actively and consciously fulfilled the competitive wish to displace her rivals—the therapist's wife in the present and her baby sister in the past. His response should have been, "Why do you call? How did you think I could help you?" Such questions reaffirm the requirement that the motives and feelings behind the call need to be examined and that the ostensible reason, that the patient is upset, is not an adequate explanation for such a call.

One of the first tasks in therapy of borderline patients is to be aware that their symptomatic testing and manipulative behaviors are often indirect expressions of anger. The indirectness of expression prevents the valuable learning about either possible retaliation or the limits of one's destructiveness from occurring. To identify the aggressive meanings and purposes behind such symptomatic behavior requires a conscientious and active effort on the part of the therapist. It is not something that is known, offered, or readily accepted by borderline patients. No one better exemplifies the acute sensitivity to the sinister meanings of patients' communication than Searles (1977, 1980). To the inexperienced or naive observer, it often seems as though such sensitivity reflects cynicism or even hints of paranoia.

Meaningful identification of the aggression behind symptomatic behaviors only occurs when the symptom itself has been delayed long enough for the affect to be experienced and directed toward the frustrating object. These symptomatic acts express and diffuse (give instinctual gratification, in the language of instinct theory) the angry reactions that might have developed. To return to the above example, the midnight caller is unlikely to recognize her anger at her therapist or rivalry with his bedmate until such time as she does not make the phone call. Many of the common problems in the early treatment of borderline patients can only be worked through when their angry meaning has entered into awareness. The patient who regresses during discharge is not only angrily protesting the loss of the hospital but is often expressing angry entitlement to more and better parenting. Moreover, staying in the hospital may be important as a act of financial and public vengeance at the parents. Although such symptomatic behaviors must be taken seriously, it is not sufficient simply to set a limit on the manipulation or to gratify the implicit demand for more protection. Such symptomatic behaviors should be actively inquired about in terms of what the patient is communicating, that is, the sadistic effort to create concern in and extract control over the caregivers. In this way, symptomatic acts become identified as communicating a request for, and protest about, what they are not getting (e.g., being held onto).

COGNITIVE EGO-DIRECTED INQUIRIES

A distinction should be drawn between this approach and the controversial issue of early confrontation and interpretation. The therapist's task is not so much to confront or interpret such behaviors, but to introduce in a deliberate and repetitious way the expectation that the patient should think about what he or she is doing before doing it. This is best done by inquiry—repeated and extensive questioning as to the reasons and the meaning behind symptomatic behaviors. Frequently, borderline patients can acknowledge that they are engaged in behaviors that they expect the therapist to disapprove of or at least that they feel frightened or guilty on account of. For the therapist to have interpreted to the midnight caller its aggressive significance toward the staff or himself or her rivals would have been a mistake. If done on the telephone, it would have gratified her wish to engage him outside the therapy; if done in subsequent appointments, it would easily be angrily denied and resisted—usually with the accusation that the therapist is grandiosely self-referential or paranoid. Careful examination of the contextual circumstances under which such behaviors occur frequently reveals the frustrations or disappointment that triggers the acts.

Nadelson (1977) and Chessick (1977) have noted that it is useful to view the rageful reactions of borderline patients as being reactive, rather than as being a result of drives. Although this is not a wholly satisfactory conceptualization of anger, I agree with it. Not only does this allow therapists to remain detached from the rageful content and thereby diminish some countertransference problems, it also encourages the patient to begin to identify such responses as symptomatic—as Chessick has suggested (1983), almost like a seizure. On occasion I have suggested to one of my patients that, at any point she began to feel righteous and indignant, it was a signal to her to pause and to consider how and to what degree an enduringly sensitive part of her neurotic makeup was being touched on. These are intermediary measures by which a part of what had been ego-syntonic character is made dystonic so that it can be better examined and understood. The therapist's first task is to draw attention to the context in which the anger appears. The emergence of anger is thus seen as the response to some painful reality. This reality then becomes the subject. Such a response calls on and preserves the ego function of reality testing and self-observation.

As I see it, then, there is an important role for the introduction of a cognitive, almost prescriptive approach by the therapist that asks borderline patients to stop, to think, and to understand what they feel angry about before acting. Eventually, this transforms such actions into matters of decision rather than impulse. This is the process by which the patients' aggressive feelings and motives become apparent and by which their expression becomes more selective.

COLLUSION VERSUS ALLIANCE

Another set of problems in the management of aggression arises in borderline patients who are already quite conscious of their rage but view it as justified. In these instances, the rage is too readily seen as caused externally or as explainable by infantile injuries and deprivations. In these latter instances, some therapists will, early in the treatment, knowingly join patients' view of themselves as having been deprived of good parenting. As a result, they may unwittingly join their patients' view of themselves as being entitled as adults. Another variation of such externalization is when patients use mental illness, usually depression, to explain and justify adult failures. The following example shows how.

The patient was a 28-year-old woman hospitalized with unremitting depression. Her depression dated to the age of 12 and she had been in ongoing psychotherapy since the age of 14. From the time she entered the hospital, she was bitterly hostile and attacking toward the staff members for what she perceived as their low class, lack of intelligence, unreasonable rules, and their wish to exploit her family's money. In the course of our initial sessions, I told her that the hospital staff's problems were not the reason why she had to come here and that it was the problems she brought to the hospital, not those she found in it, that she needed to attend to. Finally, I said she should begin by providing me with a history. She responded with rage. Her initial impulse to fire me was mollified by the advice of her former therapist and a senior consultant.

In the course of the later meetings, I learned that her depression occurred when she had her first academic failure in school. This had resulted in alienation from her academically minded father. She insistently believed that her school problems were secondary to her depression and this view had been supported by her previous therapists. When I asked whether her depression might have been secondary to the school problems (thereby suggesting that the school problems reflected some limitation in her abilities), she responded with a sudden and dangerous rage that concluded with her destruction of my desk clock. It became clear when I subsequently pressed for more information about her childhood and the events at the time her depression began that the problems in school had coincided with her menarche. Both her school problems and the menarche combined to disrupt the identification she had previously made with her father—an identification that had been critically important because of the buffer it provided in her relationship with her mother who seemed inaccessible and rejecting. Thus she suffered both a narcissistic trauma to her self-esteem and a reopening of a sense of badness associated with her failed maternal relationship. The accompanying depression had secondarily reestablished and preserved her narcissistic identification with the powerful father—as long as it provided an explanation for her school failure. This meant that, should her depression lift, she would again confront unrealistically high goals that could again only result in failure and the loss of the valued identification/alliance with the father. This explained why she responded with panic and rage to any suggestion that her depression was a result not a cause of her school problems.

The patient eventually quit therapy in the midst of a third rage reaction related to my failures to accept her demand that I conspire with her against imagined persecution of women. Despite prior discussions on the boundaries of confidentiality, she insisted that I agree to withhold information from other treatment personnel. Her discharge of me was accompanied by a return to school and defiant descriptions of how she would show me and thereby earn my appreciation. She subsequently remained in school getting good, but not excellent, grades and continued to visit—on an unannounced and unpaid basis—every few weeks to inform me triumphantly of how wrong I was.

This example illustrates a number of important issues in the management of rage in borderline patients. First, it is important to understand adult rage in more complex ways than as a reaction to inadequate parenting. It must be understood in terms of the defensive adaptations the child made to these parenting experiences. These adaptations are often deeply embedded in such patients' character structure and leave their character structure scarred and vulnerable. Moreover, although the childhood memories of parental failure may be true, they cannot be counted on to portray a complete picture. The parenting experiences become simplified by a devaluative blanket. As Kernberg (1974) has noted, this devaluation process masks the actual life insults and the angry responses appropriate to them. Without having had such an extensive history of past therapeutic failures, I doubt that I would have been emboldened to confront and challenge her conceptions as early in treatment as I did. In any event, I took up with her the fact that she was not entitled to her rage in the here and now—whatever its origin in the past—and consistently and actively pointed out to her the disproportionate and maladaptive expressions of her rage toward me and others in her immediate environment.

This example also illustrates how many borderline patients will attempt to develop a relationship with a therapist based on unrealistic premises. At the time of each of her rage reactions and at the time of her departure from treatment, she was demanding that I agree with her efforts to erase facts about herself and our prior transactions that on the basis of considerable earlier discussion, both she and I knew to be true. It was an insistent, regressive, last-ditch, and ultimately violent effort to overcome and reconstruct reality.

A third issue illustrated by this case was noted earlier (Chapter 3). Leaving treatment is not necessarily a bad outcome, just as staying in treatment is not an assurance of progress. Without exaggerating the gains she had made at the time of her leaving treatment and subsequently, they clearly reflected her having partially given up on her long-term vendetta against her family. She had resumed the business of finding a life for herself separate from them—a life that, for the first time since she was 12 years old, involved the possibility of competitive failure.

As noted earlier, it is difficult to validate the real deprivations of the past without accepting the patient's entitlement in the present. In such instances, the therapist may be unaware of the degree to which a patient's recurrent dysfunctions represent vindictive efforts to exact a price from parents or therapists for their failures. The latter may occur at the same time the patient proceeds to attend therapy regularly and view the therapist as idealized—as long as the therapist does not examine the aggressive meanings of dysfunction occurring within the therapy itself.

Other problems arise with the borderline patient whose rage is unremittingly directed at the therapist. Another example illustrates this.

A 34-year-old practicing art dealer was referred for consultation by her therapist. Treatment had reached an impasse after four years such that she became so enraged in the therapist's presence that she could not speak. In fact, she had previously changed therapists when a similar impasse had led a prior long-term therapy to be terminated. In her meeting with me as a consultant, she was at first reluctant to discuss the problem but acknowledged that she was bothered by feeling rejected by her therapist and was enraged at this feeling. At the same time, she recognized that she herself had similarly concluded that the therapy had become futile, that her behavior in it was inappropriate, and that change was needed. It was only by recognizing the latter that she said she didn't kill herself as a reaction to these rejected and rageful feelings that she had in her therapist's presence.

In the second interview, I became more aware of how she didn't look at me after entering the office—rather she turned her head away and kept her eyes downcast. I inquired about this. It turned out that she had never looked at either of her previous two therapists, that it was the only place in her life in which she behaved this way, and that she did this because "she didn't like to think of her therapist as a person." She literally saw therapists as the embodiments of her withholding, punitive parents and could not differentiate this as transference while in their presence.

I pointed out to her that in the present instance I was neither a parent nor a therapist and felt a right to the same respect she gave others with whom she conducted business. I eventually pointed out that I was doubtful that it would make sense for her to embark on another course of intensive therapy under circumstances in which her behavior seemed designed to create the same problem and which, by her own admission, was behavior within her control. She said, "Why should I look at you?" I said, "The question is what useful purpose does it serve for you to look away?" She subsequently said, "If I looked at you, it would be for your benefit!" I said there was nothing wrong in helping me and, besides, she had to work with me to make this consultation useful. She was surprised at my acknowledged self-interest and began to look at me. This pattern recurred during the next several visits and she expanded on the shameful feelings that she frequently experienced after leaving her therapist's office because of the inappropriateness of her anger toward him. The consultation was completed with a satisfactory referral for group therapy plus a less intensive individual treatment—in itself a recognition that she knew that perspective was needed in her therapy for it to become useful.

Among the issues illustrated by this example are the maladaptive functions that rage can have when it is displaced and enacted within a therapy. Here the transferential meaning (i.e., displacement from the parents) of the indirect expressions of rage were not adequately addressed. This patient was able to experience rage at her therapist as an ungiving parent only insofar as her active role in creating this distortion was allowed to continue. The patient herself was only able to sustain this distortion insofar as she didn't look at the therapist.

The patient recognized the maladaptiveness of her behavior and discontinued it. Had she not, I was quite prepared to terminate the consultation as a waste of time for both of us. For another patient who was in therapy, I eventually responded to his prolonged angry silences by stating that, even if he wanted to waste his time, I had no wish to waste mine. By sitting silently when there was work he needed to do, I was being made a collusive partner in his self-destructive procrastination. I then began to read or write during his sessions. He quickly became openly angry, but he began to talk about issues of importance. Failure to confront and limit such ongoing expressions of rage in borderline patients is experienced as an implicit agreement that their anger is justified. Thereby it does not enter into treatment as transference, and its therapeutic value is limited because it is not being analyzed. Thus not only does it contaminate the effectiveness of the psychotherapy situation, but it supports a maladaptive transfer of a sense of outrage onto the world more generally, which is not in the patient's interest.

In both of these examples, I have indicated the therapist's role as a reality anchor. The development of a working alliance within the therapy depends on some explicit agreements about the task and both the patient's and therapist's roles. This contrasts with some therapists who believe it is therapeutically harmful to provide their views on reality (Kohut and Wolfe 1978; Schwaber 1983). This latter view may be correct with patients whose life functions are not being seriously jeopardized by their distorted hopes or fears, but it is not a standard that can be employed for borderline patients in early stages of treatment.

VALIDATION

The mandate to limit the indirect expressions of anger noted above is for the purpose of exploration and discovery of the reasons behind that anger. It should not be primarily for interpretation of those reasons early in treatment. Nor should the patient's angry response to a therapist's interventions be interpreted as defensive and unrealistic without concurrent recognition that such interventions are, in fact, knowingly painful or possibly inaccurate. Again, especially during the early part of treatment, I believe it is often necessary and useful for therapists to acknowledge they had foreknowledge that their own behaviors (e.g., pointing out a painful reality, failing to get to an appointment on time) would be disturbing. Those communications are not to convey sympathy for the patient's misfortune but to convey an acceptance of responsibility for one's own aggressivity. Winnicott (1975) stresses this issue by citing the need to own up to mistakes and countertransference "hate." Likewise, it is important to identify and validate actual signs of impatience or inaccuracy or inattention when these have triggered off an angry response by a patient. The following example illustrates this.

> A concerned mother called me to raise the issue of whether some further, perhaps different, treatment might be needed for her daughter. I responded by saying that I would talk with the patient about this concern and would get back to her. After talking with her daughter, I suggested that she call her mother while she was still there and could participate on another line. The patient

promptly began a lengthy diatribe at her mother for interfering and poor judgment. It was late and I was tired. After trying unsuccessfully to interject some comments, I put my finger across my lips and went, "Shh," to my patient. She ragefully slammed down the telephone and left. She subsequently told me how she felt demeaned, how she felt I was taking her mother's side, and that she considered not coming back. I acknowledged that it had been an unfortunate indication of my impatience and a better means of getting to the issues I felt needed to be addressed should have been used. She appeared somewhat surprised and certainly mollified by this, and went on to talk about her lifelong sensitivity to instances where she felt she was not listened to and was told to wait while the interests of her parents were given center stage at her expense. This, in turn, led to a productive discussion of how her acting on feelings of anger led her to do things which then forced others to make decisions about her without her participation.

Eventually, such instances help patients to own up to their rageful responses, to be more tolerant of them, and to recognize their potential value in identifying problems, communicating distress, and even, sometimes, how anger can lead to constructive concessions from their environment.

ANGER AND THE CONCEPT OF SPLITTING

One of the characteristic features of the experience of anger in borderline patients is evident in the prior examples. They appear to have only a rather fragile capacity to maintain a reasonable and benign view of their significant others when faced with frustration, separations, or rejections. One borderline patient told me how hard she worked to "maintain a loving view of my daughter." She explained, "If I let my negative feelings out, it ruins all the positive and I can't appreciate her." When the child disobeyed, she was aware of withdrawing, feeling extremely tense, and this then would give way to suicidal impulses. Another patient responded to having had her angry motives identified by protesting, "You think that all I am is anger—that there's nothing else but that!" She then became depressed and said that, if that were true, she would kill herself. These responses speak to a very different, non-entitled reaction to being angry. Here the experience of being mad is followed by a conviction of one's "badness" and a suicidal impulse. In these instances, angry, aggressive feelings and wishes are kept out of awareness or are poorly tolerated. If owned, they are experienced as overwhelming and dissolve any sense of personal value.

These are the types of phenomena for which the concept of splitting has frequently been applied. However, the concept of splitting doesn't seem to do justice to some important aspects of the phenomena observed in these examples. To understand why borderline patients sometimes experience anger righteously and other times as indicative of their badness requires examination of whether the anger is experienced secondary to a perceived environmental failure to fill needs (i.e., when its cause is seen as external, their anger is acceptable). Other anger is expressed primarily to stake claims for one's self against sources of frustration that are impersonal; then the anger is seen as bad and unacceptable (i.e., its source is seen as internal). When the latter form of aggressiveness is thought of as expressing some adaptive aggressivity that has previously been dissociated, then its emergence may reflect therapeutic progress (i.e., healthy anger). The point is that the concept of splitting does not take into consideration the importance of what precipitates the anger—the environmental (especially interpersonal) context and the particular meaning it has to that individual. Brandschaft and Stolorow (1984) have gone so far as to say that anger in borderline patients is an iatrogenic product of therapists who do not consider the current interactional context as necessary for understanding. Among other difficulties with applying the concept of splitting to explain borderline anger is its failure to describe what accomplishes the shifts; that is, some form of ego-regulatory mechanism must be involved. Finally, the explanatory principle offered by splitting for the sudden eruption of hostility toward a significant other gives undue emphasis to idealization as an alternative to the angry and devalued view of important objects. As stated elsewhere (Chapter 2), the experience of being angry does not eradicate the capacity for a realistically ambivalent view of the therapist or other significant object. I prefer an explanation where the patients who suddenly become rageful or accusatory toward a significant other are understood to be reacting to something frustrating in their immediate interaction that signifies a form of neglect, rejection, or separation.

No doubt borderline aggression reflects a mixture of reaction and drive, yet it is the reactive aspect that is the essential component to emphasize in clinical work. In this respect, I have agreed with Kohut (1971) and Chessick (1977) who, in turn, agreed with their

predecessors—Fairbairn (1941), Balint (1968), and Modell (1963)—
that the aggressive, angry characteristics of borderline patients are
largely reactive and defensive in nature. The role of an environ-
mentally created or genetically determined excessive "aggressive
instinct" remains a viable and valuable theoretical possibility, but
it is not required to explain borderline psychopathology. In any
event, it would lack specificity because the same theoretical construct
has been used to explain other adult disorders, such as schizophrenia and depression. I largely agree with Robbins (1976) and
Meissner (1978a) in their thoughtful critiques of theories that posit
a hypertrophied aggressive drive to explain such anger.

HOW TECHNIQUES EFFECT PROCESS OF CHANGE AND OUTCOME

In the examples cited in this chapter, I have tried to show that
either to accept the validity of the patient's views or to see them
as invalid distortions both run the risk of overlooking one of the
central processes that psychotherapy can offer to borderline patients.
The most frequent problem by therapists dealing with borderline
anger is accepting too much legitimacy in the patient's anger. This
can result in efforts to diminish the frustration or accept without
intervention the prolonged but indirect expressions of anger within
the therapy. A second common problem arises in too quickly pointing out how disproportionate or unrealistic the anger is. This may
confirm the patients' convictions about their destructiveness or
prevent the patients' useful expression of aggressive impulses. Either
of these reactions can forestall sufficient investigation of the reasons
for the anger. The first reaction, legitimizing the anger, underes-
timates the patient's strengths and encourages the development of
regressive transference, which can be dangerous or result in treatment impasses. The second reaction, too much intervention, may
underestimate the patient's pathology and prevent sufficient depth
of the transference to develop. Both extremes of intervention will
essentially prevent a well-developed but contained negative transference to enter into the therapeutic work.

What is required is to stay between these extremes—to recognize
the patient's angry regression as an important indicator of a failure
to accept the therapist's importance and value (i.e, the anger is
toward someone who is felt as loved and needed), and its defensive

role in being a means of protecting the patient from more direct expressions of anger and in preserving unrealistically inflated expectations of supportive availability. In other terms, the essential therapeutic task during this period is to generate enough concern about object availability to keep the patient aware of and motivated to learn about the issues but to be sufficiently available to contain regressions within manageable and not too dangerous limits. Unremitting anger of some borderline patients in response to possible object loss can occur early in treatment and its potentially dangerous consequences (i.e., suicide attempts), negative therapeutic reactions, or further regression must be taken seriously. Usually this can be interrupted simply by the therapist's increased activity while still retaining a basic psychoanalytic position of investigation. When this fails, other sources of structure or supportive contact must be used before threatening the patient by greater frustration or unavailability. After repeatedly going through these patterns, a growing psychological awareness by patients permits greater frustration tolerance and diminishes the likelihood of self-destructive acting out. Within the context of a stronger alliance or with greater preparatory work in examining the underlying issues, more developed and object-specific expression of the angry feelings behind a patient's devaluation, manipulation, and projection can be allowed to persist without necessitating limits by the therapist (see Chapter 3).

Limiting the expression of anger while focusing on what makes the real environmental frustration so upsetting directs the therapeutic task into an ego-directed model rather than one that is corrective, cathartic, or interpretive. Central to the therapeutic progress of borderline patients is the process of learning (both through identification and cognition), which results from delay of action when it is accompanied by thoughtful consideration of both the meaning and consequences of anger. This introduces new and appropriate means for problem solving. An approach that emphasizes inquiry and self-observation diminishes interpersonal hypersensitivity and works to enlarge the ego's role in the identification and modulation of aggressive impulses. This process of neutralization is a largely neglected aspect of the management of aggression, which is important to the psychology of borderline patients and is important to the processes of change from treatment. Similarly, the recognition and acceptance of the self-serving and explicitly frustration-generating behaviors on the part of the therapist encourages patients to accept their aggressive motives without action or undue renunciation. This too is a technique that is helpful, but does not fit comfortably with either of the two alternate object-relations models of how aggression should be managed that have been offered by Kernberg or Kohut.

It should be noted that most of the discussion of the management of aggression in this chapter has concerned issues in the early phases of treatment. In the intermediate stages of treatment, different processes of psychotherapy and different techniques may be needed to help borderline patients integrate their aggression (see Chapter 3). It is conceptually intriguing, however, to recognize that the differences in the way in which aggression is managed during the early and later stages of treatment may determine some specific and incompatible benefits in outcome from treatment.

Kohut (1971) is refreshingly clear in his statements that the outcome of treatment by his methods will primarily promote the acquisition of highly valued sociocultural attributes such as empathy, creativity, humor, and wisdom. In contrast, he states that "the increase in the capacity for object love must be considered an important but nonspecific and secondary result of the treatment. . . . The more secure a person is regarding his own acceptability, the more certain his sense of who he is, more safely internalized his system of values—the more self-confidently and affectively will he be able to offer his love without undue fear of rejection and humiliation" (pp 197–198). In my experience, successful outcome primarily in the area of object love results when patients have worked through an intense but contained negative transference in which their capacity to tolerate object frustrations and separations have taught them both the adaptive potentials and the limitations of their aggression. In other words, this form of outcome involves movement from a psychological position in which borderline patients are preoccupied with the failures and limitations of others to which they respond with rage to a more advanced psychological position whereby patients recognize the maladaptive aspects of their character (which had developed in response to these failures by others) and further recognize the limitations that their character structure now imposes on them in terms of their capacity to be lovable and to love others. This type of outcome requires that patients accept the active and responsible role they have in creating recurrent interpersonal problems in the here and now. For most borderline patients, this type of outcome, I believe, can only be achieved by a treatment that follows Kernberg's recommendations of limits and confrontation about the unrealistic and overdetermined nature of ongoing rage.

This chapter has sought to illuminate the common problems in management of aggression in borderline patients and to suggest some practical forms of suggestions on useful intervention. In the process, some problems of understanding the rages of borderline patients using existing theoretical models have been identified. However, no more satisfactory model by which to understand borderline aggression and its management emerged from this review. In conclusion, I would like to complicate this discussion further by the following case example.

> In response to her therapist's vacation, Connie began work as a salesperson. As a result of her rapid success as a salesperson, she frequently missed appointments, but also felt much more self-confident. That therapist approved of this new adaptation and the patient was eventually emboldened by her success to feel sufficiently confident to accept a marriage proposal which previously she had turned down. However, once married, her inability to tolerate both her own and her husband's separations and anger quickly led to the dissolution of that marriage. This had been the precipitant for her resumption of a second course of psychotherapy. Once again, in the course of the second treatment, when the therapist went on vacation, the patient resumed work as a salesperson. Again, this precluded her regular attendance at the sessions. The therapist saw the resumption of work and subsequent inability to attend therapy regularly as an acting out that masked her feelings about his absence. He actively interpreted to her the anger behind her leaving him as she felt he had left her. In this context, the patient quit her job, but held the therapist responsible for her chronically dissatisfying sense of unproductivity.

Each therapist makes decisions about the extent to which the patient's activities are adaptive expressions of aggression and to what extent such activities reflect unfortunate displacements of affects properly contained within the therapeutic relationship. When the activity seems adaptive, but deflects energy from within the therapy, it becomes a delicate question as to when, how, and how strongly these aggressive meanings should be interpreted. The Kernberg–Kohut debate and the examples given in this chapter suggest there are significant costs to patients as well as benefits for whichever pathway a therapist pursues.

7

Psychotic Regressions in
Borderline Patients

Transient psychotic experiences are one of the central character-istics that define borderline personality disorder. Disparate clinical observations that have provided the background and basis for more recent empirical investigation into defining the borderline syndrome have focused on this characteristic. Psychologists have noted the unexpected capacity of this group of patients to regress in unstruc-tured psychological testing situations, such as the Rorschach, into a primary process mode of cognition. Psychoanalysts have noted how such patients, when misdiagnosed as neurotic, can develop transference psychoses or even regress into a more classic schizo-phrenic denouement in the context of the psychoanalytic situation. Inpatient administrators have noted how such patients may become preoccupied with paranoid concerns or regress into disorganized or withdrawn behaviors more severe than the problems that caused their hospitalization. Such observations explain how the various efforts to formulate the underlying psychological coherence of borderline personality have included lapses in reality testing as a critical feature (Frosch 1964; Kernberg 1976, 1979a; see also Chap-ter 2).

A recent series of empirical investigations has found that the presence of mild psychotic experiences provided useful discrimi-nating information in defining the borderline syndrome (Gunder-son 1977; Gunderson and Kolb 1978; Perry and Klerman 1980). Even Grinker (1979), who selected a borderline sample in his orig-inal study (Grinker et al. 1968) for the absence of psychotic experiences, has more recently indicated that the presence of brief ego dystonic psychotic experiences is particularly helpful in discriminating the borderline syndrome from a comparison group of schizophrenic patients. In light of this, it is surprising that the DSM-III criteria for borderline personality include brief psychotic experiences only as an ancillary feature. The rationale behind this remains the subject of controversy (see Chapter 1). In any event, the discriminating value of mild psychotic experiences, which was particularly evident in comparisons with nonpsychotic control groups, can be expected to be further highlighted in studies in which the borderline syndrome is delineated from other forms of serious personality disorder.

This chapter describes the types of psychotic experiences common to borderline patients, explores the context in which psychotic experiences occur, and discusses various forms of psychological intervention that prove useful in managing these psychotic experiences in both psychotherapeutic and hospital settings.

CHARACTERIZING THE PSYCHOTIC EXPERIENCES

The following description is the result of scanning the interview record of 25 patients diagnosed as having a borderline personality disorder by using the Diagnostic Interview for Borderlines (DIB) (Gunderson et al. 1981). Psychotic experiences on this sample of borderline patients can be roughly divided into the following five types.

The first type, affective phenomena, particularly involves sustained beliefs in self-worthlessness and unrealistic preoccupations with inner badness and destructiveness. Delusions associated with sinfulness or inadequacy are rare.

The second type, dissociative phenomena, includes the classic signs and symptoms of depersonalization and derealization. Research has shown that such phenomena are not more frequent but are particularly sustained in borderline patients compared with schizophrenic patients (Gunderson et al. 1975; Gunderson 1977). Common phenomena are feeling outside of one's body associated with nihilistic fears and having perceptual changes of the size and shapes of themselves and others.

It is extremely difficult to determine whether the third type, visual and auditory perceptual distortions, involves actual hallucinations. They are usually transient but are believed to be real while they are being experienced by borderline patients. They sometimes involve testing behaviors to determine their reality. Examples include: imagining the presence of someone and holding animated conversations with that person, hearing one's name being called out over and over in a clear and specifically described manner, seeing visions of demons or ghosts (one particularly colorful vision consisted of a man dressed in white who carried an ostrich), hearing one's mother's voice calling and having to turn on the light to see whether she was present.

The fourth type, paranoid beliefs, are most frequently ideas of reference that occur intermittently, sometimes becoming a part of a patient's daily life over a period of months. Sometimes these beliefs take on more organization, such as a man who believed his wife was unfaithful, would get enraged about this, but then be able to reassure himself that it wasn't so. Another patient had concerns his neighbor was spying on him but was concurrently aware that such concerns were probably unrealistic.

The fifth type involves self-boundary confusion. Not infrequently, borderline patients describe episodes when they have felt their minds can be read by other people and/or that they can read the minds of others.

The above examples illustrate the "borderline" (meaning marginal) nature of the psychotic experiences in this patient group. Others (Spitzer and Endicott 1979) have suggested that most of these experiences refer to illusions or overvalued ideas and to some disorganization of behavior, but they are not clearly psychotic in the same sense as are hallucinations or delusions that are acted on. Although the above reports were gathered from inpatients, Koenigsberg (1982) and Perry and Klerman (1980) also found that borderlines in an outpatient setting scored higher than nonborderlines on mild psychotic experiences such as episodic depersonalization and derealization, transient psychotic episodes, psychotic episodes in psychotherapy, distorted perception and ideas of others, and even the presence of psychotic thinking at the time of interview. Perhaps even more characteristic of these psychotic experiences than their content is the subjective experience, first noted by Knight (1954), whereby such patients are able to view their psychotic percepts as alien and dystonic.

All of these mild psychotic phenomena occur in the absence of drugs, yet the frequency and intensity of such experiences are increased when using psychoactive agents such as marijuana or alcohol. Likewise, borderline patients can develop more well-organized and sustained delusional ideas when they have taken other psychotomimetic agents such as LSD or mescaline (Gunderson 1977; Gunderson and Singer 1975). I believe that the appearance of serious psychotic symptoms with the use of marijuana or alcohol is a particularly strong indication for a borderline diagnosis; like the presence of sustained dissociative phenomena in the absence of drugs, however, it occurs with insufficient frequency to be counted on for diagnosis.

THE ENVIRONMENTAL CONTEXT IN WHICH PSYCHOTIC EXPERIENCES OCCUR

Frosch (1964) first underscored the capacity to lose the reality-testing function transiently but noted its generally good preservation in borderline patients. This was subsequently affirmed by Kernberg (1967, 1971). Meissner (1978a), however, notes that neither Kernberg nor Frosch make it "clear how their theoretical underpinning allows for the preservation of reality testing in one context and not in another" (p 309). In my view, as noted earlier (Chapter 2), the borderline patients' reality-testing function accurately reflects the degree to which the borderline person feels related to a primary object.

When the borderline patient feels in contact with an essentially supportive object, the sense of reality is intact. When this object tie is threatened by frustration or the possibility of loss, the relationship to reality becomes shaky, but the reality-testing capacity remains intact. When there is a felt absence of a primary object, the reality-testing function itself becomes shaky or—as in the dissociative reaction—the feeling of reality is clearly disrupted. In other words, the reality-testing function is regressively and defensively sacrificed in response to the perception that there is no single enduring and basically caring person available. It should be noted that it is not necessary that the primary object relationship be to a person; this relationship can be assumed by the external structure provided by other stable, enduring, and positive forces in the borderline patient's life, such as can be provided by work or an institution. The fluctuating reality-testing function is related to the degree of external structure—whether some of this structure is inanimate or derived from a stably present interpersonal relationship. Hence, the regression of psychological functioning with the emergence of primary-process thinking, overelaborated affects, and breakdown in reality testing has been noted repeatedly in unstructured situations as varied as psychoanalysis (Hoch and Polatin 1949; Knight 1954), Rorschach testing (Rappaport et al. 1946; Rorschach 1942; Singer 1977), and unstructured work (Frosch 1964) or school (Slavin and Slavin 1976) programs. Psychotic phenomena thus represent efforts to ward off the subjective experience of aloneness (Adler and Buie 1979a, 1979b). Under ordinary circumstances, this aspect of a borderline patient's psychology is evident in a need to have people around—even without any evident emotional contact—or in the use of radio and television as hypnotics. Under the extreme circumstances when a specific and essential object relationship has been lost, the reaction will most frequently be dangerous impulsive acts consisting of or accompanied by use of drugs or alcohol. When relief from such impulsive actions is unavailable, then the psychotic experiences described above occur.

Each of these psychotic-like experiences has object restitutive meaning; that is, they are intrapsychic means of restoring the lost object. Dissociative episodes detach the borderline person from the reality of bodily distress or the reality of the environmental situation which evoked that intolerable distress. Such dissociative episodes are accompanied by nihilistic fears, which may give rise to self-mutilation in order to confirm being alive by feeling pain. Such nihilistic fears are in the "borderline" area between an affect and a belief. Such self-mutilation is frequently accompanied by restitutive fantasies in which the absent object is either believed to be performing the act or is being punished by the act—in either event, remaining involved. The object-restitutive aspect of the visual and auditory perceptual distortions is often painfully evident because frequently a voice or an image providing soothing companionship is involved. Finally, with respect to ideas of reference, not only do these help project unacceptable self-judgments, they also allow and sustain a sense of involvement with nonspecific others at those times and under those circumstances where none is felt to exist.

Understanding the context—the "objectlessness"—in which psychotic phenomena occur in borderline patients is important to anticipate their occurrence and to guide the clinical management. I've suggested elsewhere (Chapter 3) that the resolution of the cause of these phenomena may be largely related to the nonspecific activities in psychotherapy.

MANAGEMENT OF PSYCHOTIC EXPERIENCES IN PSYCHOTHERAPY AND HOSPITALS

The following case vignette illustrates some of the principles about the understanding and management of psychotic experiences in borderline patients.

Mary is a 16-year-old identical twin whose sister, Adele, had recently been hospitalized for an overdose. Soon after Adele's hospitalization, Mary attempted to assume her sister's position working at a drug store. Shortly thereafter she began getting depressed and disorganized. She described seeing a gray-coated man whom she believed was following her, although peers with her at these times could not see him. She sometimes heard voices telling her to hurt herself and described becoming extremely anxious and temporarily disoriented when walking by boys on the street. She carried on conversations with pet animals in which she sometimes believed they spoke back to her.

At the urging of a voice which told her to do so, she took a razor blade and carved the initial of her sister, "A," on her forehead. About the actual cutting, she said she did not realize what she was doing but felt at the time she was drawing a picture of a horse on her head. After cutting herself several times, she "came to," that is, she realized she was cutting herself and immediately threw the razor away feeling surprised and frightened at what she had done.

Only at the insistence of the school authorities did her parents agree to a psychiatric evaluation, which led to her hospitalization. At the time of her admission, she spoke clearly about past events. Although she described having had visual and auditory hallucinations, these were described as transient and were viewed by her as having been due to her imagination. With respect to hearing a voice telling her to cut herself, she replied that she no longer had such a wish and viewed her having done that as "stupid." There was no indication of an overt consistent thought disorder. There was no further evidence of disorganization, hallucinations, and dissociative states during her hospitalization. When her sister, Adele, was discharged from the hospital, Mary temporarily became depressed but was able to use the hospital for structure and support, which she described as taking the place of the stability usually provided by her sister. In psychotherapy, her therapist developed the impression that, when stressed, Mary would become temporarily confused with mini-dissociative experiences in which she was only vaguely aware of her actions and could retrospectively only dimly remember the events that occurred during such times.

In general, most of the overtly psychotic-like experiences of borderline patients occur outside the hospital or psychotherapeutic context. They are common complaints leading such patients to seek psychiatric help. Occasionally they occur early in hospitalizations (before an institutional transference develops) if family support for the hospitalization is uncertain or if family availability is jeopardized by the hospitalization. Once within a therapeutic context, the need for a supportive and sustaining object has been ameliorated to a large extent, thereby diminishing the likelihood that psychotic phenomena will recur.

An instructive detail from the above case presentation concerns the failure of the patient's parents to recognize the mandate for intervening with Mary until the school authorities insisted on it. The degree to which the parents failed to be aware of their child's need helps explain how Mary could have formed her primary object tie to her sister in their stead. A life-long pattern whereby the pre-borderline child is emotionally unknown by the parents has been found to be characteristic of many of the families from which borderline psychopathology arises (Gunderson et al. 1980). When such a family system exists, it is generally not productive to attempt to use the parents as reliable and sufficiently safe external sources of structure and support. Under these circumstances, helping family members to be reconciled to this fact and the provision of a new residential long-term setting in which more consistent structure and support can be expected will be preferable.

A second family pattern that has been more frequently the focus of the limited literature about the families of borderline patients is that where the parent has served as the primary object for the pre-borderline child but, in response to the separation pressures of adolescence, withdraws support (Masterson and Rinsley 1975; Zinner and Shapiro 1975). Under these circumstances, working with the family members to modify the destructive aspects of their reactions to separation while retaining them as enabling and facilitating sources of support to the borderline offspring is the indicated approach.

Until this point, we have largely described and discussed psychotic experiences that occur outside the therapeutic context. In fact, if a patient experiences hallucinatory phenomena within a therapist's office, this would be a signal that the therapist's leverage as a primary object tie is not established. Likewise, the patient experiencing long dissociative reactions provides a mandate for the therapist to provide new and ongoing sources of external support and structure. These phenomena provide evidence that the patient's reality testing, and therefore judgment, cannot be trusted; nor can a reliable alliance with the patient be counted on. The therapist must be prepared to make unilateral interventions.

Borderline patients also have psychotic experiences that occur after a therapist or a treating institution has taken on the role of primary object. Within both contexts, borderline patients can have psychotic experiences on occasions when they feel they have lost their object or fear being too controlled and thereby in danger of losing their identity. With Mary, one should have anticipated that plans for a rapid discharge—which did not include her return to her sister and were not associated with her having continued contact with a therapist to whom a primary object tie had been established—would result in a recurrence of the types of psychotic experiences which led to her hospitalization.

The recurrence of such phenomena frequently occurs around time of discharge; these experiences are frequently seen by treating personnel as manipulations. This is inaccurate. Other borderline phenomena, such as angry devaluations and manipulative self-destructive acts, generally precede the appearance of psychotic experiences; it would be accurate to understand the purpose of such phenomena as manipulative. The failure to recognize the significance of psychotic experiences when they recur and, as a result, to push discharge under such circumstances, however, is exceedingly dangerous. It will invariably lead to desperate impulsive behaviors, such as drug taking and promiscuity—which may be self-destructive in their effects, even if not their purpose—or to a recurrence and expansion of their psychotic experiences. This is illustrated by the following example.

Sarah, a 20-year-old inpatient, was preparing to leave the hospital. In this context, over a 24-hour period, she became uncontrollably labile, with long periods of loud giggling interrupted by brief episodes of nonspecific anger. Despite insistent and repeated interventions, she appeared unable to hear or understand what was being said. This behavior came after an earlier wrist slashing, which had not deterred the staff from continuing the transition program. In response to her disorganized affective disruption, the transition from the hospital was delayed and a new aftercare program that insisted on her returning to the hall for biweekly visits was formulated. The giggling diminished and she expressed open panic about her concern that something terrible would happen to the hospital if she left it.

This example illustrates a different form of psychotic-like regression characterized by overelaborated, loosely connected affects similar to that observed in some borderline patients in unstructured test situations (Singer 1977). It also illustrates how the concrete reassurance about the continued availability of the primary object (i.e., the hospital) could terminate the psychotic episode and, in this instance, permit a successful transition to occur. The capacity to make a successful transition from the hospital for this very severely disturbed borderline patient reflected a capacity to develop a new transitional object. The use of an institution as a transitional object by borderline patients has been described by Crafoord (1977). Sarah's capacity to distort her relationship in a psychotic manner both to the hospital and to a previous therapist had proven responsive to the periodic introduction of conjoint meetings of the patient, her mother, and members of the hospital staff or her therapist. Shapiro et al. (1977) have described how transference distortions can be diminished by increasing the degree of contact between the patient and a parent—when that parent had served the function of the prior primary object—by conjoint meetings.

Within the psychotherapy situation, psychotic experiences can occur when a therapist is too impassive and inactive, as in a classic psychoanalytic situation or under circumstances where the therapist is absent (e.g., on vacations or even, in particularly sensitive patients, on weekends). The following example, similar to one cited above with respect to the hospital, occurs within the context of a psychotherapy.

Louis is a 23-year-old who had been making steady progress in therapy when he proposed to go on vacation with the expressed intent of enjoying himself for the first time in years. When the therapist expressed some support for this plan, the patient angrily demanded to know whether he would be charged for the two missed appointments. When the therapist said "no" the patient rose from his chair, became angrily accusatory about a psychiatrist in an adjoining office who he claimed alternately listened in on his sessions or made loud noises so as to interfere with them. He then sat down and declared that his therapist had been systematically overbilling for the previous six months. The therapist expressed surprise at this idea but the patient stonily and intensely made it clear there was no doubt in his mind that this

was factual. Recovering from his surprise, the therapist went on
to interpret how angry he (the patient) was at the therapist's
willingness to let him go. Undaunted by this, the patient visibly
relaxed only after the therapist indicated he would be glad to
insist on his staying in town if that's what the patient wished. It
was left that the patient could return early if he wanted to or
call if he preferred. He shook the therapist's hand on the way
out.

The intense, clear but reversible nature of this patient's paranoid
experience is illustrative. As in the previous example, reassurance
about the ongoing availability and interest—even, in this case, to
the point of expressing a willingness to provide a fictional external
control—reversed the patient's regression and allowed the patient's
separation to proceed. It should be stressed that, in both of these
examples, the interventions were successful because the institution
(in the first instance) and the therapist (in the second instance)
had established themselves as a primary object relationship. The
appearance of psychotic ideation is generally the end point of a
regressive process that can be forestalled earlier within a psychotherapy by the use of insistent and intrusive confrontation, limit
setting, or even affectual expressions on the part of the therapist
(Friedman 1975; Masterson 1976). Kernberg (1971) noted how,
when a transference psychosis occurs in borderline patients, it can
be reversed by increasing structure within the therapy or, failing
this, in the life situation outside the therapy.

On returning from vacations, therapists are particularly likely to
hear about the occurrence of mild psychotic experiences. Not only
may this be a helpful indication in revising one's diagnosis toward
the borderline category, it can provide a signal whereby future
absences can be managed so as to prevent the recurrence of these
psychotic experiences or the other more self-destructive responses
to feeling "objectless." The following are examples of the many
ways this can be done: increasing contact with other members of
a treatment team, arranging telephone contact during the intervening period, giving an address and phone number to be used on
an as-needed basis, or arranging an interim therapist.* Which if

---

*In this same way, it may be useful to consider the role that psychopharmacologic
agents have for borderline patients. They are, of course, frequently used self-
destructively. This, however, occurs on occasions when patients feel that overdosing can be used to coerce an overly frustrating object into being more supportive
or to forestall an impending loss by a primary object. Drugs can also be abused
by borderline patients under circumstances where no primary object is felt to be

any of these is optimal should be determined by the degree to which the therapist's absence can be tolerated. Employing these in response to the borderline's angry threats is only indicated when such threats are predictably followed by deeper regression into psychotic experience. Inexperienced clinicians are generally much more afraid about such options being abused than they need be.

There is yet one other circumstance in which borderline patients may become psychotic within the therapeutic context. In contrast to the above examples, which focused on the appearance of psychotic ideation in situations when a patient feels alone, borderline patients may also become psychotic when they feel too tightly controlled by their primary object. Several authors (Friedman 1969; Wishnie 1975) have warned about the regressive spiral that transpires for borderline patients within inpatient settings. They focused on how an overly nurturing milieu can lead to an acceleration of angry and self-destructive behaviors, which in turn leads to tightened restrictions as the sequence by which such regression occurs. They view such a regressive spiral as destructive and argue for short-term hospitalizations or outpatient psychotherapy as a means to avoid these. It is undoubtedly true that the regressive spiral they describe often occurs and is, in my opinion, unproductive if not destructive. It, however, is not a necessary component of either ambitious "uncovering" treatment or of long-term hospitalization, but should be seen as reflective of a treatment team with limited experience and stability (see Chapter 8).

In any event, the psychotic phenomena that emerge in these situations are usually paranoid in nature. The paranoid beliefs focus on the malevolent intentions behind restrictive policies and can

---

available as a means of blotting out the subjective experience of aloneness. However, under circumstances where a therapist has been established as a primary object for a borderline patient and the medications are used in recognition of the fact that the therapist's absence will be a source of distress, a prescription will then be experienced as an extension of the therapist that diminishes the unavailability and can have a salutory effect in preventing the serious acting out and psychotic phenomena from occurring in the therapist's absence. This is entirely independent of whatever pharmacologic action such drugs may have. Prescription of drugs becomes dangerous by a therapist who has become a primary object when it is experienced by the patient as indicative of the therapist's guilt about an absence or as evidence of the therapist's inability to understand or accept how badly such an absence will cause the borderline patient to feel. Hence, the administration of psychoactive agents to counteract or prevent psychotic experiences requires a very sophisticated and careful judgment on the part of the therapist where a misjudgment could be quite hazardous.

lead to secondary panic whereby window breaking or other efforts
to make "space" occur. The subjective experience here is of suffocation, not aloneness, and there may at times be explicit distortions
such as misidentifications or mind-reading beliefs. I have even seen
mute withdrawal with brief catatonic-like posturing on several
occasions. When such psychotic experiences occur in restricted
borderline inpatients, the situation no longer contains the potential
for the valuable working-through of a negative transference, which
is often the stated goal of such a treatment strategy.

The following case report illustrates how such psychotic beliefs
can emerge in both hospital and outpatient settings.

> Marjorie is a 31-year-old who entered the hospital after a serious
> suicide attempt. There was no evidence nor history of psychotic
> ideation. Her latent wishes for nurturance were stimulated by
> the enclosed ward and supportive attitudes of staff members. At
> the same time, she became frightened of their motives. After a
> special privilege to stay up late was revoked, she became suspi-
> cious of the envious motives of the staff and other patients—even
> fearing that the food might be poisoned. Later that day she escaped
> from the hospital and refused to return.
>
> In subsequent discussions with her therapist, she dismissed the
> more overtly paranoid concerns as temporary exaggerations but
> maintained that the jealousy toward her was real. She continued
> in intensive outpatient treatment and became paranoid once again
> approximately one year later. This time her paranoia took the
> form of fears about dangers in public places and, in fact, fears
> about practically everyone except her therapist. This occurred at
> a time when she was becoming more aware of positive feelings
> toward and longings to be cared for by her therapist. The para-
> noid concerns were sufficiently disabling that she usually confined
> herself to her house or, if she went out, she disguised herself. She
> resolved this dilemma by finding a boyfriend with whom she felt
> protected—ostensibly from the outer world but in truth more
> from her intensifying attachment to her therapist.

This exemplifies how psychotic experiences can transiently appear
in treatment contexts where the issue is not one of object loss but
one whereby different defensive needs to maintain distance are
jeopardized by the yearnings for closeness evoked by the therapy.
In both instances, the patient herself resolved the paranoid experiences by finding ways to create distance whereby she could keep
her longings in check. One could formulate the emergence of
Marjorie's paranoia either in terms of her fears of engulfment or

in terms of her fears of experiencing the emptiness and loneliness that would accompany acknowledgment of her wishes for more nurturance. In any event, the management principle is that such patients should be given the distance they wish without any threat to discontinue the treatment. Thus, in the first instance, it would have been wise had the hospital staff been less solicitous and restrictive initially and kept the door open for her to return on a flexible basis without threatening to discharge her or to reinstitute previous controls. In the second instance, although possible to interpret the protective function that the boyfriend served for Marjorie, it would have precipitated a further flight from involvement had the therapist insisted she drop that relationship because it represented an acting out of a transference that was incompatible with analyzing the transference. It took nearly a year of productive work before Marjorie willingly gave up a boyfriend and was sufficiently trusting to be less fearful about depending on her therapist and on an adjunctive partial hospital program.

SUMMARY

This chapter has described the characteristics of the mild psychotic experiences found in patients with borderline personality disorder. They generally fall into the following categories: affective, dissociative, perceptual distortions, paranoid, and self-boundary confusion. Both their frequency and their value in discriminating borderline personality disorder from other patients indicate the rationale for their being considered a core diagnostic characteristic. The theory is advanced that borderline patients develop their psychotic phenomena largely under circumstances where they have suffered the loss of a primary object whose presence is considered necessary and without whom they would experience intolerable aloneness. This explains why the psychotic phenomena that borderline patients experience usually occur outside a therapeutic context. When such phenomena occur, they are serious indicators of the need to provide more structure—either within the therapeutic context or outside of it. Means of doing this which are described include the following: diminish the degree of object loss (e.g., restrictions, family meetings, increased visits, telephone contact) or provide substitutive objects (e.g., hospitalize, interim therapist, medications). A distinction is made between the treatment implications for psychotic experiences when they occur in borderlines and the less severe borderline phenomena such as disruptive anger, devaluation, and manipulative suicide attempts, where confrontation and limits are the appropriate means of intervening. Finally, another circumstance where borderline patients become psychotic is presented: in response to contact with objects experienced as too enclosing or too intrusive. The principle of management for such circumstances is to allow the patient more control over the amount and type of contact.

8

Hospital Care of Borderline Patients

The available estimates of the frequency with which borderline patients are admitted to inpatient services come from examinations of consecutive admissions: (1) in university, private, and community hospitals, where the incidence is 10 to 24 percent (Kroll et al. 1981, 1982; Soloff 1983); (2) in tertiary private hospitals, where the incidence is 21 to 25 percent (Andrulonis et al. 1982; McGlashan 1983a); or (3) in catchment area hospitals, where the incidence is about 18 percent (Dahl, personal communication, August 1, 1982). Whatever the frequency with which borderline patients are admitted to hospital services, they are easily the most common type of personality disorder found on inpatient services, and the degree of difficulty and time required for their management is clearly disproportionate to their numbers. The present chapter is an attempt to identify issues that often make hospitalization of borderline patients difficult and to describe how such problems can be circumvented to the point that the positive benefits of a hospital course are actualized.

INDICATIONS FOR HOSPITALIZATION

The overall role of the hospital in the treatment of borderline patients is usually one reserved for the management of regressions or crises and seldom involves long-term inpatient care—as long as the patient has an active, ongoing outpatient psychotherapy (Marcus 1981;

Masterson 1976; Nurnberg and Suh 1978; Wishnie 1975). When patients are not in psychotherapy, one of the major functions of the hospital is to complete an evaluation and then to initiate and consolidate some form of ongoing outpatient therapy programs. For patients hospitalized in the context of an ongoing psychotherapy, the hospital can be used to diminish transference distortions, to intervene in response to self-destructive or antisocial acting out, or to prevent foreseeable destructive reactions to their therapist's absences or other events. Kernberg (1968) has also suggested the use of hospitalizations to contain and confront ongoing acting out that has effectively prevented meaningful outpatient therapy. In my experience, only very sensitive, psychotherapy-oriented units can do this well. Most of the time, such hospitalizations fail either because borderline patients turn their angry transference onto the unit and continues to act out within the hospital so as to render it (the hospital) impotent or because the unit sidesteps its containing role and sides with the patient's projections about the therapist. The latter may result in a change of therapist.

Even though utilization of a hospital may not be necessary, access to a hospital and a readiness to employ it are essential parts of the armamentarium therapists need to treat borderline patients. The possible need for hospitalization should be discussed with borderline patients as soon as it becomes clear that it may be needed. Therapy based on a therapist's professed commitment to keep a borderline out of the hospital, as suggested by Schmideberg (1959), is often foredoomed to fail insofar as borderline patients will test the degree to which such therapists will accept either regressive transference demands or the patient's self-destructiveness without setting limits. Paradoxically, the therapist's tolerance for either of these is likely to be experienced by borderline patients in ways that contradict their professed wishes—as a disregard for their welfare or as a reflection of the therapist's avoidance of their anger. In this regard, the employment of an enforced hospitalization in the beginning stages of treatment may provide a cornerstone for building a reasonable therapeutic alliance.

An indication for hospitalization that therapists frequently are reluctant to recognize is when their own discomfort in working with a borderline patient as an outpatient interferes with their ability to listen to material with equanimity and respond to it with the necessary flexibility. Interpretation will often be the first technique to disappear. As described elsewhere (Chapter 5), lurking in the background of such circumstances is generally a growing preoccupation by the therapist with the patient's safety—a preoccupation that is not being explicitly addressed within the therapy. Under such circumstances, if a therapist is not able to convey the cause for this anxiety in a way that the patient recognizes as being realistic (i.e., the patient denies concern about his or her own welfare), the therapist should nevertheless insist on the hospitalization solely because of its role in allowing the therapist to continue the therapy. If the patient still refused the hospitalization and is not committable, the therapy should be terminated.

A frequently overlooked and often most desirable treatment setting for borderline patients is day care. Crafoord (1977) has written about the therapeutic action of day care as being due to the movement back and forth from an institution, which provides the sustaining function of a transitional object with which separation anxieties are repeatedly evoked and reassured. Unfortunately, the value of day care is frequently diminished by the predominance of chronic patients in such programs. This has the effect of making the staff poorly prepared for or particularly intolerant of the actions of borderline patients. Such programs make the desirable milieu activities of interaction with peers and limit-setting harder to provide. Short-term (six to eight weeks) day treatment has been recommended by several authors (Adler 1973; Pildis et al. 1978). This recommendation is most valid for those borderline patients who have community supports such as jobs and have a strong therapeutic alliance. Nevertheless, for large numbers of borderline patients, long-term, properly designed, day-care programs can be life sustaining and growth producing.

SHORT-TERM HOSPITALIZATION

As noted above, for most patients who have an outpatient psychotherapy, the need for full hospitalization is intermittent and time limited. For patients without an outpatient therapist, instituting psychotherapy may be the major role of the hospital. Other goals for short-term hospitalizations are to effect environmental changes, introduce new therapeutic modalities, obtain evaluations or consultations, and contain crises as described above.

Effective short-term hospital units should contain elements of high structure, clarity, and organization (Ellsworth 1983). There should be an emphasis on order and control. The boundaries for "appropriate" behavior are clearly spelled out and contractual agreements are common. An example of a contractual agreement used at a unit specializing in borderline patients is seen in the Appendix on page 183 (courtesy of Dr. Jerold Kreisman, St. Luke's Hospital, St. Louis). This is used to establish a tone of high behavioral expectations and formal collaborations.

Structured, task-oriented groups are useful. Little emphasis is placed on emotional expressiveness, the formation of new relationships, and the sharing of problems with other patients. Nevertheless, even on a short-term unit, the flagrant negativism and devaluation that accompany separations or discharge can be convincingly identified in ways that allow more adaptive behavior and deeper psychological issues to emerge. This type of unit has a practical, business-like orientation. Patients are expected to sustain contact with people in the community and rapid triage is uniformly implemented. When possible, a discharge date is established near the time of admission.

Many writers have emphasized the importance of being able to set limits early and consistently for borderline patients (Adler 1973; Friedman 1969; Kernberg 1979b; Nurnberg and Suh 1978; Pildis et al. 1978; Wishnie 1975). This is an element of effective short-term work that is important for all patients—more so for borderline patients only insofar as they are more resourceful in illuminating the problems caused when short-term units are not so designed. Perhaps more specific for borderline patients is the role of therapeutic discharge—nonpunitively exercising the option to discharge patients who are seen as either willfully disruptive or otherwise failing to make positive use of the milieu program. This form of limit underscores the requirement of collaborative involvement and makes the hospital a valued opportunity whose availability is contingent on demonstrating an ability and willingness to work with the staff.

Some features of short-term hospitalizations of borderline patients and how they compare to long-term hospitalizations are summarized in Table 5. Much of the success or failure of short-term hospitalization will depend on good management of the admission and discharge issues and the avoidance of major staff changes, which will be discussed later.

TABLE 5. Characteristics of Short-Term Versus Long-Term
Hospitalization of Borderline Patients

Short-Term Units	Long-Term Units
Indications	
Crises (rage, overdoses)	Inadequate social supports
Consultations/evaluations	(incest, assaults,
Therapist anxiety: preventative	abandonments)
admission	Malignant self-destructiveness
Psychotic transference	Sustained depersonalization
Milieu	
Support	Containment
Structure: limits/tasks	Structure: limits/tasks
Groups (problem-oriented,	Groups (community expressive
focused)	meetings)
Clear leadership: by	Shared decision making
professionals	One-to-one meetings
Objectives	
Prevent self-destructive action	Modify manipulative patterns
Decrease anxiety	Internalize capacity for delay and
Support strengths	decrease impulsiveness
Triage to aftercare	Develop social and verbal
Modify prior therapies	communication skills
	Increase trust/dependency on
	people
	Vocational training

LONG-TERM HOSPITALIZATION

Some advocates of short-term hospitalizations do so as a result of
the harmful regressive and disruptive courses they have observed
when borderlines are given long-term hospital treatment (Friedman 1969; Wishnie 1975). Last et al. (1973) have described another
harmful course—a lengthy hospital course marked by the patient's
extreme passivity, secondary gain, and growing chronicity. Such
downhill courses have led many clinicians to advocate terminating
hospitalizations by discharge or transfer (Friedman 1969; Grunebaum and Klerman 1967; Nurnberg and Suh 1978; Quitkin and
Klein 1967; Scharf 1969). I believe such courses are not a usual or
predictable consequence of long-term hospitalization, but are the
product of poorly designed or implemented milieu programs.

Indications for long-term hospitalization for borderline patients include a more sustained and malignant pattern of self-destructiveness. This is frequently accompanied by depersonalization, but sustained dissociative experiences in themselves are frequently alleviated only by the sustained and tight holding situations such as the inpatient service can provide. In addition, long-term hospitalization is indicated for those borderline patients from very disturbed or neglectful family situations—for example, those maintaining a high level of denial despite life-endangering action, those where the patient's disability has assumed a focal role around which the parents devalue and fight, and those where actual physical abuse or incest are occurring. In such circumstances, recurrent disruptions in the patient's life can be expected and a lack of reliable support for the patient's ongoing treatment as an outpatient is predictable. Conversely, for those borderline patients who come from overinvolved, separation-sensitive families, short-term hospitalizations with sustained concurrent individual, family, and parental therapy on a long-term outpatient basis are likely to be the most desirable treatment package (see Chapter 9). Even here, however, careful evaluation of the degree to which the overinvolvement between the patient and the parents may prevent meaningful engagement in outpatient treatment is needed. When long-term hospitalization is needed, active involvement by such families should be part of the hospital program.

Goals of long-term hospitalization include all those noted for short-term stays and include four others. Long-term hospitalizations for borderline patients should attempt to modify maladaptive interpersonal patterns, to develop a greater capacity for delay of action in the face of frustrations, to enable the patients to have a more charitable view of themselves and others, and to strengthen the patients' vocational or scholastic abilities.

THE RINSLEY–MASTERSON CONTRIBUTION

The most widely cited and recognized descriptions for long-term hospital treatment that have been applied to borderline patients are the accounts by Rinsley (1965, 1967, 1971) and by Masterson (1971, 1972, 1980). Although in their original papers they discussed this from the more general perspective of residential treatment of adolescents, they subsequently identified the patients for whom their treatment recommendations were directed as having a borderline personality in its broader sense. Despite their broader definition of borderline, these recommendations about long-term treatment and its proper conduct are clearly appropriate to more narrowly defined borderline patients. The congruence of their original descriptions of residential treatment programs led to their collaborative effort to formulate the developmental origins of borderline personality (Masterson and Rinsley 1975). For purposes of this chapter, their descriptions are joined into a common account.

First, Rinsley and Masterson advocate an initial phase of hospitalization within a closed ward. This will diminish the opportunity to discharge drives and affects through action, enforce the need to become engaged with the staff, and make available the underlying significance of the previously acted-on transference to the institution/parent. Second, the patient should be separated—by force and by legal means if necessary—from his or her parents, and any contact (including correspondence) should be carefully monitored. The rationale for this is that the child/patient's psychopathology expresses the pathological family constellation, which can be understood only if it is interrupted. Third, Rinsley and Masterson advocate the concomitant initiation of psychiatric casework in order to diminish the likelihood of the family's reaction to their often profound separation anxieties by attempting to undo it or to communicate anxiety to the patient in ways that will heighten the patient's resistance to the hospitalization.

Having set such structure for the treatment program in motion, the initial phase of residential treatment has been variously termed the resistance/alienated/projective/protest phase of work. To quote Rinsley: "The major purpose of identifying, interpreting and precluding the patient's and the parents' early resistance behavior is to detach the patient from the pathogenic family and to enforce engagement with the treatment staff" (1971, p 490). It generally takes from six months to a year. Rinsley infers that the critical patient–staff interactions during this period occur around the setting of appropriate limits to contain the patient's behavior and to convey an irrevocable commitment to the separation process and the assumption of surrogate parental roles. It is also accompanied in casework with the parents by efforts to redirect their attentions and to become reconciled to the separation. The end of this phase is marked by the parents having developed sufficient trust in the treatment structure that they relinquish parental functions to the hospital and thereby end the loyalty bonds which supported the patient's ongoing resistance. From the patient's point of view, it is marked by "control of the acting out, a consequent deepening of the depression, and the spontaneous recall with appropriate affect and detached memory of the history" (Masterson 1972, p 125).

The second major phase of long-term treatment has been variously termed the working through/depressive/introjective/despair phase. At this point, the patient may appear clinically to be worse with the emergence of clinging, depression, depersonalization, and other psychotic-like experiences. Now, however, the patient is able to lean on the staff and to talk about these experiences of inner badness and past experiences related to development. Both Rinsley and Masterson suggest that much of this working through may take place in the course of individual therapy. Masterson emphasizes the importance of interpretation to clarify nuclear abandonment experiences and to work through the rage and depression associated with this. The implication is that the major function of the staff is to continue to provide a supportive, tolerant, and accepting environment in which these processes can safely proceed. Rinsley is more equivocal about the role of the individual psychotherapist, at one point suggesting that individual psychotherapy is not essential for many "symbiotic adolescents" and that staff talks can provide the corrective experience. Out of this period of regression, the patient then emerges better able to associate with the family while retaining a distinct view of the self. The patient is now ready to begin the process of separation from the hospital. The usual duration for the second phase of treatment is one year.

At the conclusion of the second phase, the patient enters the third and final stage of treatment termed the resolution/reconciliation/desymbiotization/separation phase. This phase can generally take place within outpatient or, at most, community residential treatment settings.

Rinsley (1971, p 501) summarized the overall hospital course as follows.

> In the case of the symbiotic adolescent, essentially locked within a prolonged unresolved mother/infant fusion relationship . . . the predominant therapeutic work of the resistance phase of treatment is addressed to recognition, externalization and interpretation of the adolescent's fantasies which center on reunion with megalomanic control of family members, notably the parents and especially the mother. As these occur, the residential program increasingly emphasizes progressive socialization, graduated

expansion of privileges, peer competitive participation, including residential school, occupational and recreational therapy, and increased personal responsibility.

It is important to keep the Rinsley–Masterson contribution in perspective. It is a model of intensive and ambitious treatment in sharp contrast with the literature stressing confrontation, limits, and rapid triage. I believe its application should be limited to those adolescents, or even adults, who have an extremely disruptive and destructive relationship with their parents. Hence, this approach should be employed under circumstances where conjoint treatment programs have been ruled out and where placement in a less restrictive alternative (to full hospitalization) such as a halfway house, boarding school, or day-care program have proven inadequate.

Under circumstances where careful selection for this form of long-term residential treatment has been completed, Rinsley's admonition that the treatment team must be prepared to convey a commitment to the patient in the form of consistent limits set on the family should be emphasized. Concrete evidence of this commitment to separation is invariably needed for such treatment. Once it has been firmly established, however, the exclusion of the parents from active involvement with their hospitalized offspring called for by Rinsley and Masterson may not be necessary.

One of the most common forms of resistance by families whose children have entered long-term treatment involves the effort to retain control over the treatment situation by obscuring their financial resources. This leaves both the patient and the treatment team in limbo as to their ability to work through whatever issues might be raised in the hospitalization—especially those issues relating to the patient's anger. This persistent ambiguity about the feasibility of long-term treatment speaks louder than any words of assurance that staff members can give about their commitment to treatment. It will essentially prevent any productive work from ensuing. Under these circumstances, the limit that must be set visibly (i.e., so that the patient knows of it) is a contractual agreement for underwriting the costs of a minimum length of stay, say one to two years.

A Critique

In many instances when a long-term intensive treatment program is required, the exclusion of the family from contacts with the hospitalized member is unnecessary or undesirable. The type of strict monitoring of all contact between the patient and the parents or the exclusion of the parents altogether to contacts only with the caseworker, which has been advocated by Rinsley and Masterson, should be employed under those circumstances where contact with the patient has been shown to have a demonstrably destructive effect on the patient. Even here it is preferable to attempt to get the patient to join in setting the limits on parental visits or calls. The separation should be unilaterally imposed by the treatment team only under extreme circumstances where the destructive reactions to parental contacts are visibly dangerous and where a judgment has been reached that the patient is unable to articulate the reasons for their destructive reactions or their need to have a limit imposed on these visits.

As the above comments suggest, a general warning about the Rinsley–Masterson model of treatment would be that a less unilateral, less restrictive approach be attempted each step along the way before assuming "in loco parentis" functions. For the large majority of borderline patients for whom long-term treatment is indicated, the assumption of "in loco parentis" responsibilities by a treatment team will not be necessary and should not be employed. Rather, a treatment approach giving the patient enough leeway to experience separation issues without being overwhelmed by them can be initiated from the beginning. This means that both parental contacts and the level of hall restrictions should be carefully regulated such that the separation and abandonment anxiety remains within an optimal level for learning.

Empirical Evaluations

Two recent studies have attempted to bring some empirical evidence to bear on the issue of efficacy of long-term inpatient treatment.

Masterson and Costello (1980) have done a follow-up on 31 of 59 borderline adolescents treated at Payne Whitney during the period that Masterson had been in charge of its inpatient unit. Of the other 28 patients, 6 could not be located, 9 were not evaluated extensively, and 13 were not evaluated at all because they left the program before therapeutic benefits were expected to occur (less than one year). The information available on these 28 patients all pointed to the conclusion that they were sicker initially and would do worse after discharge than the 31 patients who were followed. Table 6 summarizes follow-up evaluations, which on the average occurred four years after discharge, for the 31 patients who received a substantial "dose" (mainly greater than one year) of the Masterson inpatient program. These data indicate a broad range of outcomes. Based on Masterson's clinical experience and previous research on the course of untreated adolescents, the authors believe that these outcomes are a substantial improvement over the expected outcomes from untreated adolescents with similar problems: "Many would, no doubt, be dead, in hospitals, or in prisons" (p 100).

It was clear from this report that the better outcomes belonged to those borderline patients with higher initial ego strength, more ideal inpatient treatment experience, and far more extensive aftercare. The conclusions reached by the authors about the high benefits from the hospital treatment program must be considered controversial in the absence of control groups. The fact that only 53 percent of the original sample was followed, and that this subsample can reasonably be expected to have a better range of outcomes than the others, further precludes any firmly based optimism. Nevertheless, their report provides a valuable resource for interested readers by carefully describing the course and outcome of individual cases and thereby allowing independent judgments to be rendered about the quality of the outcomes. These case reports make it clear that a sizeable number of the patients followed up were functioning at a level that was far better than at the time of their admission and that required modest or no ongoing treatment. These good outcome cases contrast with the generally grim pictures found in previous follow-ups on less intensively treated borderline samples (Gunderson et al. 1975a; Pope et al. 1983; Werble 1970). These descriptions also leave no doubt that even the good outcome patients remain constrained by the continued and more subdued

TABLE 6. Follow-up Functional Impairment

Level of Impairment	Number of Patients	Percent
Minimal (0–10%)	5	16.1
Mild (20–30%)	13	41.9
Moderate (30–50%)	7	22.6
Severe (more than 50%)	6	19.4
Total	31	100.0

Source: Masterson and Costello 1980, p 98.

expressions of their character pathology. This study is a landmark effort to evaluate the effects of a specified and extensive residential treatment program for a borderline sample. The fact that the conclusions obtained from the study are controversial only highlights the need for future studies that build on this one in search of more definitive answers.

A more recent follow-up study has been reported by McGlashan (1984) on borderline patients given extensive residential treatment at Chestnut Lodge. These patients were diagnosed as borderline retrospectively but with methodological vigor and, along with comparison groups, were given extensive blind follow-ups 7 to 15 years after admission. There was evidence of very good functioning in the borderline group compared to comparison samples in his study. Because many patients received extensive aftercare, the specific effects of the hospitalization cannot be isolated. Nevertheless, this study joins that of Masterson and Costello in supporting the claim that there may be powerful long-term effects from the use of well-designed long-term hospitalization for selected borderline patients.

PRINCIPLES OF LONG-TERM TREATMENT

There are obvious contrasts between optimal short-term units and what would be ideal for long-term treatment of borderline patients (see Table 5). Here, there are more specific characteristics for the milieus that are particularly well suited for borderline patients as opposed to other patient groups. Such milieus should place a high emphasis on therapeutic processes, which I have elsewhere defined as involvement, structure, and validation (Gunderson 1978).

Involvement is facilitated by multiple groups in which patients are encouraged to share feelings and problems with each other and to understand behaviors within interpersonal contexts. Borderline patients profit from the opportunity to recognize the implications of such knowledge about others by becoming participants in decision-making processes. These programs, which are based on the principles of a therapeutic community as outlined by Jones (1956) or on the principles for groups described by Rice (1969), are especially likely to help with the identification and modification of maladaptive interpersonal patterns of behavior such as manipulation, seduction, and other efforts to control others. These processes are facilitated by having a stable (low turnover) staff complement composed largely of people who are contemporaries in age with the borderline patients.

Structure refers to those aspects of a milieu program that order the roles, time, and rules by which the milieu is run. Borderline patients function better when there are clear rules concerning conduct and consequences. A unit's set of privileges and restrictions, and the behaviors that lead to each, provide the scaffold for learning about maladaptive aspects of their interpersonal behaviors and especially about delay of impulsive actions. It should be emphasized that it is not in the restriction (or the privilege itself) but in the recurrent implementation of these that the borderline issues of authority, self-destructive spitefulness, and the deep sense of their own destructiveness toward others can be joined and modified. This is the arena whereby the milieu acts as a holding environment containing the aggression of borderline patients and helping with its integration and modification. The result is a corrective experience by which this aggression is experienced as less omnipotent in its effects and by which aggression by others is experienced as less sadistic. Another beneficial use of structure involves a focus on the practical issues involving relating adaptively to the larger nonhospital community. Basic practical training about common problems of daily life—such as budgets, birth control, nutrition, transportation and employment—should be considered.

Validation refers to those means by which a milieu fosters and encourages patients to operate at the fringe of their known capacities, to explore new behaviors, and to experience feelings without interference. These are formulated by ample one-to-one meetings with a staff member that manage new levels of intimacy. Once formed, such relationships should be allowed to continue on an as-needed basis after discharge. These actions of a milieu help to reinforce the sense of a stable self and a greater appreciation of one's creative capacities and limitations. This function is useful in encouraging or allowing borderline patients to express and own feelings of affection, warmth, disappointment, and loss. It is most important insofar as it assists borderline patients in reconciling themselves to the limitations on their abilities which other aspects of the hospital program or their transition into the community bring forcefully to their attention.

I believe that long-term units should ideally make some compromise between both the closed-door and open-door philosophy by maintaining an open door, but with the expectation that patients explore or explain their comings and goings from the hall. This demands the highest level of responsibility, which borderline patients are capable of while maintaining a constant focus on the issue of separation.

MANAGEMENT ISSUES

Admission

Many, if not most, of the management crises related to borderline patients revolve around admission and discharge, and the issues of separation and autonomy joined during these periods. The literature about hospital treatment of borderlines is replete with comments about the harmful, regressive spirals that borderline patients frequently become involved in within hospitals (e.g., Adler 1973; Friedman 1969; Hartocollis 1980; Wishnie 1975). The usual sequence by which this occurs is that the borderline patient seeks admission in an apparent state of desperation. This patient is then met administratively by the seemingly appropriate concern for the patient's welfare and a readiness to assume major responsibilities for that patient's life. This concern is implemented administratively by immediate restrictions on the patient. The patient then responds to this by feeling suffocated or controlled and begins to complain—either in the form of paranoid accusations about the staff's efforts to humiliate or exploit or by protesting that the problems are over and were not significant in the first place. The staff is then likely to feel betrayed or at least unappreciated for their efforts and begin to insist on the seriousness of the patient's condition. This leads to increasingly panicky reactions on the part of the patient, including "three-day notices," efforts to escape, and covert efforts within the hall to develop protective alliances. It may lead to impulsive and desperate actions, such as smashing windows to escape the subjective experience of suffocation literally. It may also lead to desperate efforts to regain some sense of control through self-mutilation (Ross and McKay 1979) or by becoming litigious and calling in lawyers. All of these reactions lead to further alienation between the staff and patient, with escalating anger and anxiety on both sides.

This sequence is particularly common on halls that have hierarchical distributions of authority whereby the "on-line" people cannot respond flexibly to borderline patients—a situation aggravated whenever those with decision-making authority are either geographically removed from the hall or feel unsupported by higher levels of hospital administration. It is also common on those long-term units that have an enforced period of restriction at the beginning of hospitalization for the ostensible purpose of "getting to know patients." Finally, it is common within hospitals where administrators are insufficiently experienced and supervised (especially common in teaching hospitals).

It follows from the above description that the earlier this regressive spiral can be interrupted, the better. The critical issue is having sufficient experience and the administrative support for the responsible staff to recognize that, although the regressive acts can be quite dangerous, they do not necessarily represent a sustained, ongoing mental state in the patient for which restricted residential care is required. The act of hospitalization itself for such borderline patients often will fill a need for holding and a sense of being cared about which can greatly affect the borderline patient's capacity to function and immediate feelings of self-worth. Under these circumstances, the fear of abandonment and the efforts to prevent it which led to the hospitalization quickly become background issues. The focus then shifts to retaining some control over their object—in this case, the hospital—in order to diminish their paranoid anxieties about being smothered, swallowed, or poisoned. These patients are now overwhelmed by a new set of fears (e.g., of becoming slavishly dependent, of being bullied, or even of ceasing to exist) and need to react against such fears by demonstrations of their capacity to maintain control. This accounts for the apparent paradox of how seemingly desperate borderline patients can respond gratefully to hospitalization and, almost before the door is closed, begin to complain about overcontrol and to demand privileges. Hartocollis (1980) has drawn parallels here to the developmental dilemma of the rapprochement subphase. This, I think, does not do justice to the more primitive paranoid or nihilistic fears that may occur.

Sensitive management of this situation requires ongoing statements of concern about the patient's welfare and a readiness to allow the patient some sense of control by decreasing restrictions when it is clear that they feel an urgency and desperation about this. When privileges are given, it is likely to be accompanied by considerable anxiety on the part of the borderline patient as concerns about aloneness, rejection, and competence again rise to the surface.

This can be dangerous when the privileges are given in an angry or rejecting way without accompanying expressions of concern by the treatment staff that it may be premature and that the patient should turn to them at the first sign of trouble. Bond (1984) advocates "paradoxical" techniques to help diminish the development of a regressive transference to institutions. He details cases in which patients' angry resistance to assuming responsibilities was reversed by joining them in underscoring and dramatizing how incompetent they are. The staff actively stress the patients' inability to function and caution against the risks of utilizing any privileges. The patients then respond, negativistically, by wanting to show the staff how much they are underestimated.

Keeping patients preoccupied by structured activities also helps to diminish concerns about containment during the early part of their hospitalization. An intensive schedule of evaluation procedures and ward activities is helpful. Lewis (1982) suggested that borderline patients should self-monitor their feeling states with scheduled reviews of these observations with staff.

Discharge

The patient's experience of abandonment and rejection makes discharge planning an equally complicated and sensitive management issue. It is a universal experience for hospital administrators to find that discharge planning frequently dissembles any sense of alliance or progress with borderline patients. Frequently, discharge plans result in a recurrence of the self-destructive behaviors that led to the hospitalization in the first place. Administrators may then be forced into prescribing rehospitalization or into heroic efforts to maintain a limit about rehospitalization—a limit that can be endangering to the patient. In the face of a hard-nosed administrative position, borderline patients may identify sensitive areas in the hospital's power structure and sustain their next self-injury within conspicuous sight of the head of the hospital, local citizen groups, or legal authorities, who will then turn with righteous indignation back toward the discharge doctor in ways painful to professional standing or pride. On the other hand, administrators who take a less hard-nosed stance and acquiesce to readmissions for borderline patients under such circumstances will often feel resentful toward the patient, as will the nursing staff who alternate between feeling exploited and devalued. This is especially so because the borderline patient who is readmitted under these circumstances will frequently disavow any wish to be there and angrily demand release. In this way, a highly volatile, hostile dependent relationship exists between such patients and the staff. This relationship frequently recreates a situation familiar to the patient from early family life and is likely to be unproductive for further treatment. Such developments usually require transfers.

There are a number of administrative means by which such problems can be made less likely, although not altogether removed. Central to these administrative methods is a recognition that a great deal of the self-destructiveness that accompanies discharge from an inpatient service is a result of the patient's perception that this is a rejection (i.e., that they are being asked to leave because the staff does not want to care for them). This interpretation is more difficult to sustain when discharge is done according to a fixed limit uniformly imposed on all patients by forces outside the staff's control; namely, termination of insurance coverage or arbitrary limits to the length of stay before mandatory transfer to another facility. This is one of the reasons why admission of borderline patients to inpatient services that have a fixed limit to the length of stay is usually preferable to admission of borderline patients to units where the length of stay is variable and individually tailored.

Whatever the structure of the hospital, it is important that the discharge plans be conveyed to the patient without concurrently recommending termination of contact with the inpatient service. In other words, when a discharge plan is set in motion and introduced to a borderline patient, it should be accompanied by strong recommendations that the patient return to the hall for an indefinite period. This again is not something that borderline patients can be expected to ask for or even express desire for. It does, however, serve to diminish greatly the sense of rejection that accompanies discharge and that leads to the spiteful self-destructiveness which so frequently complicates discharge plans. Likewise, discharge plans should be accompanied by statements explicitly indicating that the discharge does not mean that the patient is well or is not in need of considerable further treatment. Such statements will reassure such patients about the ongoing concern about their welfare and convey a valid recognition of the seriousness and long-term nature of the patient's problems, which in itself is respectful and will make self-destructive acting out a less likely mode of communication when trouble arises. Implementing these administrative structures

and supports around discharge will be sufficient to allow a relatively safe discharge and transition plan to be implemented for the
vast majority of borderline patients. In short, one does everything
possible to reassure the patient who is leaving about the continued
concern and availability of the hospital. The beneficial effects of
such activities may provide the "good mother of separation," which
some theorists feel was missing during childhood.

Paradoxically, when borderline patients enter the hospital, one
wants to convey that the door out is open; when such patients are
leaving the hospital, one wants to convey caution and reluctance.
In each instance, these administrative stances are reassuring to the
fears uppermost in the borderline patient's mind as the hospital is
entered or departed, respectively.

THREE CAUSES OF STAFF CONFLICT

It is almost axiomatic within the clinical literature that borderline
patients are frequently involved in so-called splitting of staff. It is
generally believed that such splitting occurs by virtue of splits in
the intrapsychic nature of borderline patients whereby some persons
within the object field are selected to be seen in "all good" terms
whereas others are selected to be seen in "all bad" terms (Adler
1973; Brown 1980; Hartocollis 1980; Kernberg 1967; Rinsley 1971).
Under the influence of these opposing emotional valences, the
borderline patient discloses different affects and information to
different staff members. This, in turn, results in the staff members
having rather different impressions about the patient and frequently
coming to rather divergent conclusions about the proper approach
to such a patient's treatment. The staff member who has been seen
as "all good" may hear from the patient about their previous miser-
ies and mistreatments, to which the staff member may respond
with a sympathetic view of the patient as a mistreated disabled
waif who needs kindness and tolerance. In contrast, the staff member
who has been seen under a predominantly negative affective valence
is likely to have seen the patient as angry, arrogant, or entitled due
to the patient's obvious disregard or contempt for what he or she
has to offer. Such staff members are likely to see the patient as
being in need of limits and as exploiting the hospital for secondary
gains.

There is no question that these divergent viewpoints are commonly held by staff members toward borderline patients. Adler (1973), Brown (1980), and Kernberg (1976) have attributed this to the process of projective identification. This refers to the process of projecting a quality (e.g., anger) onto a staff person, then behaving toward that person in ways (e.g., resentful) that provoke a response (e.g., avoidance) seen as confirmatory of the projection (Ogden 1982). However, an alternate explanation for the genesis of the divergent views places less responsibility on the borderline patient and more on the intrapsychic characteristics of staff members. Main (1957) wrote about the dramatic appeal such patients make to caregivers for an exclusive and corrective relationship. Subsequently, Burnham (1966) has described the strongly divergent responses which staff members—therapists—may have to such an appeal. In my experience, those who respond with sympathy and nurturance are likely to do so because of beliefs in their own specialness as caregivers or because of feelings of deprivation in their own pasts to which they have responded by a career choice based in part on reaction formations. On the other side, those who respond with intolerance and limits also often have reaction formations—for them it's a defense against their own dependent longings.

From a clinical viewpoint, there are dangers in misplaced emphasis on either of these two sources for staff disagreement. I believe that authors who attribute staff conflicts to enactments of the patient's intrapsychic life place too much emphasis on the patient's responsibility for such staff splits (Adler 1973; Kernberg 1976; Nurnberg and Suh 1978; Wishnie 1975). This has the effect of stressing the need for staff communications but contains the danger that the approach to the patient becomes guided by a ritualized pseudo-uniformity or a type of wariness ("we versus them") toward patients. Both of these effects interfere with a more genuinely responsive and empathic approach. Heavy emphasis on the staff's countertransference as responsible for disagreements (e.g., Brown 1980; Gunderson 1983a) can lead to an inhibition of the aggressiveness required to confront actively, to reality test distortions, and to limit abusiveness when such responses are warranted.

It is important in analyzing differences of opinion between staff members that no a priori theory about the origins of such disagreements be used to explain them. Hence, in addition to the alternatives described above in which a patient's intrapsychic life creates splits or in which differing countertransference issues create splits, there can be genuine differences in opinion which derive from neither the patient's perversity nor the therapists' neuroses, but which derive from the well-considered, but genuinely different perspectives thoughtful staff may have about the same phenomena. This variation on the Stanton-Schwartz phenomena (1954) needs to be addressed no less rigorously than disagreements based on the aforementioned causes.

Obviously, splitting within staff occurs more often on halls where there is a low premium placed either on introspection or on staff communication. Such splitting is greatly diminished by the presence of frequent staff and patient community meetings in which a common pool of clinical observations about the interactions between patients and various staff can be shared. It also is more likely to occur when staff are either inexperienced or new. Staff can recognize more easily when a patient is distorting their interactions with someone when they have worked together with the other staff member sufficiently long to know that person's usual style of relating. They can also more easily recognize when a patient's view of the other staff member is correct. Experienced staff have been burned enough by their own countertransference issues—whether in the direction of withholding or nurturing—that they are tolerant and even appreciative of other staff whose countertransference issues complement and balance the patients' overall exposure.

DISCUSSION

The number of contributions to the literature on hospital treatment of borderline patients has proliferated greatly during the past 10 years. A review of this literature indicates areas of emerging consensus and debate. Important generalizations that can be drawn from the literature include the following five points.

First, the general role of the hospital in the overall treatment of borderline patients is that of a backup to outpatient treatment, which provides an essential service during periods of crisis. Beyond this there is general agreement about the indications for hospitalization. To these I have added the role of the hospital as a means of containing the therapist's anxiety.

Second, hospitalization of borderline patients involves two common types of regression. One of these is the hazards of regression into an angry, combative, negativistic stance vis-à-vis administrative rules or into a more childlike, even psychotic, demand for nurturance. Virtually everyone has described the dangers of such downward spirals.

Third, ubiquitous staff conflicts complicate the hospital experience. Here there is general agreement about the content of the staff conflict; namely, the contrast between viewing borderline patients as waifs in need of nurturance or as manipulators in need of limits.

Fourth, with respect to proper inpatient treatment, easily the clearest consensus regards the need for early and consistent imposition of firm limits. These limits do not necessarily mean restrictions and, in fact, may be better imposed by limiting access to a facility. Limits are used to enforce progressive expectations that borderline patients utilize their available ego functions maximally. Such limits need to be set on patient behavior and on the amount and type of staff availability.

Fifth, milieu programs must emphasize interpersonal issues— confronting maladaptive interpersonal patterns and providing new strategies or models for managing the frustrations inherent in interpersonal involvement.

Having reviewed these areas of agreement, it is also clear that the literature portrays areas of persisting disagreement. One of the major issues that can be inferred from the literature concerns the claims for the value of long-term hospitalization. Some authors seem to feel that it is contraindicated because of the kinds of disruptive regressive experiences that accompany long-term hospitalizations. In contrast, others believe that long-term hospitalization contains the possibilities of growth experiences that exceed or accelerate what can be accomplished in outpatient treatment alone.

There is also disagreement about the causes of the patient regressions that occur within hospitals. Some authors emphasize the degree to which it is an inevitable by-product of the supportive and containing functions of a hospital. Others emphasize (as have I) the degree to which such regressions reflect poor management within the hospital. Still others (see Chapter 9) emphasize that such regressions are related to vicissitudes in the relationships to primary objects (parents, spouses, therapists) which have little to do with the hospital itself. Valuable research could be done to assess how closely such inpatient regressions correlate with milieu type, administrative interventions, or the vicissitudes in nonmilieu relationships.

There is also a disagreement between competing explanations for intrastaff disagreements. Some emphasize the importance of the patient's projections as cause for splitting; others emphasize staff countertransferences as an explanation for such staff conflicts. From a research point of view, the relative power of these two alternate explanations (i.e., one which holds the patient's inner life responsible and the other which largely holds the psychology of the caregivers as responsible for the phenomenon of splitting) could be tested. If the former hypothesis is predominantly true, then the selection of objects as good or bad would occur more or less randomly. In contrast, if the latter hypothesis is predominantly true, one would expect that the same staff members would currently appear as "all good" and "all bad" to a series of borderline inpatients. I have drawn attention here to the sometimes neglected degree to which such staff conflicts stem from having roles that lead to different observations and from having different past professional experiences. Here staff disagreements are amenable to correction by education. Clearly the implication of this is that staff conflicts are overdetermined and need to be examined without theoretical preconceptions.

As of now, there has been little empirical research brought to bear on the issue of hospital treatment. In the absence of it, the questions raised by this review are unlikely to reach further resolution. Alternative explanations are unlikely to be persuasive to people with differing viewpoints and experiences. Both the frequent use of hospitals by borderline patients and the controversies surrounding their treatment make it timely in the decade ahead to initiate empirical studies in this area.

9

Multimodal Treatment

Implicit in this chapter is the statement that the basic treatments of individual psychotherapy and hospitalizations for many borderline patients are not optimal by themselves. Other forms of treatment, such as family, drug, or group, should be considered in the development of the treatment program of a borderline patient. There is, as yet, no widely recognized point of view that these other types of therapy can by themselves be the exclusive form of treatment for borderline patients, or even that they should be employed for all borderline patients in conjunction with other treatments. Thus it requires clinical judgment to employ these therapies selectively.

Some major controversies about treatment have been described in previous chapters on psychotherapy (Chapters 3 and 4) and hospital care (Chapter 8). In both of these areas, however, there is considerable clinical literature and tradition to draw on and some debates have been brought into clear focus. This chapter deals with other forms of treatment about which less has been written and where the ranges of practice are sufficiently undefined so that focused controversies have not emerged. Most of these treatments are set against a backdrop of individual psychotherapy or hospitalization or both. Hence many of the issues involve the interface or integration of those background treatments. Before moving into these new areas of family therapy, pharmacotherapy, and group therapy, this chapter will first discuss issues related to the integration of individual psychotherapy and hospital treatment.

153

THERAPIST–MILIEU INTERACTION

"Fit"

Friedman (1975) and more recently Gordon and Beresin (1983) have discussed the influence of theory on technique in the treatment of borderline patients. They have outlined discrepant approaches that could roughly be characterized as exploratory and supportive (or reconstructive versus adaptational). Gordon and Beresin have described how, when a therapist and an inpatient service hold contrasting views of the appropriate approach, misunderstandings and conflict that are harmful to patient care arise. They point out that units that emphasize adaptation, structure, and limits will often be misunderstood by therapists who look for the hospital to provide a holding environment in which regressive issues may get worked through. Conversely, units that tolerate regression and encourage the expressiveness of patients may seem to create or encourage iatrogenically the borderline patient's pathology in the eyes of therapists who have been involved in a structured, ego-supportive, adaptationally oriented therapy. Empirical support for the importance of the "fit" between such milieu goals and either insight-oriented or supportive psychotherapeutic approaches has already been demonstrated with schizophrenic patients (Frank and Gunderson 1984). In addition to underscoring the importance of a good fit between therapist and inpatient unit, the implications of this observation are that, in its absence, clarity of expectations and treatment philosophies may help to identify and stave off conflicts and misunderstandings.

Therapist–Administrative Splits

A related source of staff conflict involves therapists and hall administrators. The literature is divided between advocates for therapist–administrator (TA) splits and those who oppose it. The reason for opposition involves the encouragement TA splits give to the patients "splitting" off either their positive or negative transference (Adler 1977; Brown 1980; Kernberg 1976). Moreover, TA splits are more complicated—they take time for patients to understand the power arrangement and they require additional communication between the therapist, who may know the patient best, and the administrator, who is often too busy or impatient for advice. The borderlines' propensities to devalue and an inpatient service's desire to feel special combine to leave an admitting therapist feeling excluded and like a failure. Administrators must be sensitive to this possibility and actively intercede to include therapists on halls where TA splits exist.

One of the most important benefits of TA splits is that they provide a natural mechanism by which to consult on psychotherapy. Too often, junior administrators are reluctant to provide the perspective that senior therapists need—especially when such therapists are reluctant to request it. Other positive benefits of TA splits are the preservation of the therapist's neutrality and the greater outside perspective that can be offered therapists (Brown 1980; Johansen 1980). Borderline patients are frequently involved in struggles to get therapists to assume responsibilities for their lives. One function of the hospital is to demonstrate the limitations of the therapist's ability to take such responsibility. This function is undermined by the therapist's administrative activity. In my view, the advantages of the TA split outweigh its disadvantages mainly in long-term hospitalizations. Here there are needs for consistent, centrally organized milieu policies and staff approaches. This is not possible when each patient has a different administrator. Moreover, the insight-oriented role of therapists in long-term institutions is preserved and supported by allowing this role to remain separate from the administration.

FAMILY INTERVENTIONS

Types

The judicious planning of family interventions requires a careful assessment of the character of the family's relationship to the designated patient. Much of the descriptive and dynamic literature characterizing families of borderlines has been reviewed earlier (Gunderson and Englund 1981). These primarily clinical accounts have now been complemented by reports from a series of empirical studies (Bradley 1979; Frank and Parris 1981; Gunderson et al. 1980; Soloff and Millward 1983; Walsh 1977). These reports have led me to conclude that within the varied family constellations from which borderline psychopathology can arise, there are two

distinct characteristics that can help clinicians plan family interventions. One pattern characterized by overinvolvement has been
emphasized by investigators who observed families within treatment contexts (Masterson and Rinsley 1975; Zinner and Shapiro
1975). This pattern was also observed in the original empirical
study by Grinker et al. (1968) and has recently been confirmed by
Soloff and Millward (1983). The second and more common pattern
is characterized by neglect. This pattern emerged from empirical
studies on patients whose families were not selected on the basis
of being in treatment (Gunderson et al. 1980; Walsh 1977). These
two family patterns (i.e., overinvolvement and neglect) have different implications for the planning of family interventions.

In the overinvolved type families, resistance to separation as
described by Masterson and Rinsley (1975) is apparent. Shapiro et
al. (1975) expand on this by describing a process whereby the
parents in such families emphasize both the hostile and fearsome
aspects of separation and thus respond with either hostility or fear
to their adolescent's efforts to separate. Thus they project independence onto their offspring when it does not exist and view it as bad
when it does exist, thereby promoting infantilization. In the clinical
situation, such families often present with obvious apprehensions
about their borderline offsprings' welfare. They are likely to be
involved in soul-searching already, and they eagerly seek involvement in the treatment program. Borderline offspring in such families are often actively struggling with dependency issues by a denial
of any dependent neediness or by anger at their parents for having
made them dependent, or both. In any event, whether denied or
reviled, these dependent needs are still actively being gratified by
the patient's family.

These overinvolved type families require ongoing, active family
participation in treatment. If a hospital does not involve them, they
will become actively hostile to the treatment. Efforts to exclude the
family from involvement heighten the separation anxiety of the
family and lead them to withhold support for the individual treatment. Even should such parents support an individual treatment,
the borderline patient will feel as if their involvement with a therapist will lead to a loss of dependent gratifications—a loss which
they are unprepared for without a substitute source such as only
an institution can provide. The Masterson and Rinsley description
of inpatient care (see Chapter 5) documents how efforts to treat

these separation-resistant families without concurrent skilled family therapy required long-term residential treatment.

In a series of papers, Shapiro (Shapiro 1978b, 1982; Shapiro et al. 1975, 1977; Shapiro and Kolb 1979) has described factors that cause the family therapy of such families to provide benefits beyond those available in individual therapy. He summarizes these as follows:

> 1) the stage of adolescence itself and the shared family regression that recapitulates and allows for the reworking of earlier conflicts; 2) the adolescent's continuing need for family support during this period; 3) the powerful effects of new experience with his parents on strengthening the adolescent's still flexible character structure; and 4) the possibility of reintegration of projected and acted out conflicts into a modification in parental functioning. (Shapiro 1982, p 215)

In bringing about such positive benefits, Shapiro advocates a conjoint family therapy of 1½ hour meetings each week, which is complemented by individual therapy of an exploratory psychoanalytic type and by parental couples treatment. It is the couples therapist and the individual therapist who act as co-therapists for the conjoint meetings. A description of this model of family treatment, its rationale, and its processes provide the only clearly defined and well-thought-out model for family therapy in the literature. One of its important characteristics is the emphasis it gives to affective expression within a family. The co-therapists make ongoing and deliberate efforts to help the family members own and express feelings toward each other that were previously denied, acted-out, or misdirected. Consistent with the clinical literature from individual psychotherapy, the most problematic affects are related to anger. A second characteristic, underscored by Mandelbaum (1977), is the use of family therapy to identify and make explicit covert alliances, disagreements, or power foci within the families.

Families who are characterized by the neglect pattern present themselves differently in the clinical setting and require different forms of treatment intervention. Neglect includes families in which parental functions of support, attention, and limits are absent. This may be due to active disregard for the children or the passive inattention secondary to distractions. In many instances, neglectful parents will not be responsible for the borderline patients having sought treatment. In fact, they may be very angry at the fact that their offspring has either solicited or been sent for treatment. This event is likely to be seen either as a weak dependent act or as self-indulgent attention getting. In contrast to the overinvolved type of family, the parents here will be overtly resentful toward any expressions of dependency by their children. Borderline patients from such families are likely to be overtly concerned with issues of being cared about or, if this is denied, they may defensively portray their families in blandly ideal terms. Under these circumstances, family therapy is not only unwelcome, but is probably contraindicated. Explosive, angry recriminations often make such therapy unworkable (e.g., Stone 1983b). Here the patient should be seen in individual psychotherapy that is kept separate from the family while the parents meet in a more supportive, less exploratory context. Meetings with the parents of borderline patients should focus on education about the nature of their offspring's difficulties. This will diminish the suggestion that the parents are responsible agents in the development of their offspring's difficulties. Here, in order for the parents to support their offspring's treatment, it may be important that they feel reassured that the treatment is directed toward helping the patient develop more independence and is not directed at blaming them.

These two basic approaches to family involvement can be applied routinely within hospital or day care centers. The role of family involvement for outpatient borderline patients is less routine and often less conspicuous. Nevertheless, as described elsewhere (Chapter 7), such visits may be the most effective means of containing psychotic transferences or addressing certain resistances based on the theme of parental malevolence or based on claims of financial restraints. Shapiro (1982) and Langs (1978) warn of the potential that family meetings may be used to dissipate transferences that are better centered and eventually integrated within the individual therapy. There is no doubt that countertransference processes may too readily precipitate a turn to family. Yet the more common problem in my experience is a therapist's readiness to keep family members out of treatment at times when the therapy is jeopardized. Such reluctance can be based on accepting the patient's views about the family as reality rather than as invariably altered by both projections and the transference. The reluctance can also be due to an underestimation of the importance of family interactions in the patient's ongoing difficulties.

Family Issues and Hospital Treatment

Whatever the nature of the borderline patient's family, it is critical that the hospital team actively seek to involve and inform the family about the patient's treatment progress and program. Failure to do this in ways that keep the borderline patient's family actively supportive of continued hospitalization leads to a sequence that creates major management problems and often leads to premature termination of treatment.

Typically, this unfortunate sequence begins with the distraught family bringing their borderline son or daughter to the hospital either because of their own intolerance of the patient's behavior or at the recommendation of some other authority. Once the admission is completed, however, the unattended-to parents may easily revert to a position vis-à-vis the hospital whereby they ask the hospital to justify and explain the reason for ongoing hospitalization while openly sympathizing with their child's complaints about the food, roommates, restrictions, or other aspects of the hospital program. This undoes the benefits of the limit they imposed by the hospitalization and supports the patient's resistance. This supports the patient's illusion of being a mistreated waif and misrepresents the family as now opposing the hospitalization rather than being responsible for it. To the patient, this often causes the hospital to be seen in one or the other of two misleading roles: either as coercively insisting on the patient's separation from parents who are reluctant to let their offspring go or as saving the patient from parents whom the hospital sees as malicious. This sequence is very common with borderline patients, although not unique to them. It needs to be addressed early and often in hospitalization in order to maintain the parents as allies with the hospital treatment goals and to maintain their sustained participation as responsible parents on whom the success of the treatment depends.

This sequence is much more common when borderlines are admitted to long-term units than when they are admitted to short-term units. On short-term units, parents frequently remain in the role of advocating and encouraging continued hospitalization because of their recognition that the problems at home are likely to return. Insofar as this position (i.e., of support for the hospitalization) is not intended as abandonment and is accompanied by ongoing involvement by the family, it, in itself, becomes a reality-buttressing and an emotionally supportive reason for a rapid return of function by hospitalized borderline patients. For this reason, family visits should not only be allowed, but should be required for most borderline patients early in their hospitalization. Depending on the particular family dynamics and the degree of rage and impulsivity on the part of the patient, these visits may need to be for limited periods of time. The contrast between this and Rinsley's approach has been noted earlier (see Chapter 8).

A common problem related to integrating family involvement has been described by Johansen (1979). He noted that the borderline's tendency to devalue past caregivers—most notably the parents—may be accompanied by an idealization of the current treaters that goes unaddressed. This, he states, may be due to an unconscious effort to avoid the patient's anger. It also is likely to conform with any grandiose preconceptions about special caregiving capacities among the treaters. In any event, it will have the unfortunate effect of alienating the family. Houch (1972) earlier described a similar sequence whereby the missionary zeal of psychotherapists unwittingly leads to ignoring the importance of spouses, which, in turn, can lead either to sudden withdrawal from the hospital or divorce. The following case vignette illustrates these issues:

Mrs. L was an attractive 23-year-old who had developed symptoms of severe non-endogenous depression and suicidal ideation in the two months prior to her admission to a day care program. At the time of this admission, she had recently relocated as a result of her husband's work. She had one similar episode of depression at the time that she began college.

The patient's depression and suicidal ideation responded rather rapidly to the supports available within the milieu. She appeared eager for attention and appreciative of the opportunity to discuss the difficulties in her marriage. She described her husband as insensitive and punitive. In fact, he appeared to be a somewhat rigid and compulsive man who viewed the patient's treatment with suspicion.

The patient was assigned a psychotherapist who rather openly sympathized with the patient's complaints about her husband. He was impressed with her depression and quickly began a course of antidepressants. The administrator felt alienated from the therapist, whom he felt had been unilateral and arbitrary in his administration of the medication. Moreover, the administrator felt the therapist's expressed sympathy to the patient acted to undermine his own efforts to set limits on the patient's increasing dependency on the day hospital. He advised the patient that her husband needed to get into therapy and he met with the husband to encourage this. Eventually, the husband agreed to begin an individual psychotherapy of his own. From the start, the patient and her husband were seen by a social worker in couples treatment, which was directed at helping the husband to channel his frustrations about the wife's absences and the treatment team's ineffectiveness more constructively.

Although the patient's depression quickly appeared to lift, all efforts to mobilize her toward either more responsible community activities (as an employee, housewife, or sexual partner for her husband) were met with a recurrence of her suicidal ideation and eventually by minor self-destructive acts. She complained openly that she thought she had to choose between her marriage and her treatment program and the needed support and attention it provided. Despite her husband's compliance with the treatment program, he remained resentful of the claims it made on his wife's time and affections. He felt alienated and scapegoated. These feelings became more prominent in his individual therapy, which invited him to think of his own needs. Eventually, the patient's conflicting loyalties were resolved by her decision to withdraw from the treatment program altogether.

The social worker and the patient's therapist both saw the depression as being the result of her introjected and justified anger at the husband. The administrator disagreed with this, but, because he was active in supporting the husband's treatment, this provided unwitting support for the patient to externalize her problems onto her husband. The therapist, the administrator, and social worker were all young males who were actively competitive with each other. Their competitiveness toward each other got displaced onto the husband who accurately perceived himself as scapegoated and rightly perceived the treatment as a rival. The patient articulated her dilemma accurately as being faced with a need to give up the passive gratifications that abounded in the treatment situation or her healthier aspirations to make her marriage work.

Lost from view was the fact that her earlier depression had been precipitated by separation from her parents when she had originally gone to school and in the present instance too when she was relocated with her husband. It was the parental transference which was being gratified by the hospital and which made transitions from it feel so perilous.

The implicit acceptance of the role of being a "better" caregiver, illustrated in this example, poses burdens on a staff which can only lead to disillusionment. It also encourages the basic sense of entitlement of the borderline patient in ways that are destructive.

It cannot be overemphasized that an inpatient program must be aware of the critical role that a borderline patient's primary relationships have on causing or reversing the regressions of borderline patients (see Chapter 2). In this regard, Lewis (1982) has pointed out how frequently a patient's behavior within hospitals can only be understood by recognition of vicissitudes in the relationship to the therapist. This is certainly true when the therapist has assumed a role of primary object. However, in my experience, it is far more common to overlook the importance of relationships to nontreatment personnel in the family. The noisy impulsive activities and the immediate emotional demandingness of borderline patients are often examined solely from the viewpoint of reactions to the immediate treatment situation and readily overlook the communications concurrently but more quietly taking place with primary objects outside the treatment setting. One common example of this is how, even in short-term hospitalizations, the patient's discharge resistance is seen solely as an effort to avoid separation, maintain dependent gratifications, and so on. These are important but may overlook the degree to which the hospitalization has gratified and expressed sadistic wishes for vengeance (by shaming or financially straining) on a family seen as withholding.

PHARMACOTHERAPY

There is a rapidly growing interest in the possible effectiveness of a variety of medications for borderline patients. Paralleling the changes within psychiatry more broadly, during the last decade there has been a shift from seeing borderline patients as exclusively treatable by psychodynamic psychotherapy toward a readiness to employ drug treatments. Whereas pharmacotherapy with borderline patients was rare and relatively frowned on 10 years ago, now it is commonplace. Even in outpatient settings, the majority (63 percent) of a series of patients had prior exposure to psychotropic medications (Skodol et al. 1983). This is so despite the fact that there are still no prospective controlled studies to support the usage of any particular type of chemical intervention. In the absence of such information, the claims for efficacy of pharmacotherapy have grown at the same time the variety of agents for which such efficacy is claimed have proliferated. At this time, there are advocates for the use of tricyclic antidepressants (Akiskal 1981), MAO inhibitors (Klein 1977), low doses of phenothiazines (Brinkley et al. 1979; Serban 1984), lithium (Rifkin et al. 1972), and carbamazepine (Tegretol) (Schatzberg 1983). The limited research in this area has received numerous reviews in recent years (Brinkley et al. 1979; Cole and Sunderland 1982; Gunderson and Elliott 1984; Klein 1977; Liebowitz 1983; Soloff 1981). The safest generality to emerge from existing studies is that borderline patients with specific affective or psychotic symptoms should receive drug therapy (i.e., antidepressants or neuroleptics) appropriate to those symptoms (Cole et al. 1984). Tegretol appears to have its greatest value in limiting the overtly destructive impulsive actions of borderline patients.

Many clinicians have warned about the usual ineffectiveness (Last et al. 1973; Sarwer-Foner, 1977) or the actual harmfulness (Dyrud 1972; Friedman 1969; Havens 1968; Ostow 1962; Schnick and Freedman 1974) of pharmacotherapy for borderline patients. The inpatient period is a good time to test pharmacotherapies under relatively controlled conditions in which the likelihood of destructive acting out is diminished and whereby the side effects and response can be more carefully monitored. One argument in favor of TA splits is that an administrator may more safely prescribe drugs than a therapist insofar as the former has a less volatile or intense transference relationship. This may also be true for the outpatient in psychotherapy, where drugs prescribed by someone else may have less dangers associated.

The combination of psychopharmacologic and psychotherapeutic treatments, like all other combined treatments, is complicated in borderline patients by the possibility of creating destructive splits. Borderline patients may see pharmacological and psychotherapeutic approaches as incompatible and feel forced to take "loyalty vows" that preclude an optimally comprehensive approach. Borderline patients often angrily renounce one approach and idealize the other so as to avoid the possibility of displeasing (betraying) whomsoever they target their hopes on and for the sake of achieving a more simplified view of both their own problems and how these problems might be solved. Psychotherapists and psychopharmacologists need to be aware of this tendency and to discourage borderline patients from these temptations actively by both educational and interpretive means. This is less apt to be done when the patients' efforts to simplify their problems coincide with the belief systems of the professionals involved; that is, either that psychotherapy is an expensive, dependency-generating treatment given by needy "do-gooders" or that drug therapy is a simplistic, sedation-generating treatment reflective of an impersonal and intolerant approach to patients. In truth, both groups could justifiably note that the other's treatment is only rarely very successful.

It is clearly better if everyone involved takes the more clinically (and scientifically) sound approach of basing their approach on several common foundations: (a) that the origins and treatment of borderline personality is multidetermined and incompletely understood; (b) that there is almost surely a role for both psychological and biological causes and treatments; (c) that the relative role of psychological and biological factors will vary from patient to patient in their explanatory power and therapeutic effectiveness; and (d) that both psychotherapeutic and psychopharmacologic treatments have a common backdrop—the establishment of a stable and supportive relationship. Nevertheless, even with these basic foundations for treatment planning, it often will take considerable time before the integration of treatment is possible—time during which, if a drug or psychotherapy is forced on an unwilling patient, the result will only be destructive acting out.

For Patients Already in Psychotherapy

Some of the complexities of introducing pharmacological treatment to a patient in psychotherapy are illustrated by the following case:

> After a disappointing sexual liaison, Andrew, a borderline patient in intensive outpatient psychotherapy, requested an additional appointment on a weekend. When his therapist insisted that the reasons for this request be examined, Andrew walked out. He overdosed at the time this appointment was to have taken place and called a colleague of the therapist's who arranged for his admission. The inpatient administrator expressed concern about the patient's depression and recommended a course of antidepressant therapy. The subsequent education Andrew received about the presumed biogenetic origins of depressions directly contrasted with the views of his therapist. The therapist viewed the overdose and the consequent hospitalization as an angry, manipulative reaction to his failure to meet at the time requested. Andrew dismissed the therapist's interpretations as egocentricism and told him and the hall staff that the therapist's wish to be important had blinded him to providing appropriate treatment.
>
> The patient was at no time, before or after his hospitalization, clinically depressed and the drug therapy failed to have any discernible effect. However, the introduction of the drugs helped

to support his denial of both the hostility behind the overdose and even a sense that he had responsibility for making the suicide gesture. Andrew literally said, "My depression made me do it."

When Andrew subsequently left this therapist to seek other treatment, he felt relieved to find a new therapist who made it a precondition of treatment that he not take any medication. This reflected a return to the more long-standing antipathy toward pharmacotherapy that Andrew had always maintained because of the loss of control he feared.

The existing literature indicates that patients in psychotherapy should be given a careful assessment of their potential to benefit from pharmacotherapy. The existing data support the idea that some borderline patients get better on drugs, but not all. The first question to be asked is whether there is a discrete symptom picture of types (i.e., either melancholic vegetative depressive symptoms or psychotic-like cognitive symptoms) that are usually responsive to pharmacotherapy. This was not carefully done for the patient described above.

The second question to be asked in assessing the need for drug treatment is whether patients have sufficient supports in their life situation and stability in their personality functioning to make reasonable compliance likely. Even borderline patients who show clear symptomatic improvement with drug treatment are subject to the same problems of compliance—especially when they become outpatients—that beset psychotic patients, with the added caveat that they may more consciously and resourcefully want to manipulate their symptom appearance for purposes of interpersonal gain. Andrew was compliant with his prescribed drugs as long as it seemed to support his denial and to express his retaliatory anger at the therapist.

A second issue to be addressed for the borderline patient already in psychotherapy are countertransference issues involved in the inclusion of a drug therapy. Does it feel like an admission of personal failure? Does it involve injury to one's ideological beliefs? The patient in the example above was quick to use this possibility to attack his therapist. If so, can these attitudes be harnessed to make the introduction of a drug treatment useful to the patient? In other words, is the psychotherapist able to support the treatment in a way that discourages the patient from thinking that it is an act of disloyalty? Borderline patients can readily believe that accepting drug treatment will be a traumatic blow to their therapist's esteem. An even more important countertransference issue is whether the introduction of a drug treatment reflects either a growing sense of desperation and hopelessness or an outright wish to get rid of the patient. Maltsberger and Buie (1974) have aptly described such dramatic and sometimes dangerous countertransference feelings toward borderline patients.

A third area to be assessed before administering drug treatment to a patient in psychotherapy involves the transference. Here I will point to some common reactions that can be anticipated and that need to be addressed. The introduction of drugs to an ongoing psychotherapy always raises as an issue the patient's fear of the therapist's loss. Borderline patients will see it as an effort to decrease the intensity of the relationship, as if the therapist is saying "you are too much for me." If this reaction is not identified, it is likely to be acted on by withdrawal or some more openly self-destructive act. Until the issue has been clarified and the patient feels reassured on this issue, the introduction of the pharmacotherapy should be delayed.

A second transference issue relates to a disillusionment that may accompany the introduction of pharmacotherapy. Borderline patients often seek psychotherapy with the idea that it will provide nurturance or other parenting experience, which they believe is needed because of failures of their biological parents. They may adamantly resist the introduction of drugs insofar as they reflect a noninterpersonal cause to their problem; that is, they would, and often have, gladly sacrificed their own welfare as a means of acting out their vendetta against their parents. Two points need to be made about this. First, the construction of such a psychotherapy is distorted and needs to be actively and aggressively addressed by the therapist. Second, under such circumstances, the introduction of drugs is probably doomed to fail and certainly is not the best vehicle by which to address such a transference distortion. The patient may respond by leaving treatment or by acting out with the drugs prescribed under these circumstances.

Another transference issue that is common in the introduction of drugs is that they threaten the patient's sense of control. Many borderline patients will resist pharmacotherapy for this reason—especially when they feel that their control of other areas in their life is tenuous. The case vignette above illustrates this issue dramatically.

Issues in Adding Psychotherapy to Pharmacotherapy

There is a relatively recent, growing development in the treatment of borderline patients suggesting that they can be treated primarily with pharmacotherapy and a minimal, but secondary, amount of counseling or supportive psychotherapy. This is especially likely for those borderline patients who present with obvious depressive symptomatology or eating disorders for which the pharmacotherapeutically oriented psychiatrist is most likely to feel optimistic. Just as with the patient who begins by receiving psychotherapy, a thoughtful assessment should be given to the patient receiving primarily pharmacotherapy as to whether more intensive or more exploratory psychotherapy should be added. The pharmacotherapist should consider whether there are ongoing familial, interpersonal, or work problems that can't or aren't being addressed within the present pharmacotherapeutic regimen. Is the patient interested in working on these problems? If the answer is yes, then the additional assessment should be made as to whether there are sufficient supports (financial and social) for this patient to undertake a more exploratory therapy (see Chapter 3). Equally important, are there skillful and motivated mental health professionals available to deliver this added service?

If the pharmacotherapist concludes the patient would profit from the addition of an exploratory form of psychotherapy, the pharmacotherapist must then review the same sorts of issues that the psychotherapist has with respect to the addition of a new therapy. The first area to be examined involves the countertransference issues that may be involved in making such a recommendation. Here too it can feel like a personal failure. In fact, this is a common occurrence for the pharmacotherapist who has been involved in a sometimes increasingly desperate effort to treat such patients effectively. This can involve moving from one drug to another with multiple dose changes and multiple side effects complicating the administration. Not only is this course bound to be frustrating, but it is often accompanied by the explicit or implicit message to the borderline patient that there must be something that will work to alleviate the problems and that it is essential that it be found because there is no reasonable recourse. This bind may be most extreme when the pharmacotherapist has introduced ideas such as "chemical imbalance" to explain the need for therapy. This pattern is illustrated by the following case example:

Joan was an attractive 20-year-old who had been referred for pharmacotherapeutic evaluation. It soon became apparent that she was enmeshed in a difficult family situation and that a variety of self-mutilative behaviors and suicidal impulses reflected a danger to the patient requiring hospitalization. Within the safer confines of the hospital, the pharmacotherapist energetically and enthusiastically began a course of antidepressants, which had ambiguous effects. The ambiguity of the effects was due to the fact that much of the patient's symptomatic behavior recurred as the time for discharge planning approached. As a result, a second course of a different medication was embarked on and her hospitalization was prolonged.

The patient became deeply attached to the pharmacotherapist, who was available day and night and was openly and obviously concerned about her general welfare while taking seriously each nuance of her somatic complaints. Whereas the therapist saw her as a forlorn and needy girl, the nursing staff soon developed a different impression about the patient based on her hostility and manipulativeness. When the suggestion was made that a psychotherapist be added to the treatment program, both the patient and her doctor were openly resistive. The patient and her family were exceedingly grateful for the doctor's heroic efforts on her behalf—both with respect to medications, optimism, and availability, and with respect to his helping her in her struggles with the inpatient staff. Joan knew that his devotion was unusual and she realistically expected that a new doctor would be unlikely to provide similar support. The pharmacotherapist felt as if he would be abandoning a patient clearly dependent on him and toward whom he had made a commitment. Moreover, he still held out hopes that her problems could be alleviated by further pharmacologic experimentation.

In this case, the limitations of the drug effects and the characterological and familial problems were much more apparent to everyone else than to the pharmacotherapist. This set the stage for a very problematic referral. The flip side of the above countertransference situation is the pharmacotherapist, who, as a result of such escalating efforts to salvage a borderline patient from misery, develops such antipathy for the resistant, angry, and often times noncompliant patient that the therapist in fact is eager to get rid of such a patient. Here again, Maltsberger and Buie's (1974) admonitions apply. The hostility toward the patient that lies behind the transfer to a psychotherapist further undermines the patient's hope and implicitly expresses a devaluation of the psychotherapy as a secondary treatment or last resort.

As this discussion of countertransference suggests, the pharmacotherapist also needs to be sensitive to transference issues when the introduction of an exploratory psychotherapy is recommended. Will the patient feel as if this recommendation means that the pharmacotherapist has given up? Will it be experienced as an abandonment or a confirmation of the patient's hopelessness? The enthusiasm and hope that a pharmacotherapist provides are important ingredients in their therapeutic effects that must be recognized. As a result, the introduction of an exploratory therapist appropriately needs to convey realistic disappointment, but should not contain hints of rejection. Ongoing contacts with the patient are important during the introduction of the psychotherapy and until it is well established.

Many borderline patients may cling to a pharmacotherapist because of a fearful reluctance to open their personal and internal lives up for review. This in turn often reflects a basic fear that something irreversibly wrong will be discovered in them or reflects fear of developing a relationship in which they would be expected to become dependently vulnerable. Here the pharmacotherapist can be very helpful with explanations about the necessarily slow process by which self-revelations occur and about the degree to which a patient is required to be a collaborating participant in the psychotherapy. In other words, their fears that the psychotherapist will see right through them or wish to take control over them are unrealistic. Obviously, the pharmacotherapist who has relied on a concept of "chemical imbalance" will have a hard time introducing a psychotherapist without admitting error. In such instances, it is best to do so, anticipating and bearing the patient's resulting anger and disillusionment, and to make sure the next borderline patient profits from what has been learned.

To summarize, the most useful generalities that emerge from this discussion of introducing a psychotherapy or a pharmacotherapy are the need for caution and flexibility in introducing change. Rejection and separation issues are likely to contaminate the transfer or addition of a different form of treatment. Although such contamination is less severe when the therapist has remained modest in claims and ambition for the treatment being provided, it is nevertheless true that the hope for a cure is an intoxicating ingredient of most treatments that helps sustain patients through difficult periods. Thus, such changes require time for working through. Rarely should changes be planned to occur quickly or suddenly.

GROUP THERAPY

Within the immense literature on group therapy, relatively little has been devoted specifically to the borderline patient (Horwitz 1977, 1980). Nevertheless, it is common clinical wisdom that group therapy is a valuable adjunct to ongoing individual psychotherapy. A major reason for the discrepancy between the widely held view that groups are useful for borderline patients and the relatively little literature is the difficulty in getting the borderline patient to enter or remain in a group therapy. As a result, most of the experiences with borderline patients in groups derives from inpatient or substance abuse treatment settings where participation is required or reinforced. It is largely because borderline patients perform well in such groups and seem to profit from the experience that there is such widespread optimism about the role of group therapy in their treatment.

Borderline patients generally seek treatment that involves an exclusive relationship with a caregiver toward whom they have invested great hopes. As a result, they do not welcome the prospect of sharing the therapist with others. For the patient already in an individual psychotherapy where the group therapy is recommended as a supplementary treatment, all of the same transference and countertransference issues (e.g., abandonment, loyalty, hope) that were discussed with respect to adding pharmacotherapy apply equally. Because of these issues, the vast majority of borderline patients for whom group therapy is recommended do not follow through.

It may improve the chances of success if the group therapy is linked to the individual therapy from the beginning. Participation in an ongoing group is made a contingency for an individual psychotherapy. Under these circumstances, borderline patients are more likely to attend the group long enough to become involved and attached to the group, at which point it becomes viable in its own right without the contingency required to get there in the first place.

There are a number of benefits for borderline patients who do participate in group therapy that are different but complementary to benefits from individual psychotherapy. The presence of peers within the group therapy situation allows confrontations about maladaptive interpersonal or impulsive patterns to occur with less likelihood of their being written off as being in the service of some power or controlling need of an authority. When other borderline patients are in the group, they are especially perceptive in identifying such patterns. The second ramification of being in a therapy involving peers is the earlier introduction of issues of rivalry and envy than occurs in individual psychotherapy alone. Thirdly, most groups maintain an explicit mission of growth and independence, which helps to identify and make dystonic the dependent gratifications that are a major part of the borderline patient's function. The common pattern in borderline patients whereby they live a very dependent life while overtly denying their neediness can be actively confronted within group therapies. Peers may more effectively and forcefully raise questions, for example, about the reasons why someone at the age of 23 still has laundry done by parents or has failed to seek out paid employment. Finally, group therapy provides a set of peers with whom communications of feelings and personal problems may be productively experimented with. It is a corrective experience in itself to find that problems can be talked about and feelings expressed without harmful repercussions. This supportive aspect of the group is especially valuable for the patient in individual psychotherapy who can turn to it in times of stress within and outside the psychotherapy.

There is some controversy about the ideal composition of groups for borderline patients. Stone and Weissman (1984) have agreed that borderline patients profit from having group therapies that include other borderline patients. They suggest that in outpatient settings, the isolated borderline patient is too likely to feel alienated from healthier group members and as a result will drop out. On the other hand, Wong (1980) has argued against having too many borderline patients in the same group. He emphasizes the disruptive potential of the interpersonal demandingness and affective lability, which need stronger egos in the group and within an individual therapy to tame and stabilize such disruptions. Some clinicians have attempted to develop groups composed exclusively of borderline patients. Obviously, a group therapist who undertakes this is assuming a difficult task in which multiple extra-group contacts can be anticipated. Roth (1980) points out the strains and countertransferences for therapists who have too many borderline patients in their groups. Probably such a group should be undertaken only if the participants are in concurrent individual therapy (e.g., Shaskin 1971). Whatever the benefits for the borderline patient might be, both psychotic and neurotic patients profit from having borderline members in their groups. The efforts by borderline patients to enact their transference wishes and the availability and strength of their angry affects provide a helpful counterposition to the inhibitions of affect and action that characterize many psychotic or neurotic patients.

Given the frequency of borderline patients in both inpatient and outpatient settings, the almost universal belief that group therapy is a useful adjunctive treatment for the majority of them, and the relatively low cost of this treatment, a great deal more should be learned about it. As it is, enormous problems persist in getting borderline patients to agree to enter into a group therapy and then to maintain them there with or without concurrent individual therapy. As with other arenas of treatment for borderline patients, there is a need for more careful delineation of samples, descriptions of the group treatment itself (e.g., frequency, duration, composition, techniques), and parameters of change before the role of this treatment can be more confidently stated.

REHABILITATION THERAPY

Many psychotherapists either overlook or greatly underestimate the ongoing vocational or educational disabilities of their borderline patients. Such needs are often overlooked within inpatient units because of the common appearance of social awareness in borderline patients and because of the noisy management issues and stormy interpersonal problems with which hospital staffs are confronted and can become preoccupied. The actual work performance both historically (Gunderson 1977) and prognostically (McGlashan 1983b; Pope et al. 1983; Werble 1970) is poor. Even the most optimistic of these reports (McGlashan 1984) documents serious morbidity in employment (48 percent of the time employed) for the first nine years after an extensive treatment was initiated.

Under circumstances where the borderline's life and therapies seem so flooded with action, work or school seems beyond reach rather than as a desirable and healthful complement to the psychotherapist or milieu staff. The reasons for this are highly complex, but for purposes of this chapter, it is sufficient to note that the therapist and other members of the treatment team can enter into this situation by helping to structure the other hours of a patient's day and focusing on the need and value for work in the general welfare of a person's life. While the work experience itself provides a valuable buttressing effect in stabilizing and structuring a person's daily work and supporting also a sense of self-esteem, it also provides a model for a task orientation and frustration tolerance that reinforces and works complementarily with the needs of a viable psychotherapy. Finally, it functions as an alternative geographic placement for borderline patients on inpatient services, which regularly and meaningfully directs attention to the separation issues and the conflicts about assuming adult responsibilities that are central to their psychopathology and to the hospital's mission in offering to assist them.

Evaluation of rehabilitation needs for the dysfunctional borderline patient should consider whether this dysfunction reflects defective learning which requires rehabilitation or whether it reflects a regressive retreat from the patient's current life or treatment situation. When the dysfunction is regressive, its maladaptive aspects need to be identified and interpreted. At times when it is clear that the dysfunction is acting out, it can make sense to make continuation or initiation of a therapy contingent on the patient's utilizing available work skills. Sometimes this can be accomplished by insisting on a patient's participation in bill paying.

By virtue of developmentally based reaction formations or acquired identifications with their therapist, many patients seek careers in the health services. For many borderline patients, these occupations become stabilizing and rewarding occupations. This is worth stating largely because the prospects of such a result may seem very bleak at first and occasionally lead treating persons to try to steer borderline patients away from such fields.

EXPRESSIVE THERAPIES

Several articles have been written in recent years about the role of art therapy for borderline patients (Brenner 1982; Mottai 1982; Obernbreit 1982). All describe the troublesome problems presented by the impulsivity and magical thinking of such patients, and emphasize the need for limits, structure, and consistency. Most of the time, art therapy is used adjunctively to individual psychotherapy. An eloquent account of this process is provided by Naevestad (1979). For some borderline patients, the expressions of their internal life are more easily conveyed into the exterior world by pictures. This, in turn, may facilitate the verbalization process in the psychotherapy in the same way that dreams do.

10

The Term *Borderline*

This book has repeatedly addressed the dilemmas that characterize the interface between borderline patients and those in the mental health field who attempt to treat them. These dilemmas are at the heart of why such patients have commanded so much attention, why the term *borderline* remains appropriate in describing them, and why the diagnosis of borderline personality disorder has earned a place in the present diagnostic lexicon.

The major advocates for inclusion of borderline personality as a diagnosis have been those who have been involved with their treatment. The impetus has not come from the studies of their genetics, course, biological markers, or laboratory tests. Nor could convincing arguments for the development of this diagnosis be derived from the persistent efforts to formulate their intrapsychic characteristics or developmental pathogenesis. The argument for the merit of borderline personality as a diagnosis rests largely on whether the diagnosis can accurately predict the occurrence of treatment dilemmas discussed in this book as being to some extent specific to these patients. If the diagnosis does predict these dilemmas and they are to any extent specific to this patient group, the diagnosis fulfills a valuable clinical function. This will be so regardless of whether studies of family pedigree or pharmacologic responsiveness or even course of illness suggest similarities or overlap with other diagnostic groups.

What then are the predictable and specific clinical dilemmas that, I believe, validate the borderline diagnosis? The first dilemma, within the diagnostic process itself, is the fluctuating levels of psychological performance and the accompanying changes in phenomenology. I have argued here that it is less the specificity of these phenomena and more the sensitivity of these phenomena to changes in the interpersonal context that is central to the border-line's psychopathology.

The second dilemma of diagnostic significance is the urgent appeal made for help. This plea, repeated over and over again in the course of treatment, is for an exclusive helping relationship, and it is often accompanied by overt or covert devaluation of previous helpgivers. Out of this grow two predictable treatment complications. First is the countertransference responses to this urgent plea for an exclusive helping relationship, and second is the sequence whereby the help that is offered is viewed as inadequate. This pattern has led to the description of borderlines as "help-rejecting complainers." The patient who calls a suicide prevention center and announces gaspingly that he or she has just taken an overdose, but then refuses to discuss the cause, seek medical care, or give an adequate address creates this dilemma so quickly and stressfully that the diagnosis of borderline personality is axiomatic and becomes permanently imprinted on the call's recipient.

A third dilemma that the diagnosis of borderline personality predicts is the development of strongly oppositional views of the patient by different persons in or outside the treatment situation. More specifically, some people will view the borderline patient as a deprived waif, whereas others will view the borderline patient as an entitled bully. Sometimes these views appear sequentially— the superficial appearance of being a waif gives way to recognition as a bully. Therapists exposed to borderline patients over time may find their views alternating between such views. I have tried to dissect the anatomy of such polarized views and its consequences (Chapter 8).

The fourth and fifth predictions about borderline patients deal with their special sensitivity to separations and loss. One can predict with confidence that experiences of separation will be accompanied by behavioral regression, with the specter of self-destructiveness becoming covertly or explicitly an issue (Chapter 6). The experience of actual object loss will likewise be accompanied by a behavioral regression that contains not only the potential for self-destructiveness but also psychotic experiences (Chapter 7).

The sixth and seventh predictable dilemmas have to do with

response to treatment. Here one can predict that borderline patients will either leave or regress harmfully within an unmodified psychoanalytic treatment (Chapters 3 and 4). The seventh dilemma is that borderline patients will either abuse or find limited relief from purely pharmacologic treatment (Chapter 8). With the widespread acceptance of these clinical predictors, there has been a decline in the misapplication of psychoanalysis to such patients, but a paradoxical growth in the prescription of drugs for such patients—mirroring the shifts in psychiatric practices but also, I think, an unwarranted psychotherapeutic nihilism.

Related to these observations are predictive statements about the long-term morbidity of this disorder. The diagnosis of borderline personality is predictive of a significant morbidity in both interpersonal relations and role performance. Short-term treatments may have an effect on function and affect but cannot be expected to have enduring impact on the borderline patient's character pathology (i.e., the sense of self and expectations for relationships). However, despite the high level of functional morbidity, such patients are probably more responsive to long-term interventions than patients with some other forms of serious character pathology (e.g., schizoid, antisocial, or paranoid characters).

The term *borderline* itself has been the subject of repeated attacks. Originally, it was attacked because the term was used to imply diagnostic uncertainty (the so-called wastebasket diagnosis a la Knight 1953). The implication was that, if diagnostic clarity were obtained, the patients on whom this designation had been employed would actually fit some other already-defined neurotic or psychotic group. This has not been the case and at this point there are few opponents to its placement within the personality disorder axis. The second attack, paradoxically, came from the opposite direction. This critique derives from a concept of borderlines as a stable and identifiable form of character pathology and argues that the term *borderline* should be abandoned because it suggests, incorrectly, a marginal or atypical relationship to schizophrenia or the affective disorders (Loranger et al. 1982). As a result, it is argued that the term *borderline* should be jettisoned in favor of a more descriptively accurate and diagnostically distinct term.

A third criticism is that the term *borderline personality* has come to have such a broad utilization that it lacks the desirable and scientifically mandated specificity implied by making this category a discrete personality disorder.

In fact, the authors of DSM-III originally suggested the term *unstable personality disorder* as a replacement for *borderline personality*. This term was immediately besieged because it failed to recognize the stable intrapsychic structures that made this personality so difficult to change. Because the term *unstable* implied variability or transiency, these critics argued that it was even more misrepresentative than *borderline*. In any event, this effort ended abruptly when it was found that no one employed the unstable category in field trials. This result was, in fairness, more a testimony to the strength of the clinical tradition associated with the term *borderline* and the reluctance of the psychiatric community to adopt abrupt changes than it is an argument against the scientific and long-term wisdom of employing a new term for this category.

The confusion between the concepts of borderline personality organization and borderline personality disorder unfortunately remains. Given the problems found in trying to rename the latter, I think it is wise to drop the former; that is, to discontinue use of the term *borderline personality organization*. The concept, however, of a single type of intrapsychic organization which many patients with serious character pathology have in common remains accurate and valuable. I believe that Rinsley's (1982) recent effort to rename this concept as *self disorders* is helpful and appropriate. Meissner's (1984) term *borderline spectrum* is another effort, but one that only perpetuates the tendency for *borderline* to have multiple meanings.

The strongest reason for maintaining the term *borderline* comes from the clinical dilemmas themselves with which the name is associated. The fact is that these patients are often marginal, ambiguous, and unstable. First of all, despite the descriptive discriminability that has been documented on borderline patients vis-à-vis those with major psychoses, the differential diagnostic problems remain a reality (Chapter 1). There are borderline patients and schizophrenic patients for whom, on a nonphenomenologic basis, discrimination is not easy. This is so, for example, when looked at in terms of psychological tests or in terms of morbidity in role performance. Similarly, from a nonphenomenologic point of view, there remains an ambiguous relationship to the major affective disorders for at least some borderline patients. Some borderline patients have family pedigrees or responses to antidepressants that seem to link them to the affective disorders. From an intrapsychic point of view, the issue of whether the character structure of borderline patients is psychotic (having been organized around fixed idiosyncratic beliefs) is often unclear even after extensive evaluations or treatment.

More important than these residual diagnostic problems, however, are the reasons for maintaining the term *borderline* that derive from the persistent clinical dilemmas to which caregivers are called on to respond. The borderline patient's most characteristic and defining psychopathology only becomes evident on the verge of separations. Moreover, their internal lives are preoccupied with maintaining the thin border between the panics associated with object loss and those associated with being overwhelmed, dominated, or fused. This preoccupation must be recognized and shared by therapists. Invariably, the residuals of one's own separation experiences (e.g., reluctant, angry, incomplete, abrupt) are brought back for review by the exposure to borderline patients.

The polarizations (good/bad, all/nothing, now/never) within borderline patients repeatedly evoke polarized responses from their environment. To survive and be helpful in the midst of such demands, the therapist must consistently see the unrealistic side of the patient's view without responding as if its opposite contained a more rational perspective. Truth must always be perceived as being somewhere in a grey zone that is never completely clear, never fully attainable, and, above all, never completely satisfactory. Here I feel we come closer to the reason why the term *borderline* has persisted despite the many criticisms that can be leveled against it. The experience of uncertainty—of vacillating between helplessness and exhortation, of being unsure what is actually in the patient's best interest versus one's own, of not even knowing whether one's feeling responses should be owned as countertransference or be viewed as the result of the patient's projections—is a continuous reminder of the thin border of attachment and rationality within ourselves, a border that is constantly threatened by the demands by such patients to provide availability, clarity, certainty, and direction where, in fact, none exists or is possible.

A special tension surrounds the treatment of borderline patients deriving from the "borderline"—meaning unclear—level of responsibility which such patients can be expected to accept. It is evident, insofar as these patients often seem unable to function as outpatients but not to need full hospitalization, that they remain in between and perhaps best served by half-way houses or by partial hospital programs. Ambiguities about level of responsibility are a

source of tension in virtually all of the treatment dilemmas described
in this book. The decade ahead, stimulated in part by the Hinckley
trial, can be expected to explore this issue in much more depth. As
I have indicated, I believe where the line is drawn in terms of
holding patients responsible versus assuming responsibility for them
is a delicate clinical problem and one that is necessarily somewhat
subjective and arbitrary. This, then, is another "borderline" with
which clinicians are familiar. It is a line that also seems to resonate
with retaining the term *borderline* for this patient group.

The above rationale for the use of the term *borderline* makes
clear that no textbook or recipe can adequately prepare a clinician
to work successfully or comfortably with such patients. In addition
to the need for a militant recognition of the inherent complexities
of the dilemmas for which borderline patients demand answers,
there are other qualities needed in such therapists. Of these is a
flexibility that goes along with seeing each of the problems that
are presented within a treatment as being to some extent unique
and in need of a creative solution. No other patient group displays
such a spectrum of functional competence. From a technical point
of view, a therapist ranges from the early phases of the treatment,
where repeated limits and behavioral monitoring are required, to
the later stages of treatment, in which a more passive stance accompanied by an equally militant demand for borderline patients to
explore their internal life responsibly are required. No other patients
so routinely require the full gamut of technical interventions as do
these. It leaves the therapist no place to hide behind such self-
definitions as "I am a psychoanalyst" or "I am a hospital psychiatrist" or "I am a self-psychologist" or "I am a behavior modifier"
and so on. Allegiance to any isolated technical approach simply
restricts the ability to work with such patients altogether or restricts
one's usefulness to a limited aspect of the total problem.

There is a more central issue, which identifies therapists who
can or do work with borderline patients well. This is an abiding
curiosity about the dark side of human nature. With respect to
borderline patients, this means that either the borderline patients'
views of themselves as deprived waifs in search of a good mother
or the therapists' views of themselves as good persons governed by
altruistic motives are equally viewed as less than half true. It is the
darker side of themselves and others that occupy the interest and
attention of such therapists. This means that such therapists must
recognize and be comfortable with the aggressive motives behind

their own and their patients' behaviors. There must be a genuine recognition of one's own controlling, sadistic, and envious motives, which seeks their exposure in others, not for the purposes of judgment, but rather for the sake of sharing a common bond. It means an interest—even an impatience—to engage borderline patients with the negative transference issues. It means a comfort with the financial and time restrictions that become the battlegrounds in which meaningful engagement of such patients occurs.

The development as a therapist suited for work with borderline patients involves the transformation in one's view of the subject. It is akin to the changes Waldo Leopold or Sigrid Olsen described in their evolution as naturalists. Each got interested in ecology for reasons that they later abandoned. One was a guide interested in the habits of wildlife; the other was a conservationist interested in the preservation of resources. Both eventually came to love the natural order of life, which included both the need for predation and the succession of generations. Time and again, borderline patients proffer therapists the prospect of sharing a more ideal world in which human motives are uniformly benign and in which personal pain is considered unfortunate and cruel. So readily does this join one's own illusions that a bond is sealed before it is recognized. Borderline patients are so essentially tragic that it is difficult to do otherwise. In the same way, it is difficult more generally for anyone to be content with what is real, let alone to prefer life with its inherent hard edges. It is at the heart of treating borderline patients to know that the separations about which patients complain so obliquely and destructively are neither cruel nor undesirable.

This is the final reason why *borderline* seems an apt term. It reflects the precarious balance of both positive and negative forces in the personality of borderline patients. Their rages and compassions are equally intense. The border between being motivated by perversity (the pleasure in hurting) and by defensiveness (the wish to avoid hurt) is inherently ambiguous. The judgments of whether a person is psychotic and whether a person is responsible for his or her own actions are inherently unclear—partial and intermittent. These force a therapist to evaluate and adjust constantly. At its best, it means that the treatment of such patients contain the most informative and enriching experiences within the mental health field.

APPENDIX

Description and Patient Participation Form: Department of Psychiatry Comprehensive Treatment Unit

Your physician has determined that your psychiatric illness would best be treated by a specialized program called "The Comprehensive Treatment Unit." This program requires your commitment to getting well and also your active participation and cooperation. A brief description of the treatment program is outlined below:

1. You must be informed and willing to participate in the program.
2. This program is structured to provide more intensive therapy for the problems which brought you to the hospital.
3. You must agree to participate in the following:
   a. Group Therapy—Meets three days a week for one hour.
   b. Community Meeting—Meets once a week for one hour. This meeting consists of all nursing, activities therapy, social service, and pastoral care staff available from the unit meeting with all the patients from the unit. It will be a meeting to discuss problems encountered in the hospital setting which have to do with living together and relating to one another. There will usually be a physician present and possibly your own doctor will attend this meeting.
   c. Other activities may be designated as a part of your Treatment Program by the Treatment Team. These include:
      1. Self-Awareness—Meets three days a week for one hour.
      2. Relaxation Group—Meets twice a week for one hour.
      3. Assertiveness Training—Meets three days a week for one hour.
      4. Out-Trips—Occur two to four times a week.
      5. Family Group—Meets once a week.
4. Any suicide attempts or attempts to leave the hospital or the program will have to be reviewed with you by the Treatment Team (including your physician), and a decision will then be made regarding your continued participation in this program.

- -

I have read the above treatment program outline recommended by my doctor, and I feel that I understand the treatment plan suggested. I agree to participate in this program.

_____   _____
Patient's Signature   Date

_____   _____
Physician's Signature   Nurse's Signature

183

References and Bibliography

Abend S, Porder M, Willick M: Borderline Patients, Psychoanalytic Perspectives. New York, International Universities Press, 1983

Adler G: Hospital treatment of borderline patients. Am J Psychiatry 130:32–35, 1973

Adler G: Regression in psychotherapy: disruptive or therapeutic? Int J Psychoanal Psychother 130:32–35, 1975

Adler G: Hospital management of borderline patients and its relation to psychotherapy, in Borderline Personality Disorders: The Concept, the Syndrome, the Patient. Edited by Hartocollis P. New York, International Universities Press, 1977

Adler G: The myth of the alliance with borderline patients. Am J Psychiatry 136:642–645, 1979

Adler G: The borderline-narcissistic personality disorder continuum. Am J Psychiatry 138:46–50, 1981

Adler G, Buie D: Aloneness and borderline psychopathology: the possible relevance of child development issues. Int J Psychoanal 60:83–96, 1979a

Adler G, Buie D: The psychotherapeutic approach to aloneness in borderline patients, in Advances in Psychotherapy of the Borderline Patient. Edited by LeBoit J. New York, Jason Aronson, 1979b

Akiskal H: Sub-affective disorders, dysthymic, cyclothymic and bipolar II disorders in the borderline realm. Psychiatr Clin North Am 4:25–46, 1981

American Psychiatric Association: Diagnostic and Statistical Manual for Mental Disorders, 3rd ed. Washington, DC, American Psychiatric Association, 1980

Andrulonis P, Glueck B, Stroebel C, et al: Borderline personality subcategories. J Nerv Ment Dis 170:670–679, 1982

Arkema P: The borderline personality and transitional relatedness. Am J Psychiatry 138:172–177, 1981

185

Balint M: The Basic Fault: Therapeutic Aspects of Regression. London, Tavisock, 1968

Baron M: Schizotypal personality disorder: family study. Unpublished paper presented at the 136th Annual Meeting of the American Psychiatric Association, held in New York in May 1983

Barrash I, Kroll J, Carey K, et al: Discriminating borderline disorder from other personality disorders: cluster analysis of the diagnostic interview for borderlines. Arch Gen Psychiatry 40:1297–1302, 1983

Berkowitz D, Shapiro R, Zinner J, et al: Family contributions to narcissistic disturbances in adolescents. International Review of Psychoanalysis 1:353–362, 1974

Bond T: Paradoxical intention in the treatment of borderline patients. Psychiatry, 1984 (in press)

Boyer L: Analytic experiences in work with regressed patients, in Technical Factors in the Treatment of the Severely Disturbed Patient. Edited by Giovacchini P, Boyer L. New York, Jason Aronson, 1982, pp 65–106

Bradley S: The relationship of early maternal separation to borderline personality in children and adolescents: a pilot study. Am J Psychiatry 136:424–426, 1979

Brandschaft B, Stolorow R: The borderline concept: pathological character of iatrogenic myth? in Empathy. Edited by Lichtenberg J, Bornstein M, Silver D. The Analytic Press, Hillsdale, NJ, 1984

Brenman M: On teasing and being teased and the problem of moral masochism. Psychoanal Study Child 7:264–285, 1952

Brenner S: The hospitalized borderline patient: development, dynamics, and indicators for art therapy, in Art Therapy: A Bridge Between Worlds. Falls Church, Va, American Art Therapy Association, 1982, pp 62–63

Brinkley J, Zeitman S, Friedel R, et al: Low-dose neuroleptic regimens in the treatment of borderline patients. Arch Gen Psychiatry 36:319–326, 1979

Brown L: Staff countertransference reactions in the hospital treatment of borderline patients. Psychiatry 43:333–345, 1980

Buie D: The abandoned therapist. Int J Psychoanal Psychother 9:130–134, 1982

Buie D, Adler G: The definitive treatment of the borderline personality. Int J Psychoanal Psychother 9:51–87, 1982

Burnham D: The special problem patient: victim or agent of splitting? Psychiatry: Journal of the Psychiatric Study of Interpersonal Processes 29:105–122, 1966

Burstein E: The quantitative study: psychotherapy outcome. Bull Menninger Clin 36:3–85, 1972

Carpenter W, Gunderson J, Strauss J: Considerations of the borderline syndrome: a longitudinal comparative study of borderline and schizophrenic patients, in Borderline Personality Disorders: The Concept, the Syndrome, the Patient. Edited by Hartocollis P. New York, International Universities Press, 1977

Carr A, Goldstein E, Hunt H, et al: Psychological tests and borderline patients. J Pers Assess 43:582–590, 1979

Charney D, Nelson C. Quinlan D: Personality traits and disorder in depression. Am J Psychiatry 138: 1601–1604, 1981

Chessick R: Intensive Psychotherapy of the Borderline Patient. New York, Jason Aronson, 1977

Chessick R: Intensive Psychotherapy of a borderline patient. Arch Gen Psychiatry 39:413–419, 1982

Chessick R: Problems in the intensive psychotherapy of the borderline patient. Dynamic Psychotherapy 1:20–32, 1983

Chodoff P, Lyons H: The hysterical personality and "hysterical" conversion. Am J Psychiatry 114:734–740, 1958

Cole J, Sunderland P: The drug treatment of borderline patients, in Psychiatry 1982 [Volume 1 of Psychiatry Update]. Edited by Grinspoon L. Washington, DC: American Psychiatric Press, 1982, pp 456–470

Cole J, Salomon M, Gunderson J, et al: Drug therapy in borderline patients. Compr Psychiatry 25:249–262, 1984

Conte H, Plutchik R, Karasu T, et al: A self-report borderline scale: discriminative validity and preliminary norms. J Nerv Ment Dis 168:428–435, 1980

Cornell D, Silk K, Ludolph P, et al: Test-retest reliability of the diagnostic interview for borderlines. Arch Gen Psychiatry 40:1307–1310, 1983

Crafoord C: Day hospital treatment for borderline patients: the institution as transitional object, in Borderline Personality Disorders: The Concept, the Syndrome, the Patient. Edited by Hartocollis P. New York, International Universities Press, 1977, pp 385–397

Crumley F: Adolescent suicide attempts. JAMA 241:2404–2407, 1979

Dickes R: The concepts of borderline states: an alternative proposal. Int J Psychoanal Psychother 3:1–27, 1974

Dyrud J: The treatment of the borderline syndrome, in Modern Psychiatry and Clinical Research. Edited by Offer D, Freedman D. New York, Basic Books, 1972, pp 159–173

Ekstein R: Children of Time and Space, of Action and Impulse. New York, Appleton-Century-Crofts, 1966

Ekstein R, Wallerstein J: Observations on the psychology of borderline and psychotic children. Psychoanal Study Child 9:344–369, 1954

Ellsworth R: Characteristics of effective treatment milieus, in Principles and Practice of Milieu Therapy. Edited by Gunderson J, Will O Jr, Mosher L. New York, Jason Aronson, 1983, pp 87–123

Fairbairn W: A revised psychopathology. Int J Psychoanal 22:271, 1941

Fairbairn W: Object relationships and dynamic structure. Int J Psychoanal 27:30, 1946

Falloon I, Boyd J, McGill C, et al: Family management in the prevention of exacerbations of schizophrenia. N Engl J Med 306:1437–1440, 1982

Frances A, Cooper A: Descriptive and dynamic psychiatry: a perspective on DSM-III. Am J Psychiatry 138:1198–1202, 1981

Frances A, Clarkin J, Gilmore M, et al: Reliability of criteria for borderline personality disorder: a comparison of DSM-III and DIB. Am J Psychiatry 141:1080–1083, 1984

Frank A: Linking specific and nonspecific factors in psychotherapy: the relationship between treatment techniques and the development of a therapeutical alliance. Manuscript in preparation.

Frank A, Gunderson J: Matching therapists and milieus: effects on engagement and continuance in psychotherapy. Psychiatry 47:201–210, 1984

Frank H, Paris J: Recollections of family experience in borderline patients. Arch Gen Psychiatry 38:1031–1034, 1981

Friedman H: Some problems of inpatient management with borderline patients. Am J Psychiatry 126:299–304, 1969

Friedman H: Psychotherapy of borderline patients: the influence of theory on technique. Am J Psychiatry 132:1048–1052, 1975

Frieswyk S, Colson D: Prognostic considerations in the hospital treatment of borderline states: the perspective of object relations theory and the Rorschach, in Borderline Phenomena and the Rorschach. Edited by Kwawer J, Lerner H, Lerner P, Sugarman A. New York, International Universities Press, 1980, pp 229–255

Fromm-Reichmann F: Principles of Intensive Psychotherapy. Chicago, University of Chicago Press, 1950

Frosch J: The psychotic character: clinical psychiatric considerations. Psychiatr Q 38:1–16, 1964

Frosch J: Psychoanalytic considerations of the psychotic character. J Am Psychoanal Assoc 18:24–50, 1970

Frosch J: The relation between acting out and disorders of impulse control. Psychiatry: Journal for the Study of Interpersonal Processes 40:295–314, 1977

Giovacchini P: Character disorders: with special reference to the borderline state. Int J Psychoanal Psychother 2:7–36, 1973

Giovacchini P: Treatment of Primitive Mental States. New York, Jason Aronson, 1979

Gordon C, Beresin E: Conflicting treatment models for the inpatient management of borderline patients. Am J Psychiatry 140:979–983, 1983

Gordon D, Gunderson J: Psychological test performance of borderline patients: a review. Manuscript in preparation.

Graff H, Mallin R: The syndrome of the wrist cutter. Am J Psychiatry 124:74–79, 1967

Grinker R: Diagnosis of borderlines: a discussion. Schizophr Bull 5:47–52, 1979

Grinker R, Werble B: The Borderline Patient. New York, Jason Aronson, 1977

Grinker R, Werble B, Drye R: The Borderline Syndrome: A Behavioral Study of Ego Functions. New York, Basic Books, 1968

Grunebaum H, Klerman G: Wrist slashing. Am J Psychiatry 124:524–534, 1967

Gunderson J: Characteristics of borderlines, in Borderline Personality Disorders: The Concept, the Syndrome, the Patient. Edited by Hartocollis P. New York, International Universities Press, 1977

Gunderson J: Defining the therapeutic processes in psychiatric milieus. Psychiatry: Journal for the Study of Interpersonal Processes 41:327–335, 1978

Gunderson J: Empirical studies of the borderline diagnosis, in Psychiatry 1982 [Volume 1 of Psychiatry Update]. Edited by Grinspoon L. Washington, DC: American Psychiatric Press, 1982, pp 414–437

Gunderson J: Discussion of "Problems in the intensive psychotherapy of the borderline patient" by Chessick R. Dynamic Psychotherapy 1:33–34, 1983a

Gunderson J: Interfaces between psychoanalytic and empirical studies of borderline personality disorder. Unpublished paper presented at the Annual Meeting of the American Psychoanalytic Association, held in New York on 15 December 1983b

Gunderson J: DSM-III diagnoses of personality disorders, in Current Perspectives on Personality Disorders. Edited by Frosch J. Washington, DC, American Psychiatric Press, 1983c, p 20–41

Gunderson J: Engagement of schizophrenic patients in psychotherapy, in Attachment and the Evolution of a Self. Edited by Akabana Y, Sacksteder J, Schwartz D. New York, International Universities Press 1984 (in press)

Gunderson J, Singer M: Defining borderline patients: an overview. Am J Psychiatry 132:1–10, 1975

Gunderson J, Kolb J: Discriminating features of borderline patients. Am J Psychiatry 135:792–796, 1978

Gunderson J, Englund D: Characterizing the families of borderlines. Psychiatr Clin North Am 4:159–168, 1981

Gunderson J, Carroll A: Clinical considerations from empirical research, in Psychosocial Intervention in Schizophrenia. Edited by Stierlin H, Wynne L, Wirsching M. New York, Springer-Verlag, 1983, pp 125–142

Gunderson J, Elliott G: Interface of borderline and affective disorders. Am J Psychiatry, 1984 (in press)

Gunderson J, Carpenter W, Strauss J: Borderline and schizophrenic patients: a comparative study. Am J Psychiatry 132:1257–1264, 1975a

Gunderson J, Schulz C, Feinsilver D: Matching therapists with schizophrenic patients, in Psychotherapy of Schizophrenia: Current Theory, Research and Practice. Edited by Gunderson J and Mosher L. New York, Jason Aronson, 1975b, pp 343–360

Gunderson J, Kerr J, Englund D: The families of borderlines: a comparative study. Arch Gen Psychiatry 37:27–33, 1980

Gunderson J, Kolb J, Austin V: The diagnostic interview for borderline patients. Am J Psychiatry 138:896–903, 1981

Gunderson J, Siever L, Spaulding E: The search for a schizotype. Arch Gen Psychiatry 40:15–22, 1983

Gunderson JG, Frank AF, Katz HM, et al: Effects of psychotherapy in schizophrenia, II: comparative outcome of two forms of treatment. Schizophr Bull, 1984 (in press)

Hartocollis P: Long-term hospital treatment of adult patients with borderline and narcissistic disorders. Bull Menninger Clin 44:212–227, 1980

Havens L: Some difficulties in giving schizophrenic and borderline patients medications. Psychiatry 31:44–50, 1968

Hoch P, Polatin P: Pseudoneurotic forms of schizophrenia. Psychiatr Q 23:248–276, 1949

Horner A: Stages and processes in the development of early object relations and their associated pathologies. International Review of Psychoanalysis 2:95–105, 1975

Horwitz L: Clinical Prediction in Psychotherapy. New York, Jason Aronson, 1974

Horwitz L: Group psychotherapy of the borderline patient, in Borderline Personality Disorders: The Concept, the Syndrome, the Patient. Edited by Hartocollis P. New York, International Universities Press, 1977, pp 399–422

Horwitz L: Group psychotherapy for borderline and narcissistic patients. Bull Menninger Clin 44:181–200, 1980

Horwitz L: Clinical and projective assessments of borderline patients. Unpublished paper presented at a symposium on The Borderline Patient: A Multiaxial View, held at the Department of Psychiatry, University of Miami School of Medicine, in Key Biscayne, Florida, on 26 March 1982

Houck J: The intractable female patient. Am J Psychiatry 129:59–63, 1972

Jacobson E: Contribution to the metapsychology of cyclothymic depression, in Affective Disorders. Edited by Greenacre P. New York, International Universities Press, 1953

Johansen K: A theoretical basis for the management of the hospitalized borderline patient. Current Concepts in Psychiatry 5:8–16, 1979

Johansen K: Separation of therapist and administrator in hospital treatment of borderline patients. Hosp Community Psychiatry 31:259–262, 1980

Jones M: The concept of a therapeutic community. Am J Psychiatry 112:647–650, 1956

Kendler K: Diagnostic approaches to schizotypal personality disorder: an historical perspective. Unpublished manuscript, 1984

Kendler K, Gruenberg A, Strauss J: An independent analysis of the Copenhagen sample of the Danish Adoption Study of Schizophrenia, II, the relationship between schizotypal personality disorder and schizophrenia. Arch Gen Psychiatry 38:982–984, 1981

Kernberg O: Countertransference. J Am Psychoanal Assoc 13:38–56, 1965

Kernberg O: Borderline personality organization. J Am Psychoanal Assoc 15:641–685, 1967

Kernberg O: The treatment of patients with borderline personality organization. Int J Psychoanal 49:600–619, 1968

Kernberg O: Prognostic considerations regarding borderline personality organization. J Am Psychoanal Assoc 19:595–615, 1971

Kernberg O: Contrasting viewpoints regarding the nature and psychoanalytic treatment of narcissistic personalities: a preliminary communication. J Am Psychoanal Assoc 22:255–267, 1974

Kernberg O: Borderline Conditions and Pathological Narcissism. New York, Jason Aronson, 1975

Kernberg O: Object-Relations Theory and Clinical Psychoanalysis. New York, Jason Aronson, 1976

Kernberg O: The structural diagnosis of borderline personality organization, in Borderline Personality Disorders: The Concept, the Syndrome,
the Patient. Edited by Hartocollis P. New York, International Universities Press, 1977, pp 87–121

Kernberg O: Two reviews of the literature on borderlines: an assessment.
Schizophr Bull 5:53–58, 1979a

Kernberg O: Overall structuring and beginning phase of treatment of
borderline and narcissistic patients, in Parameters in Psychoanalytic
Psychotherapy. Edited by Goldman G, Milman D. Dubuque, Iowa, Kendall/
Hunt, 1979b, pp 215–236

Kernberg O: Developmental theory, structural organization, and
psychoanalytic technique, in Rapprochement: The Critical Subphase of
Separation-Individuation. Edited by Lax R, Bach S, Beuland J. New York,
Jason Aronson, 1980, pp 23–28

Kernberg O: Problems in the classification of personality disorders.
Unpublished paper presented at Clinical Grand Rounds, held at New
York Hospital, Cornell Medical Center, Westchester Division, on 11
September 1981a

Kernberg O: Structural interviewing. Psychiatr Clin North Am 4:169–195,
1981b

Kernberg O: Cited in Medical World News. February 1983

Kernberg O: Supportive psychotherapy with borderline conditions, in Critical Problems in Psychiatry. Edited by Cavenar J, Brodie H. Philadelphia,
Lippincott, 1982, pp 180–202

Kernberg O, Burstein E, Coyne L, et al: Final report of the Menninger
Foundation's psychotherapy research project: psychotherapy and
psychoanalysis. Bull Menninger Clin 34:1–2, 1972

Kernberg O, Bauer S, Blumenthal R, et al: Diagnosing borderline personality organization: a pilot study using multiple diagnostic methods. J
Nerv Ment Dis 169:225–231, 1981a

Kety S, Rosenthal D, Wender P, et al: The types and prevalence of mental
illness in the biological and adoptive families of adopted schizophrenics,
in The Transmission of Schizophrenia. Edited by Rosenthal D, Kety S.
New York, Pergamon Press, 1968, pp 345–362

Kety S, Rosenthal D, Wender P, et al: Mental illness in the biological and
adoptive families who have become schizophrenic: a preliminary report
based on psychiatric interviews, in Genetic Research in Psychiatry. Edited
by Fieve R, Rosenthal D, Brill H. Baltimore, Johns Hopkins University
Press, 1975, pp 147–165

Kibel H: The importance of a comprehensive clinical diagnosis for group
psychotherapy of borderline and narcissistic patients. Int J Group
Psychother 30:427–440, 1980

Klein D: Psychopharmacology and the borderline patient, in Borderline
States in Psychiatry. Edited by Mack J. New York, Grune & Stratton,
1975, pp 75–92

Klein D: Psychopharmacological treatment and delineation of borderline
disorders, in Borderline Personality Disorders: The Concept, the Syndrome,

the Patient. Edited by Hartocollis P. New York, International Universities Press, 1977, pp 365–384

Klein M: The Psychoanalysis of Children. London, Hogarth Press, 1932

Klein M: Notes on some schizoid mechanisms. Int J Psychoanal 27:99–110, 1946

Klein M: Mourning and its relation to manic depressive states, in Contributions to Psychoanalysis. Edited by Klein M. London, Hogarth Press, 1950

Knight R: Borderline states. Bull Menninger Clinic 17:1–12, 1953

Knight R: Management and psychotherapy of the borderline schizophrenic patient, in Psychoanalytic Psychiatry and Psychology. Edited by Knight R, Friedman C. New York, International Universities Press, 1954

Kobele S, Schulz S, VanKammen D: Diagnostic interview for borderlines successfully excludes other diagnoses. Unpublished manuscript, 1981

Koenigsberg H: A comparison of hospitalized and nonhospitalized borderline patients. Am J Psychiatry 139:1292–1297, 1982

Koenigsberg H, Kernberg O, Schomer J: Diagnosing borderline conditions in an outpatient setting. Arch Gen Psychiatry 40:49–53, 1983

Kohut H: The Analysis of the Self. New York, International Universities Press, 1971

Kohut H: Thoughts on narcissism and narcissistic rage. Psychoanal Study Child 27:360–400, 1972

Kohut H, Wolfe E: The disorders of the self and their treatment: an outline. Int J Psychoanal 59:413–425, 1978

Krohn A, Mayman M: Levels of object representations in dreams and projective tests. Bull Menninger Clin 38:445–466, 1974

Kroll J, Sines L, Martin K, et al: Borderline personality disorder: construct validity of the concept. Arch Gen Psychiatry 38:1021–1026, 1981

Kroll J, Carley K, Sines L, et al: Are there borderlines in Britain? A cross-validation of U.S. findings. Arch Gen Psychiatry 39:60–63, 1983

Langs R: The Therapeutic Interaction: A Synthesis. New York, Jason Aronson, 1977

Langs R: Interventions in the bipersonal field, in Technique in Transition. New York, Jason Aronson, 1978, pp 627–678

Last U, Lowenthal U, Klein H: Borderline patients in a chronic ward. Arch Gen Psychiatry 28:517–521, 1973

Leff J: Developments in family treatment of schizophrenia. Psychiatry 51:216–232, 1979

Lerner P, Lerner H: Rorschach assessment of primitive defenses in borderline personality structure, in Borderline Phenomena and the Rorschach Test. Edited by Kwawer J, Lerner H, Lerner P, Sugarman A. New York, International Universities Press, 1980

Lewis J: Early treatment planning for hospitalized severe borderline patients. Psychiatric Hospital 13:130–136, 1982

Lichtenberg J, Slap H: Notes on the concept of splitting and the defense mechanism of the splitting of representations. J Am Psychoanal Assoc 21:772–787, 1973

Liebowitz M: Is borderline a distinct entity? Schizophr Bull 5:23–28, 1979

Liebowitz M: Psychopharmacological intervention in personality disorders, in Current Perspectives on Personality Disorders. Edited by Frosch J. Washington, DC: American Psychiatric Press, 1983, pp 68–93

Loranger A, Oldham J, Tullis E: Familial transmission of DSM-II borderline personality disorder. Arch Gen Psychiatry 39:795–799, 1982

Mack J: Borderline states: an historical perspective, in Borderline States in Psychiatry. Edited by Mack J. New York, Grune & Stratton, 1975

Mahler M: A study of the separation-individuation process and its possible application to borderline phenomena in the psychoanalytic situation. Psychoanal Study Child 26:403–424, 1971

Mahler M, Kaplan L: Developmental aspects in the assessment of narcissistic and so-called borderline personalities, in Borderline Personality Disorders: The Concept, the Syndrome, the Patient. Edited by Hartocollis P. New York, International Universities Press, 1977, pp 71–86

Main T: The ailment. Br J Med Psychol 30:129–145, 1957

Malan D: Individual Psychotherapy and the Science of Psychodynamics. London, Butterworths, 1979

Maltsberger J, Buie D: Countertransference hate in the treatment of suicidal patients. Arch Gen Psychiatry 30:625–633, 1974

Mandelbaum A: The family treatment of the borderline patient, in Borderline Personality Disorders: The Concept, the Syndrome, the Patient. Edited by Hartocollis P. New York, International Universities Press, 1977, pp 423–438

Mann J: Time-Limited Psychotherapy. Cambridge, Harvard University Press, 1973

Mann J, Semrad E: Conversion as process and conversion as symptoms in psychosis, in On the Mysterious Leap from the Mind to the Body. Edited by Deutsch F. New York, International Universities Press, 1959, pp 131–154

Marcus E: Use of the acute hospital unit in the early phase of long-term treatment of borderline psychotic patients. Psychiatr Clin North Am 4:133–144, 1981

Marmor J: Orality in the hysterical personality. J Am Psychoanal Assoc 1:656–675, 1953

Masterson J: Treatment of the adolescent with borderline syndrome (a problem in separation-individuation). Bull Menninger Clin 35:5–18, 1971

Masterson J: Treatment of the Borderline Adolescent: A Developmental Approach. New York, John Wiley & Sons, 1972, p 125

Masterson J: The splitting mechanism of the borderline adolescent: developmental and clinical aspects, in Borderline States in Psychiatry. Edited by Mack J. New York, Grune & Stratton, 1975

Masterson J: Psychotherapy of the Borderline Adult. New York, Brunner/Mazel, 1976

Masterson J, Costello JL: From Borderline Adolescent to Functioning Adult: The Test of Time. New York, Brunner/Mazel, 1980

Masterson J, Rinsley D: The borderline syndrome: the role of the mother in the genesis and psychic structure of the borderline personality. Int J Psychoanal 56:163–177, 1975

McCully R: Certain theoretical considerations in relation to borderline schizophrenia and the Rorschach. Journal of Projective Techniques 26:404–418, 1962

McGlashan T: The borderline syndrome, I: testing three diagnostic systems for borderlines. Arch Gen Psychiatry 40:1311–1318, 1983a

McGlashan T: The borderline syndrome, II: is borderline a variant of schizophrenia or affective disorder? Arch Gen Psychiatry 40: 1319–1323, 1983b

McGlashan T: The Chestnut Lodge follow-up study, II: long-term outcome of borderline personalities. Arch Gen Psychiatry 41:586–601, 1984

Meehl P: Schizotaxia, schizotypy, schizophrenia. Am Psychol 17:827–838, 1962

Meissner W: Notes on some conceptual aspects of borderline personality organization. International Review of Psychoanalysis 5:297–311, 1978a

Meissner W: Theoretical assumptions of concepts of the borderline personality. J Am Psychoanal Assoc 26:559–578, 1978b

Meissner W: The Borderline Spectrum: Differential Diagnosis and Developmental Issues. New York, Jason Aronson, 1984

Michels R: A debate on DSM-III. Am J Psychiatry 141:539–553, 1984

Millon T: Disorders of personality, DSM-III: Axis II. New York, John Wiley & Sons, 1981

Modell A: Primitive object relationships and the predisposition to schizophrenia. Int J Psychoanal 44:282–291, 1963

Modell A: The holding envrionment and the therapeutic action of psychoanalysis. J Am Psychoanal Assoc 24:285–308, 1976

Moras K, Strupp H: Pretherapy interpersonal relations, patients' alliance, and outcome in brief therapy. Arch Gen Psychiatry 39:405–409, 1982

Morris H, Gunderson J, Zanarini M: Transitional objects and borderline patients. Unpublished paper presented at the 137th Annual Meeting of the American Psychiatric Association, held in Los Angeles on 6 May 1984

Mottai P: The adolescent borderline patient in art therapy, in Art Therapy: A Bridge Between Worlds. Falls Church, Va, American Art Therapy Association, 1982, pp 18–20

Nadelson T: Borderline, rage and the therapist's response. Am J Psychiatry 134:748–751, 1977

Naevestad M: The Colors of Rage and Love. London, Whitefriars Press, 1979

Nurnberg H, Suh R: Time-limited treatment of hospitalized borderline patients. Comparative Psychiatr 19:419–431, 1978

Obernbreit R: Object relations theory and the language of art, in Art Therapy: A Bridge Between Worlds. Falls Church, Va, American Art Therapy Association, 1982, pp 57–59

Ogden T: Projective Identification and Psychotherapeutic Technique. New York, Jason Aronson, 1982

Ostow M: Drugs in Psychoanalysis and Psychotherapy. New York, Basic Books, 1962

Perry J: Which borderline? An empirical comparison of clinical descriptions. Unpublished manuscript, 1981

Perry J: The borderline personality disorder scale: reliability and validity. Arch Gen Psychiatry, 1984 (in press)

Perry J, Klerman G: the borderline patient. Arch Gen Psychiatry 35:141–150, 1978

Perry J, Klerman G: Clinical features of the borderline personality disorder. Am J Psychiatry 137:165–173, 1980

Perry J, Cooper S: A preliminary report on defenses and conflicts associated with borderline personality disorder. Draft manuscript presented before the Panel on Borderline Personality Disorders and the Fall Meeting of the American Psychoanalytic Association, held in New York on 16 December 1983

Pildis M, Soverow G, Salzman C, et al: Day hospital treatment of borderline patients: a clinical perspective. Am J Psychiatry 135:594–596, 1978

Pine F: On the concept "borderline" in children: a clinical essay. Psychoanal Study Child 29:341–368, 1974

Pope H, Jonas J, Hudson J, et al: The validity of DSM-III borderline personality disorder. Arch Gen Psychiatry 40:23–30, 1983

Quitkin F, Klein D: Follow-up of treatment failure: psychosis and character disorder. Am J Psychiatry 124:85–91, 1967

Rado S: Theory and therapy: the theory of schizotypal organization and its application to the treatment of decompensated schizotypal behavior, in Psychoanalysis of Behavior, Vol 2. Edited by Rado S. New York, Grune & Stratton, 1962

Rappaport D, Gill M, Schaefer R: The Thematic Apperception Test, in Diagnostic Psychological Testing, Vol 2. Chicago, Year Book Medical Publishers, 1946

Reich W: On the technique of character analysis, in Character Analysis, 3rd ed. New York, Simon and Schuster, 1949, pp 39–113

Rice A: Individual, group and intergroup processes. Human Relations 22:565–584, 1969

Rifkin A, Quitkin F, Carillo C, et al: Lithium carbonate in emotionally unstable character disorder. Arch Gen Psychiatry 27:519–523, 1972

Rinsley D: Intensive psychiatric hospital treatment of adolescents. Psychiatr Q 39:405–429, 1965

Rinsley D: Intensive residential treatment of the adolescent. Psychiatr Q 41:134–143 1967

Rinsley D: Theory and practice of intensive residential treatment of adolescents. Adolesc Psychiatry 1:479–509, 1971

Rinsley D: An object relations view of borderline personality, in Borderline Personality Disorders: The Concept, the Syndrome, the Patient. Edited by Hartocollis P. New York, International Universities Press, 1977

Rinsley D: Borderline and other self disorders. New York, Jason Aronson, 1982

Robbins L: The psychotherapy research project of the Menninger Foundation, I: orientation. Bull Menninger Clin 20:223–225, 1956

Robbins M: Borderline personality organization: the need for a new theory. J Am Psychoanal Assoc 24:831–853, 1976

Rorschach H: Psychodiagnostics, 5th ed. Bern, Hans Huber, 1942

Rosenthal D, Wender P, Kety S, et al: The adopted-away offspring of schizophrenics. Am J Psychiatry 128:307–311, 1971

Ross R, McKay H: Self-Mutilation, Lexington, Mass., Lexington Books, 1979

Roth B: Understanding the development of a homogeneous identity-impaired group through countertransference phenomena. Int J Group Psychother 30:405–426, 1980

Sargent H: The psychotherapy research project of the Menninger Foundation, II: rationale. Bull Menninger Clin 20:226–233, 1956a

Sargent H: The psychotherapy research project of the Menninger Foundation, III: design. Bull Menninger Clin 20:234–238, 1956b

Sarwer-Foner G: An approach to the global treatment of the borderline patient: psychoanalytic, psychotherapeutic, and psychopharmacological considerations, in Borderline Personality Disorders: The Concept, the Syndrome, the Patient. Edited by Hartocollis P. New York, International Universities Press, 1977, pp 345–364

Scharf P: The inpatient treatment of a borderline personality disorder. Psychiatric Opinion 6:37–43, 1969

Schatzberg A: Brain imaging in atypical depressions. Unpublished paper presented at the McLean Hospital Symposium on Atypical Depressions, held in New York City on 1 May 1983

Schick J, Freedman D: Research in non-narcotic drug abuse, in American Handbook of Psychiatry, 2nd ed. Vol 6. Edited by Hamburg D, Brodie H. New York, Basic Books, 1974, pp 552–622

Schmideberg M: The borderline patient, in American Handbook of Psychiatry, vol. 1. Edited by Arieti S. New York, Basic Books, 1959, pp 398–416

Schulz C: All or none phenomena in the psychotherapy of severe disorders, in The Psychotherapy of Schizophrenia. Edited by Strauss J, Bowers M, Downey TW, et al. New York, Plenum Press, 1980

Schwaber E: Construction, reconstruction, and the mode of clinical attunement, in The Future of Psychoanalysis. New York, International Universities Press, 1983, pp 273–292

Searles H: Integration and differentiation in schizophrenia: an overall view. Br J Med Psychol 32:261–281, 1959

Searles H: Dual and multiple identity processes in borderline ego functioning, in Borderline Personality Disorders: The Concept, the Syndrome, the Patient. Edited by Hartocollis P. New York, International Universities Press, 1977

Searles H: Psychoanalytic therapy with the borderline adult: some principles concerning technique, in New Perspectives on Psychotherapy of the Borderline Adult. Edited by Masterson J. New York, Brunner/Mazel, 1978, pp 43–65

Searles H: Countertransference and Related Subjects: Selected Papers. New York, International Universities Press, 1979a

Searles H: Jealousy involving an internal object, in Advances in Psychotherapy of the Borderline Patient. Edited by LeBoit J, Capponi A. New York, Jason Aronson, 1979b, pp 347–403

Searles H: Psychoanalytic therapy with borderline patients: the development in the patient of an internalized image of the therapist. Unpublished lecture presented at The Fifth O. Spurgeon English Honor Lecture, held at Temple University School of Medicine, Philadelphia, on 25 April 1980

Searles H: Some aspects of separation and loss in psychoanalytic therapy with borderline patients, in Technical Factors in the Treatment of the Severely Disturbed Patient. Edited by Giovacchini P, Boyer L. New York, Jason Aronson, 1982, pp 155

Serban G: A response of borderlines to small dosage neuroleptics. Am J Psychiatry 1984 (in press)

Shapiro E: The psychodynamics and developmental psychology of the borderline patient: a review of the literature. Am J Psychiatry 135:1305–1315, 1978a

Shapiro E: Research on family dynamics: clinical implications for the family of the borderline adolescent. Adolesc Psychiatry 6:360–376, 1978b

Shapiro E: The holding environment and family therapy with acting-out adolescents. Int J Psychoanal Psychother 9:209–226, 1982

Shapiro R, Zinner J: Family organization and adolescent development, in Task and Organization. Edited by Miller E. New York, John Wiley & Sons, 1975

Shapiro E, Kolb J: Engaging the family of the hospitalized adolescent: the multiple family meeting. Adolesc Psychiatry 7:322–342, 1979

Shapiro E, Zinner J, Shapiro R, et al: The influence of family experience on borderline personality development. International Review of Psychoanalysis 2:399–411, 1975

Shapiro E, Shapiro R, Zinner J: The borderline ego and the working alliance: indications for family and individual treatment in adolescence. Int J Psychoanal 58:77–87, 1977

Shaskan D: Treatment of a borderline case with group analytically oriented psychotherapy. J Forensic Sci 2:195–201, 1971

Sheehy M, Goldsmith I, Charles E: A comparative study of borderline patients in a psychiatric outpatient clinic. Am J Psychiatr 137:1374–1379, 1980

Shein H, Stone A: Psychotherapy designed to detect and treat suicidal potential. Am J Psychiatry 125:1247–1251, 1969

Shye S (ed): Theory Construction and Data Analysis in the Behavioral Sciences. San Francisco, Jossey-Bass, 1978

Siever L, Gunderson J: Genetic determinants of borderline conditions. Schizophr Bull 5:59–86, 1979

Siever L, Gunderson J: The search for a schizotypal personality: a review. Compr Psychiatry 24:199–212, 1983

Siever L, Insel T, Uhde T: Biogenetic factors in personalities, in Current Perspectives on Personality Disorders. Washington, DC, American Psychiatric Press, 1983, pp 42–57

Sifneos P: Manipulative suicide. Psychiatr Q 40:525–537, 1966

Sifneos P: Short-term Psychotherapy and Emotional Crisis. Cambridge, Harvard University Press, 1972

Singer M: The borderline diagnosis and psychological tests: review and research, in Borderline Personality Disorders: The Concept, the Syndrome, the Patient. Edited by Hartocollis P. New York, International Universities Press, 1977

Singer M, Larson D: Borderline personality and the Rorschach test: a comparison with acute and chronic schizophrenics, normals and neurotics. Arch Gen Psychiatry 38:693–698, 1981

Skodol A, Buckley P, Charles E: Is there a characteristic pattern to the treatment history of clinical outpatients with borderline personality? J Nerv Ment Dis 171:405–410, 1983

Slavin M, Slavin J: Two patterns of adaptation in late adolescent borderline personalities. Psychiatry: Journal for the Study of Interpersonal Processes 39:41–50, 1976

Soloff P: Pharmacotherapy of borderline disorders. Compr Psychiatry 22:535–543, 1981

Soloff P, Ulrich R: The diagnostic interview for borderlines: a replication study. Arch Gen Psychiatry 38:686–692, 1981

Soloff P, Millward J: Psychiatric disorders in the families of borderline patients. Arch Gen Psychiatry 40:37–44, 1983

Soloff P, Millward J: Developmental histories of borderline patients. Unpublished manuscript, 1983

Spitzer R, Endicott J: Justification for separating schizotypal and borderline personality disorders. Schizophr Bull 5:95–104, 1979

Spitzer R, Endicott J, Gibbon M: Crossing the border into borderline personality and borderline schizophrenia: the development of criteria. Arch Gen Psychiatry 36:17–24, 1979

Spitzer R, Williams J, Skodol A: DSM-III: the major achievements and an overview. Am J Psychiatry 137:151–164, 1980

Spitzer R, Skodol A, Williams J, et al: Supervising intake diagnoses. Arch Gen Psychiatry 39:1299–1305, 1982

Stanton A, Schwartz M: The Mental Hospital. New York, Basic Books, 1954

Stanton A, Gunderson J, Knapp P, et al: Effects of psychotherapy on schizophrenic patients: the design and implementation of a controlled study. Schizophr Bull, 1984 (in press)

Stone L: Notes on the noninterpretive elements in the psychoanalytic situation and process. J Am Psychoanal Assoc 29:89–118, 1981

Stone M: The borderline syndrome: evolution of the term, genetic aspects, and prognosis. Am J Psychother 31:345–365, 1977

Stone M: Contemporary shift of the borderline concept from a subschizophrenic disorder to a subaffective disorder. Psychiatr Clin North Am 2:577–594, 1979

Stone M: The Borderline Syndromes. New York, McGraw-Hill, 1980

Stone M: Diagnosis, genetics and personality aspects of borderline patients. Unpublished paper presented at Hillside Medical Center, New Hyde Park, New York, on 3 December 1982

Stone M: Psychotherapy with schizotypal borderline patients. J Am Acad Psychoanal 11:87–111, 1983a

Stone M: Negative outcome in borderline states, in Above All Do Not Harm. Edited by Mays D, Franks C. New York, Springer, 1983b

Stone M, Weissman R: Group therapy with borderline patients, in Contemporary Perspectives in Group Psychotherapy. Edited by Slavinska-Holy N. London, Routledge & Kegan Paul, 1984 (in press)

Stone M, Kahn E, Flye B: Psychiatrically ill relatives of borderline patients: a family study. Psychiatr Q 53:71–84, 1981

Sugarman A: The infantile personality: orality in the hysteric revisited. Int J Psychoanal 60:501–513, 1979

Sugarman A: An object relations understanding of borderline phenomena on the Rorschach. Unpublished paper presented at the conference Current Developments in Projective Techniques, held at Yale University, New Haven, Conn, in May 1981

Sugarman A, Lerner H: Reflections on the current state of the borderline concept, in Borderline Phenomena and the Rorschach Test. Edited by Kwawer J, Lerner H, Lerner J, Sugarman A. New York, International Universities Press, 1980

Tahka V: Psychotherapy as phase-specific interaction: towards a general psychoanalytic theory of psychotherapy. Scandanavian Psychoanalysis Review 2:113–132, 1979

Torgersen S: Genetic and nosologic aspects of schizotypal and borderline disorders: a twin study. Arch Gen Psychiatry 41:546–554, 1984

Vaillant GE: A debate on DSM-III. Am J Psychiatry 141:542–545, 1984

Volkan V: Primitive Internalized Object Relationships. New York, International Universities Press, 1976

Volkan V: Six phases of the psychoanalytic psychotherapy with borderline patients. Unpublished paper presented at Dialogues on Borderlines, held at the Institute of Pennsylvania Hospital, Philadelphia, on 3–4 April 1981

Waldinger R, Gunderson J: Completed psychotherapies with borderline patients. Am J Psychotherapy 38:190–202, 1984

Wallerstein R: Psychoanalysis and psychotherapy: relative roles reconsidered. Unpublished paper presented at the Boston Psychoanalytic Society and Institute Symposium, held in Boston on 29 October 1983

Walsh F: The family of the borderline patient, in The Borderline Patient. Edited by Grinker R, Werble B, New York, Jason Aronson, 1977

Weiner I: Borderline and pseudoneurotic schizophrenia, in Psychodiagnosis in Schizophrenics. New York, John Wiley & Sons, 1966, pp 398–430

Wender P, Rosenthal D, Zahn T, et al: the psychiatric adjustment of the adopting parents of schizophrenics. Am J Psychiatry 27:1010–1018, 1971

Werble B: Second follow-up of borderline patients. Arch Gen Psychiatry 23:3–7, 1970

Will O: Human relatedness and the schizophrenic reaction. Psychiatry, 22:205–223, 1959

Willett A, Jones A, Morgan D, et al: The borderline syndrome: an operational definition. Unpublished paper presented at the 20th Annual Meeting of the American Psychiatric Association, held in Honolulu in May 1973

Winnicott D: Transitional objects and transitional phenomena. Int J Psychoanal 34:89–97, 1953

Winnicott D: The depressive position in normal emotional development, in Collected Papers Through Pediatrics to Psychoanalysis. New York, Basic Books, 1958

Winnicott D: Hate in the countertransference, in Through Pediatrics to Psycho-Analysis. New York, Basic Books, 1975, pp 73–82

Wishnie H: Inpatient therapy with borderline patients, in Borderline States in Psychiatry. Edited by J Mack. New York, Grune & Stratton, 1975, pp 41–62

Wong J: Combined group and individual treatment of borderline and narcissistic patients: heterogeneous vs. homogeneous groups. Int J Group Psychother 30:389–404, 1980

Zales M: Character Pathology: Theory and Treatment. New York, Brunner/ Mazel, 1984

Zanarini M, Gunderson J: Diagnostic Interview for Borderlines, 3rd ed. Manuscript in preparation

Zetzel E: The so-called good hysteric. Int J Psychoanal 49:256–260, 1968

Zetzel E: A developmental approach to the borderline patient. Am J Psychiatry 128:867–871, 1971

Zinner J, Shapiro E: Splitting in families of borderline adolescents, in Borderline States in Psychiatry. Edited by Mack J. New York, Grune & Stratton, 1975

Index